"In the providence of God, Greek philosophy was available precisely at a time when the early church thought carefully about the Trinity, incarnation and other important topics. For centuries, Jerusalem and Athens have been friends. But today there is suspicion and outright rejection of Greek thought in the church. In my view, this attitude rests on confusion about Greek philosophy and its relationship to Christian teaching. With the publication of *When Athens Met Jerusalem,* we finally have an authoritative guide to these themes. Reynolds's work is an interesting read, accessible to a nonspecialist and teeming with content. This book should be required reading for all undergraduates in Christian colleges, laypeople and pastors who need to be reacquainted with the important relationship between Jerusalem and Athens."

J. P. Moreland, Distinguished Professor of Philosophy, Biola University, and coauthor of *Philosophical Foundations for a Christian Worldview*

"John Mark Reynolds writes with the artistry of a true poet and the insight of a true scholar. His passion for teaching shines through the pages of this book."

Nancy Pearcey, author of *Total Truth: Liberating Christianity from Its Cultural Captivity*

"To create the great civilization of Christendom, of which we are all the heirs, it was necessary to fuse the divine revelation given to the Hebrews (Jerusalem) with the philosophical brilliance of the Greeks (Athens). Now, in order to save the best elements of that civilization, those two great traditions must be united again. In this charming book, one of today's leading Christian educators explains how Christian thought has again become an exciting intellectual adventure."

Phillip E. Johnson, Professor of Law Emeritus, University of California—Berkeley, and author of *Darwin on Trial* and *Reason in the Balance*

"'Close to the truth,' ah, so close, writes John Mark Reynolds about one of the best ancient Athenian philosophers. That's what Athens has to do with Jerusalem. That's what Plato has to do with Christendom and eventually with Christianity today. The story of the origins of Christian thinking that Reynolds tells is not the one we often hear from the pulpit. There is no bashing of intellectuals, no rejection of the machinations of the mind in favor of the intuitions of the heart, no substitution of faith for the role of thinking. Reynolds himself was brought back to Christ through the reading of Plato's *Republic.* Astonishing? Yes, but read Plato as Reynolds does and it all makes sense. Written with the passion of a lover of truth and the Word of Truth found finally in Christ, this book will challenge any student of either the ancient Greek philosophers or the beliefs of the early church."

James W. Sire, author of *The Universe Next Door* and, with scientist Carl Peraino, *Deepest Differences: A Christian-Atheist Dialogue*

"John Mark Reynolds is the most stimulating lecturer on the interplay of classical and Christian thought I have ever heard. I have been longing for him to write a book capturing his brilliant ideas on the topic. It is a great blessing that this book has finally arrived—and *When Athens Met Jerusalem* does not disappoint. It is one of the finest and yet most readable treatments ever in print."

Craig J. Hazen, Ph.D., founder and director of the Christian Apologetics Program, Biola University, and editor of *Philosophia Christi*

"This is a bold, original, salutary book, written with great passion, wonderful wit and deep love. Reynolds argues, convincingly I think, that Athens and Jerusalem, the classical and the Christian cultures, cannot live apart and are both in danger of perishing unless they are brought together in creative harmony. What is so unusual and so compelling about this appeal is that equal weight and equal appreciation are given to both classical learning and Christian faith. Reynolds has indeed accomplished the truly remarkable feat of replacing the ages-old deadlock between reason and revelation, or faith and reason, with a loving and respectful marriage between the two, and thus foretells of and foresees a new beginning for classical civilization and a revitalization of Christian teaching."

Alfred Geier, Associate Professor of Classics, University of Rochester

"It must be a treat to sit in John Mark Reynolds's classroom. In its verve and intelligence, *When Athens Met Jerusalem* is the next best thing. I wish I had read a book like this when I was a student. The need is even greater today, when even the teachers turn against reason, and every day makes clearer that Jerusalem is Athens's best friend."

J. Budziszewski, University of Texas at Austin, and author of *The Line Through the Heart: Natural Law as Fact, Theory, and Sign of Contradiction*

WHEN ATHENS MET JERUSALEM

An Introduction to Classical and Christian Thought

JOHN MARK REYNOLDS

IVP Academic

An imprint of InterVarsity Press
Downers Grove, Illinois

InterVarsity Press
P.O. Box 1400, Downers Grove, IL 60515-1426
World Wide Web: www.ivpress.com
E-mail: email@ivpress.com

InterVarsity Press® is the book-publishing division of InterVarsity Christian Fellowship/USA®, a movement of students and faculty active on campus at hundreds of universities, colleges and schools of nursing in the United States of America, and a member movement of the International Fellowship of Evangelical Students. For information about local and regional activities, write Public Relations Dept., InterVarsity Christian Fellowship/USA, 6400 Schroeder Rd., P.O. Box 7895, Madison, WI 53707-7895, or visit the IVCF website at <www.intervarsity.org>.

Design: Cindy Kiple
Images: Monica Farling/iStockphoto

ISBN 978-0-8308-2923-1

Printed in the United States of America ∞

 InterVarsity Press is committed to protecting the environment and to the responsible use of natural resources. As a member of Green Press Initiative we use recycled paper whenever possible. To learn more about the Green Press Initiative, visit <www.greenpressinitiative.org>.

Library of Congress Cataloging-in-Publication Data

Reynolds, John Mark, 1963-
   When Athens Met Jerusalem: an introduction to classical and
   Christian thought/John Mark Reynolds.
     p. cm.
   Includes bibliographical references and index.
   ISBN 978-0-8308-2923-1 (pbk.: alk. paper)
   1. Christianity—Origin. 2. Philosophy, Ancient. 3.
   Christianity—Philosophy. I. Title.
   BR129.R49 2009
   261.5'1—dc22
                2009000457

P	16	15	14	13	12	11	10	9	8	7	6	5	4	3	2	1
Y	22	21	20	19	18	17	16	15	14	13	12	11	10	09		

To Three Who Made It Possible:

Al Geier, Father of My Logos

J. P. Moreland, Friend and Mentor

Phillip Johnson, Way Maker and Godfather

And to the Hidden Fourth, My Hope

CONTENTS

PREFACE

CHRISTIANS ARE NOT IN HEAVEN YET, but we do live in Christ's kingdom: Christendom.

Christendom was born, in part, out of the intellectual influence of Greco-Roman and Jewish thought. Greco-Roman thought developed over eight centuries of intellectual history. The story of Greek philosophy and how it helped prepare the way for Christendom has not recently been told from a Christian perspective in a sympathetic and accessible manner. *When Athens Met Jerusalem* tells this story of Greco-Roman intellectual preparation for the coming of the Christ.

When the apostle Paul stood on Mars Hill in Athens (Acts 17:16-34), he faced a listening audience prepared by centuries of discussion. Because Paul understood the intellectual baggage and issues of his day, he was able to impact and change the direction of that discussion. Paul changed the Greek and Roman intellectual world that day.

Anybody who lives in a place with a Christian heritage, even if that heritage lies mostly in the past, needs to understand the relationship that developed between Christian ideas and Greek philosophy. To do that, one first needs to understand the development of Greek and Roman thought. Christian theology has shaped and is still shaping many places in the world, and it was the Greeks who contributed a philosophical language to Christianity.

The church fathers are incomprehensible without knowledge of Greek philosophy. Thomas Aquinas, whose ideas still shape much of Christian philosophy and theology, relied heavily on an interplay of Greek categories, vocabulary and concepts. The Protestant Reformers, especially the classically educated Calvin, also were deeply influenced by Greek thought.

Of course, Christians did not just copy Greek ideas. They accepted some, modified others and freely used Greek categories and vocabulary. When they rejected Greek ideas, as they often did, even that rejection shaped Christendom by helping to define what it is *not*.

For non-Christians, such cultural ignorance is dangerous. Christianity and ancient Greek thought are built into the "operating system" of the West. Like using a computer without knowing anything about the operating system, unless you are lucky such ignorance is likely to cause harm.

Other areas of culture, such as literature, music and art, assume a working knowledge of Greek and Roman ideas. It is hard to make sense of the paintings of Rossetti without knowing something about Plato. The Narnia books by C. S. Lewis are even better when the reader can trace the author's masterful use of classical philosophy. Even the Disney film *Pocahontas* makes use of lines borrowed from Greek philosophers, leaving little doubt that Greece pervades Western pop culture.

Finally, Christendom was born in a time much like the start of the twentieth century. Religious uncertainty and change were in the air. Old ideas had failed spectacularly, but new ideas had not yet taken their place. Christians faced a cultural, political and social environment that was both attractive and, at least in part, hostile to the gospel. How they were able to not only survive but also thrive and create a better, more appealing culture is a good lesson for all Christians today. Even non-Christians, who may be swayed by facile attacks on the cultural importance or benefits of Christianity, can utilize such knowledge for better and more constructive conversations with the billion human beings who are followers of Jesus.

ACKNOWLEDGMENTS

I WOULD LIKE TO THANK Fieldstead and Associates for the grant that made the initial research for this book possible. Howard and Roberta Ahmanson had the vision to make the Torrey Honors Institute and this book reality.

Paul Spears and Fred Sanders, colleagues and leaders at the Torrey Honors Institute at Biola University, patiently listened to these ideas. Much of the good here is due to them, though the errors are my own.

John Mark N. Reynolds

INTRODUCTION

Athens and Jerusalem

ON THE AREOPAGUS

The view from the Acropolis of twenty-first-century Athens showed a group huddled together on the ancient Mars Hill, reading in the blazing heat of the midday summer sun. I sat with forty students from the Torrey Honors Institute of Biola University reading the seventeenth chapter of Acts. The blue sky of Greece stretched over us, and it was hot, but we did not want to leave that scene or stop our conversation. Behind us on the Acropolis were the shining white ruins of the Parthenon, the temple dedicated to Athena. To our right was the marketplace where a man named Socrates asked the impertinent questions that killed him. To our left was the place where the first and perhaps some of the greatest theater ever produced saw light. Before us in the distance was the tumultuous sea that Homer pictured in his *Odyssey*.

This hill was the final goal of our trip to Europe, but not merely because of the great history and culture of Greece. We were on a pilgrimage to Athens mostly because of the sermon that was preached here by a Jewish rabbi, Saint Paul, when he brought the gospel to Greece. We came for the ancient church, still standing, that lifts up the cross in the center of the pagan marketplace. We came to sit under the highest hill in Athens, with its great chapel dedicated to Saint George the dragon slayer. We knew that Saint Paul, too, had slayed a great serpent: the idolatry of Greece. Paul's victory changed everything. We knew we were children from the marriage of two cultures. On Mars Hill, we were standing at the birthplace of our true country: Christendom.

Christianity was born out of Judaism. One cannot understand the second covenant without grasping the first. The great spiritual revelation of God to Moses and to the Jewish people is the unalterable core of Christian belief.

In God's great providence, Christianity was born at a time when Greek and Roman thought dominated the ancient world and influenced everyone and everything—including the Jews and Judaism. Christendom, the culture of Christians after Jèsus' life, death and resurrection, was the product of Christians making sense of both Greek and Jewish heritages. This is the story of the Greek heritage of Christendom.

THE REALLY ANCIENT WORLD

The Greeks had a bible of sorts, a primary set of documents foundational to the way they thought. The *Iliad* and the *Odyssey,* written down by the legendary poet Homer, gave the Greeks fixed stories about humans and gods that could be used to form a coherent view of reality. Homer's masterful and moving poems shaped the language and the direction of the culture. His religion became the basis for some of the first unifying social structures in Greece, including the rise of the great oracle at Delphi.

Homer is a hidden part of many conversations in the modern world. He lurks in the basement of ideas with his notion (shared by another early Greek writer Hesiod) that chaos may be at the bottom of everything. Homer taught human beings to fear the gods—not in the Judeo-Christian sense of awe and love, but in terms of terror. His great study of the Trojan War, the *Iliad,* begins in war and ends there. His is a hard view of reality, skeptical about progress for humans who are born into pointless struggle with gods and nature, a torment that does not even end in death.

While the oracles of the Homeric gods may have been officially silenced, the intellectual possibilities presented by Homer have not. When a modern is skeptical and hopeless about finding real goodness, truth or beauty, then he or she imitates Homer. It is a terrifying and stultifying vision. Some ancient Greeks recognized that there was a problem with merely relying on the poetic imagination to guide their society. Without denying the beauty of Homer, Greeks who loved the truth began to think about the foundations of their culture.

THE LOVE OF WISDOM AND THE WAY
OF CONVERSATION

Thinking may be hard at first, but it is addictive with practice. People created in God's image will ask questions, and questions demand answers. Answers seem to be what questions are *for,* but the Greeks soon realized that the first answers were not the end of the process. Good answers lead to better questions, and these questions keep the process of learning alive. It is possible to find a single truth, but one truth has a tendency to lead to the search for another, just as eating one honest-to-goodness potato chip generally demands a second.

People began to question the old answers, sometimes finding them satisfying and sometimes not. Crudely at the start, men like Thales tried to describe the world more rationally. These first thinkers were often dogmatic themselves, but they lacked the power to impose their thoughts on their successors. This led to an explosion of different ideas that stood in contrast to the stagnation of the Homeric view.

Sadly, philosophy was no more lucrative in ancient times than it is today. Developing a new theory of "everything" provided no pay for the first philosophers, but teaching the students of the rich did. The philosophers learned that cleverness sells, but too much contention with the establishment does not. They became Sophists, willing to sell their skills, especially in rhetoric, for money. Sophists were willing to *say* anything, but they were not willing to encourage their students to *act* on those teachings. They were daring talkers but prudent actors.

One of these teachers, Socrates, refused to play by these wicked rules. He would not limit his questions or his actions in order to fit into conventional Greek society. Socrates taught through conversation and the skillful use of questions. These questions were not just for the sake of talking but for finding a good life to live.

Socrates' daring got him killed by the religious and academic establishment, but he left behind an inspired generation of students to carry on his legacy. The greatest of these students was Plato, a writer equal to Homer in imagination and power, and one of greatest philosophers who ever lived. Plato captured conversational learning in his dialogues. In these writings he challenged readers to interact with characters in his stories and so find a philosophical way of living. His dialogues challenged the power of the traditional Homeric despair, but did so indirectly, thus preserving Plato's life and school against the criticisms of the powerful supporters of the old gods. Plato began to be the master of those who doubt and dare to follow their doubts to new and dangerous ideas.

Plato's best student was the philosopher Aristotle. If Plato was the master of the question, then Aristotle was the expert of the declarative sentence. Aristotle was "the master of those who know."[1] He pioneered formal logic and examined the natural world in the most systematic manner up to that point in history. He also consciously reflected on those thinkers who came before him and tried to respond to their ideas in his own writings. In this way, Aristotle was the forerunner of modern scholars who do not start their investigations as if nothing came before them but begin their own work aware of the "great conversation" they are joining. Interesting things happened in philosophy after Aristotle, but no figure matched the gigantic influence of Socrates, Plato and Aristotle.

Eventually philosophy stagnated because it lost track of the conversation and struggled to unite the needs of all classes of people. Tyrants like Alexander the Great, Aristotle's most famous pupil, made freedom of inquiry even more difficult. Philosophy became private or fell prey to strange and irrational religion. The desire to do philosophy did not dry up, and in fact it grew in centers like Alexandria, but the quality was low. Ideas after Aristotle multiplied but did not progress. There is a great deal of water in a swamp, but it doesn't go anywhere. The man who had the answer to this stagnation was Saint Paul.

THE CULTURE OF ATHENS AND JERUSALEM

Christianity in the East and the West formed cultures that had roots both in the classical world of Greece and Rome and in the faiths of Jerusalem, Christianity and (less comfortably) Judaism. This is true in the Christian West, where both Greek and Jewish thought shaped the architectural ideas that produced the cathedrals of Paris. The parliamentary government of Britain has roots in both the democracy of Athens and the law of Moses.

It is also true in the Christian East. Eastern Christendom formed a new empire that shielded Western Europe from invasion and destruction. For one thousand years the great capital city, Constantinople, main-

---

[1]Dante *Inferno* 4.131.

tained unbroken study of both ancient biblical and pagan texts. It honored both the "inner wisdom" of the faith and the "outer wisdom" of the Greeks and Romans. Constantinople evangelized an entire commonwealth of states that stretched from the Balkans to Russia.

This fusion of Athens and Jerusalem can be seen in the buildings and the books of cities in Britain, Ethiopia, Romania and the United States. It is no accident that the United States Supreme Court is housed in a building with biblical references carved onto a structure built in the classical style of Rome and Greece.

Athens and Jerusalem became partners very early in the history of the church. A group of Jewish disciples of Jesus were confronted by the fact of his resurrection, and they went on to preach the good news to the Roman Empire—basically the whole world in which they lived. Rome was dominated by the ideas of Greece, which in turn had been dominated by the ideas of Athens. Religion and philosophy had a Greek flavor in every part of the empire. How did the church deal with the massive intellectual and cultural heritage of this classical civilization?

One reaction was to reject "secular learning" to keep the church pure. Theology had nothing to learn from philosophy. "What has Athens to do with Jerusalem?" thundered Tertullian, a champion of keeping the two far apart.[2] A great deal as it turned out, since Tertullian's own writings echoed Greek philosophy on nearly every page.

Judaism itself had been influenced by Greek learning. There was no "pure" stream of knowledge that did not run through Athens. The very Greek language that the early Christians used to communicate their message was soaked in centuries of classical thought. Trying to pry Athens and Jerusalem apart usually led to inconsistency and heresy.

Tertullian ended up trapped in the heresy of Montanism, which taught that Jesus was going to land the New Jerusalem in a remote backwater of the Roman Empire. Private revelations to wild prophets stood on par with Scripture. Jerusalem without Athens becomes a weird place.

Sometimes the church went to the other extreme and worshiped Athens. Persecution made this rare, but it was still a problem. Origen, one

---

[2]Tertullian *Prescription Against Heretics* 7.

of the greatest Christian thinkers of the early church, often pinned his understanding of Scripture more on his Neo-Platonic philosophy than on the biblical text. His literary analysis of the text of Genesis often found hidden spiritual meanings invisible to anyone not brought up on Neo-Platonic philosophy. This excessive devotion to Plato caused Origen to develop a defective view of Christ and his nature. Jerusalem could not be reduced to a suburb of Athens without endangering the faith.

Mainstream Christians, such as Augustine in the West and Basil in the East, found a middle way. Jerusalem gave the basic, rational, religious truth on which to build an understanding of the world. It was the starting place for wisdom. Athens gave the technical language and categories to help define and extend this truth. Jerusalem gave the world truth; Athens gave it a valid way to express that truth. Out of this creative harmony came the classical Christian civilizations that shaped most of the world in which we live.

ATHENS AND JERUSALEM SEPARATE

For centuries these two cities, Athens and Jerusalem, provided the boundaries for intellectual and cultural growth. They formed one new kingdom. Tensions between the rationalism of Athens and the faith of Jerusalem always existed, but each recognized the contributions made by the other. Eventually, however, the citizens of both cities grew restless.

One product of classical Christian civilization was modern science. Secular, scientific answers seemed to make religious truth and boundaries not only unnecessary but stifling. Athens began to pull away from Jerusalem. In the process, what was best in the old Greek and Roman tradition was also discarded. The moderation and humility so prized by the ancients was forgotten. Science would answer all questions and solve all problems. The old classical Christian civilization began to crumble.

Others have noted the decline of this classical Christian culture.[3] The sort of society that produced John Chrysostom, Thomas Aquinas or C. S. Lewis no longer exists. Christians on the right and on the left have foolishly taken joy in the destruction.

---

[3]See Phillip Johnson, *Reason in the Balance* (Downers Grove, Ill.: InterVarsity Press, 1995).

Some Christians have moved to Athens while keeping a summer home in Jerusalem. For them, the rationalism of Athens, by now reduced mainly to science, dictates the nature of reality. Jerusalem provides these accommodating Christians with personal peace, as religion is seen as a vacation from the harsh realities of a Neo-Darwinian world. They allow for a shadowy divine providence to be unseen behind it all.

Jerusalem is allowed this marginal existence as long as it promises never to interfere with science. Statements such as "God created the heavens and the earth" (Genesis 1:1) are reduced to "spiritual" truths with no physical content. Even some Christian colleges are dominated by this spirit. Religion is kept firmly in line, and faculty members are petrified of their Athenian masters. Jerusalem, like many vacation homes, is filled with yesterday's furniture. No one lives there; they just hang out there on weekends and holidays.

Other Christians have condemned Athens and left it to burn. They do not mourn the death of classical Christian culture. These pious souls have locked themselves inside Jerusalem and are not coming out until the war is over. Armed with Bible verses, they glare over the walls and leave the rest of the world alone. When the world returns the favor, they complain that the truth is being ignored.

I once spoke in a church about the sinful hatred many Christians have for Athens. After my talk, an older person came up to me and said that this hatred was a sign of revival! In her view, Christianity should be all about feeling and never about thinking. Thinking, she thought, leads to doubting, and doubting is a way of life in apostate Athens.

Such faithful Christian folk try to avoid reasoning altogether, only to end up reasoning badly. Any attempt to understand the Bible requires reason. Christians often go on for years after their conversion with a fully functioning mind but no guidance on how to use it. They have questions. They try not to reason them out, so they simply reason without training. Trapped within these walls, an inbred Jerusalem becomes a bit crazy.

STUDYING ATHENS WHILE LIVING IN JERUSALEM

Christians must recapture the middle way of Augustine and Chrysostom. Athens and Jerusalem are not two cities, but two districts in one city: the city of God.[4] There are hopeful signs that such a revival can happen. Sales of classical tales have reached bestseller lists in the Christian community. Christian day schools and a few colleges have seized on the classical model. A progressive conservatism that preserves the best of the past while using modern tools has a growing number of supporters. When allowed to coexist, Athens and Jerusalem create a cultural explosion. They have done so in the past and will do so again, if an attempt at revival is made soon.

Christians must act quickly, for Athens and Jerusalem are dying and each needs the other to thrive. Athens has been sacked by secular barbarians who chain rationalism to materialistic science. Science can do useful things, but it knows nothing about truth, goodness and beauty. Science cannot subsume virtue to its limited methods, so it must deny the existence of virtue if scientists wish to control all knowledge.

Athens, the rational mind, does not by itself have the resources it needs to deal with the most important things. The ancient Greeks knew this, which was why so many of them were eager to embrace Christianity. We are learning the same lesson again, the hard way. The fashionable cynicism called postmodernism is merely the tired realization that rationalism without faith ends up destroying its own foundations.

Jerusalem, too, is sick. Its inbred residents, who cannot even do the sort of classical theology that produced their own creeds, sit in their ghetto talking only to themselves. Ironically, her ruling class is often composed of absentee landlords. They live in Athens and only show up in Jerusalem to collect their tithes. These rulers reject the creeds, since Athens has rejected both the religion and the classical thought behind them, but cannot substitute much of anything in their place. So the church offers the spectacle of evangelicals who believe the Bible contains errors and Anglican bishops who do not believe in God.

Neither secular nor Christian culture has modern or postmodern answers. Real accommodation between Jerusalem and a scientific or postmodern Athens is impossible. Some contemporary theologians try to dialogue with postmodernity, but this is impossible without denying

---

[4]Augustine *City of God* 1.pref.

their Christian heritage. The creeds are written in elegant and precise Greek. They make bold assertions about God and reality. The early Christians could do this because they believed their ideas were true. Move very far from those ideas as the mainstream church has understood them, and basic orthodoxy and Christian identity come into question. To be truly Christian, after all, was to believe some things and not to believe others. That very idea, however, makes conversation with those who deny logic in their religion impossible.

It is an odd world. The rationalists believe that Christian doctrines are false. The postmodernists think that all doctrines have only an "inner" or personal truth. Christians are too afraid of losing to engage in the discourse, so Athens cannot hear what Jerusalem has to say.

Yet they are like a married couple that begins to look alike after many years of marriage. The very shape of theological discourse has a Greek tone. Jerusalem cannot praise the nature of the Holy Trinity without echoing the language of pagan philosophers. Athens has discovered that it cannot go it alone either. Science without God, intellect without theology, is rapidly becoming anti-knowledge. If you cannot know *the* truth, then even small "truths" can be called into question. Athens and Jerusalem cannot live apart.

Any hope of reviving Christian cultures must begin by understanding what they are and from whence they come. At one time every educated person was familiar with both Greek and Christian foundational ideas, but no longer. The renewed study of the ancients, both Greek and Christian, is vital for any new beginning for classical civilization.

Knowledge of ancient Athens is vital for Christians. Some see it as the starting place for the flowering of new classical Christian civilizations. Human reason, unscarred by an irrational desire to rid itself of Christianity, will flourish. As Christians move toward the classical model, they must also be aware of the mistakes and dangers along the path. We cannot just reclaim the Academy, we must remake it. Modern Athens is not what it once was.

Ancient Athens has been harmed by modernity every bit as much as ancient Jerusalem. The irony is that secularists have no more use for old books and writers than the most anti-intellectual Christians. One can graduate with an advanced degree from elite colleges in the United States without having read a single classical author, or at least with any care.

As humans have remodeled and destroyed ancient Athens, they have also sacked Jerusalem. It was, after all, a man hostile to both classical and Christian ideas who, while sitting by a lake in Switzerland, developed the ideological formula that has captured the times. He knew that fallen human beings were interested in personal peace, often at any cost. He understood that contemporary people were driven by economic desires and believed that the promise of a place to call one's own could be an adequate substitute for religion. This philosophy would gain appeal in democratic, capitalistic, totalitarian and socialistic societies. Lenin summed up the spirit of his age in 1917 with his revolutionary call to reduce human happiness to "Peace, Bread, and Land."[5]

Classical and Christian thinkers did not agree, knowing that goodness is often better than peace bought at the price of allowing evil. They knew that the quest for truth was more important than personal affluence. Whether in the monastic community or in compassionate capitalism, they knew it was the truth, not wealth, that would set humans free. Finally, classical and Christian humanists believed that "stuff" could not satisfy if there was no beauty. Mere consumption or production was not enough. There were standards of beauty to which every civilization should aspire. Classical Christian civilizations answered this age with a cry for "the good, the true and the beautiful."

Christians are not alone in this longing. Every human is created in the divine image and can become like God by his mercy. The image of God in every human being longs for him to return home. We are all homesick. Though far from home, a few gifted souls know what they are missing. The longing for the good, the true and the beautiful leads to love. This love is the way of wisdom. The love of wisdom was not exclusive to ancient Greece, but Greeks first recognized what it was and pursued it continuously. When English speakers use the word *philosophy,* which is derived from Greek and means "love of wisdom," they honor that heritage.

---

[5]April 1917.

1

BUILDING ATHENS

Philosophy Before Socrates

✣

PRE-SOCRATIC PHILOSOPHY

The ideas of Athens had founders, people known as philosophers. Socrates may be considered the first great philosopher, but these were his ancestors. These pre-Socratic philosophers began the process of thinking about the world in a systematic and rational manner.

The pre-Socratics lived so long ago that most of their work is forgotten. These first philosophers started writing during the early part of the sixth century before Christ. The people of Israel were creating the Old Testament, thus building the divine foundations for Zion, while the pre-Socratics were laying the foundation for Athens. These men began the long conversation about the role of faith and reason in the good life. If Christians are going to cultivate a relationship with philosophical Athens, they must begin with the founding fathers of that city.

Old ideas often show up in new places, seemingly without warning. These half-forgotten concepts are like recessive family traits that can pop up unexpectedly. It can bring a pleasant surprise, like the first red-haired daughter in two generations, or it can be dangerous, like a son born with hemophilia. The ideas of the pre-Socratics have been with Western civilization so long that it is easy to forget them. Sometimes pieces of these ancient systems of thought lie buried in a book only to be revived later. Handed down like recessive traits, they can appear many generations later with interesting results. Many of the ideas of the New Age movement can be traced back to the pre-Socratic philosophers. Is everything full of "gods"? The pre-Socratic Anaximander thought so long before the local psychic hotline got interested.

Other pre-Socratic ideas have made their way into the Christian faith. Many Christians sing the old hymn "This Is My Father's World." They may not realize it, but when they sing of the "music of the spheres," they are repeating a bit of Pythagorean philosophy. Is that good or bad? To answer that question, Christians must understand what the Pythagoreans believed and how it came into the Christian faith.

Is the foundation for Athens—for Western civilization—sound? There may be cracks buried deep in the basement walls that have helped to undermine Western culture. We can only find answers by learning what the great-grandparents of modernity believed.

BEFORE PHILOSOPHY:
HOMER, HESIOD AND MYTHOLOGY

Ancient people without God were like schoolchildren without teachers. They were ready and eager to learn, but they did not have even the basic categories to make a start. Everything had to be learned. Even the Jewish people, with the advantage of divine guidance, took centuries to learn basic lessons about the nature of creation. Think how difficult the lessons about idol worship were for the Hebrews, even with God's close oversight. For the Greeks and other pagan peoples, the task began only with the common grace from God's divine image within humans. It is not surprising that they made mistakes. It is a miracle that they did so well. To study the Greek thinkers before their contact with Christianity is to see the best that human reason and imagination is capable of without divine revelation.

When God appeared to Moses in the burning bush and said, "I AM," he answered some vital questions. The Jews learned that God was real and that he had something to say. Over time, God also revealed himself as the Creator and the only true God. Just as important to human history, he was good. He was not deceitful or whimsical. Humans could rely on him. God's universe was good.

The Greeks did not have the luxury of this divine shortcut to the truth. Left to themselves, the Greeks saw two options: either the world was at bottom chaotic, or it was orderly. A chaotic world may seem livable for a while, but then "stuff happens." There is no sense complaining about it, though it might make a person feel better to do so. There is no reason to complain when chance produces unexpected outcomes that humans do not like. In a chaotic world, there is no ultimate reason for anything. There is no design, no plan.

Even a wise person looking at the apparent futility of human existence can easily decide that meaning is an illusion. An entire culture can decide that there is no ultimate truth, goodness or measure of beauty. Stuff happens and then you die. Before philosophy, Greek religion bought into this realism born of despair that had no end.

The Greek afterworld was a place of darkness and gloom. Humans, even great heroes like Achilles, became gibbering shades when they died. The dead Achilles would rather be a living swineherd. All human glory is nothing in the ultimate resting place, the Stygian gloom of the Greek afterlife. Hope convinces humans that there is a chance to beat the fate of all mortals, but hope is always a fraud.

This is the world of Greek mythology. The gods, including the most powerful, Zeus, were neither creators nor good. They were themselves the offspring of other darker gods. Hesiod, who compiled some of the seminal stories of the gods in his *Theogony,* saw everything springing from chaos and night. Zeus himself was not the first of the gods, nor would he be the last; he was one of many. The intrigue and bickering of the gods on Mount Olympus rivaled that of the most dysfunctional household. There was no justice in the actions of Hesiod's gods. Power was everything, and the gods acted on their whims. If they lusted, they raped or wooed. It made no difference to them.

Homer, the greatest Greek poet and mythmaker, pictured gods who used humans as playthings in the famous Trojan War. The war began with a petty quarrel between the gods to determine which of the female deities was the fairest, and it grew to swallow up human heroes. The irrationality of the war was matched by the futility of human existence itself. Mortal man was doomed to die. Unlike the beasts, humans were aware of their own immortality, but strive as they might, they could not overcome it.

Humans could not escape their fate no matter how powerful their passions. The first word of Homer's *Iliad,* the magnificent poem about the Trojan War, can be translated "divine wrath." The Greek hero Achilles possesses this godlike passion and was the ideal warrior. His anger, so potent it condemns hundreds of Greeks to death, does nothing but destroy everything he loves. He is a man with only one weakness, the famous Achilles' heel, but that is enough. He falls. He is merely a man.

Goodness and beauty are also without power or ultimate meaning in the Homeric world. In the *Iliad,* the Trojan hero, Hector, is the most sympathetic of the heroes. He hates the endless war and knows that Troy is doomed to defeat. He fights for honor and to protect his beloved wife and son for as long as he can. He knows they will die as slaves, and he cannot bear the thought. Homer shows the great love between Hector and his wife in a passionate encounter between the two on the walls of Troy. Though Hector loves his wife, his son and his city, it is all futile. He will die. Nothing can save him.

This point is made even more clearly in Homer's *Odyssey.* The Greek hero Odysseus tries to return home at the end of the Trojan War. Odysseus is a warrior sick of war, whose victory has proven hollow. Odysseus wants nothing more than to go home, but the gods force him to do more great deeds. The warrior eventually sees his home again, but only after many sorrows. There is no good reason for his torment. It is simply the will of the gods and the bad fortune of Odysseus.

In one part of his journey, Odysseus visits Hades and sees the hopeless fate of the human dead. He recognizes that all the fame won in the Trojan War means nothing in the face of death. Is the answer to become a god? Even if it were possible, Homer shows that it would not suffice. The goddess Calypso holds Odysseus for ten years. She desires him and wishes to keep him with her on her island. Yet when Calypso offers Odysseus immortality, he declines it. The goddess offers him every pleasure without end, but Odysseus sits "sobbing great tears"[1] on the edge of her pleasure-

---

[1] Homer *Odyssey* 5.83.

filled island. Humans cannot be happy in the life of the gods because they are not built for divine pleasures. Those things cannot satisfy. They need their own place, even if that place cannot last long.

These earliest Greeks, faced with a world of chaos, produced great art and great literature. They did not produce great philosophy or great science. Their worldview gave them no reason to look for the underlying order and meaning that is necessary to motivate great thinking. The literature of Homer formed a bible for the ancient Greeks. His ideas were everywhere, saturating every level of Greek culture.

Some Homeric fundamentalists actually claimed that all knowledge was to be found in the *Iliad* and the *Odyssey*. Want to know the proper way to drink wine? There is a passage in Homer linking wine drinking with onions, so that is how it should be done! Most Greeks did not go so far, but Greek art, literature and drama often were centered on Homeric themes and characters. If Christians are people of the Book, the earliest Greeks where people of the epic poem.

The world of Hesiod and Homer was the world of myth. Mere storytelling had to suffice to explain the human condition in a world where truth was as changeable as the will of the gods. The hard, certain truths of mathematics and science were foreign to a culture steeped in mystery, dread and doubt. If this world had a certain beauty, it was in the courage and moderation with which the Greeks faced what they feared was true. The gods and blind fate were whimsical and often evil. One faced them with resignation and perhaps a moderate piety that would draw neither their love nor their hatred, since both were equally fearful.

This pessimism about the world led to small-scale thinking. Despite their common cultural core of Homer, language and history, the Greeks resisted unification. Local gods were worshiped in local ways. The Zeus of Athens had different traits from the Zeus of Thebes. What else could one expect when the gods lacked firm character? Religion was not tied to history because history itself was simply the pliable means to justify the power of a particular dynasty. If you wanted to rule a Greek city, you could always claim that some god raped your grandmother, thus picking up the semidivine status you would need to claim the rights of a ruler.

Ethics and politics in Greek cities had a local take as well. The hometown rules, if they worked for the city, were good because they were the hometown rules. The rules in the next town might be different. Athens came to value art and commerce, while Sparta learned to despise them. Which city was correct? The Homeric response would be, "My city is correct for me."

The Greeks never abandoned the idea that their own city-state, or polis, was everything that mattered. In a senseless world, the individual could find higher meaning only in the company of like-minded individuals. This extended family, which in the early days was actually related by blood, was what gave the solitary Greek purpose. A man or woman might die, but the polis would go on. Everything, even the polis and the Olympian gods, would be supplanted in the end, but till then the polis might endure for many generations. Greeks came to prefer death to exile from their own polis. Like the weeping Odysseus on Calypso's island, a Greek who had to live in another city still knew he or she was not home. A common cultural heritage and language were not enough to unify ancient Greece.

Moderns who try to return to the worship of the old Greek gods do not realize what these gods were like before the coming of philosophy and Christianity. Having forgotten Christianity and abandoned reason, people are returning to the chaotic gods of the past. They hope to be liberated from sexual inhibitions, patriarchy and a host of other perceived ills of Western culture, but what they get is a return to chaos and irrationality. There may be the appearance of beauty, but there is no basis on which to build a universal culture.

THE IONIAN MIRACLE

The philosophers tried to free Greek culture from the dreadful fear that chaos was at the bottom of the world order. By thinking rationally about the world, they hoped to establish that it was a cosmos—an orderly place—not chaos. Did humans live in a universe, having one rule or guiding principle, or did they live in a "multiverse," where rationality had no long-term place? At first glance the world looked chaotic, but on deeper reflection the design, order and unity of the cosmos was seen. Paganism, the worship of the old gods, could not survive that assault. By the time of Christ, most educated Greeks worshiped the old gods merely out of civic obligation. The masses may have believed the myths, but thoughtful people had long ago rejected their truths as literal. This process of liberation did not begin in the city of Athens but in the coastal region of Ionia.

Because Greek culture was based in the small political unit of the polis, it tended to split and multiply. By the fifth century B.C., small Greek cities could be found all over the Mediterranean world. There were important Greek cities, such as Syracuse and Locri, in Sicily and Italy, and Greek settlements would eventually reach as far north as southern Russia. But the heart of Greek culture remained the coastal area surrounding the Aegean Sea, including the area that forms the modern nation of Greece. In the fifth century B.C., however, it was the Greek cities on the coastal region of Asia Minor (modern-day Turkey) that had intellectual leadership. The ancients called this collection of cities Ionia. They were the center of Greek cultural life until conquest by the Persian Empire sapped their strength. The first recorded philosophers lived in this region.

Not much is known about the first philosophers of Ionia, and none of their works have survived to the present day. Everything that is known about them comes from quotations of their works in other writings. There are important summaries of pre-Socratic views in the writings of Aristotle, and some important quotations survive in the work of Aristotle's disciple Theophrastus. Given the treatment these writers gave those whose works are still available, such as Plato, one cannot have great confidence that these summaries were always done fairly. Later writers had their own agendas to advance, and they were not above bending the views of earlier philosophers either to support their own arguments or to make others more easily refuted.

Studying the pre-Socratics is like putting together an intellectual jigsaw puzzle. One quotation here is matched to a fragment of an idea there and then connected to a citation in another work. The result often says more about the modern writer than about the actual thinking of the pre-Socratic philosopher being studied. Still, some things are known about the pre-Socratics that give us important insights about the shift from Homer to philosophy. The pre-Socratics did not complete this transformation of Greek culture, but they did begin it.

THALES: ESCAPING CHAOS

In the year 585 B.C. an Ionian philosopher named Thales accurately predicted an eclipse of the sun, and philosophy was born. His prediction was remarkable because it was not just a lucky guess but part of a well-ordered cosmology. Thales was not just interested in telling myths about the world. He wanted to find some unifying principle that would provide a rational basis, a foundation, for further investigation. This began a quest that would last for the next century: the search for an *archē,* or foundational point.

If one decides on the basic truth that the world is a cosmos and not chaos, then one is still left with two important questions: What is the basis or pattern for this unity? How does this unity come to be? The ability to explain why it is so is an important distinction between the merely mythical and the rational explanation of events. A rational explanation is often simple, objective and universal. Unlike Homeric religious explanations, such reasoning opens up an idea for use in other circumstances.

Greek myths were by nature local, intended to explain the details of a particular phenomenon by making up a story around the object in question. A particular mountain had that exact shape because of what some god did in a battle with the Titans. If some new fact about the mountain became known—for example, that it contained gold—the new detail was added to the story: the god bled on the mountain, and his immortal ichor was transformed into gold. This myth may have provided a reason for the shape of the mountain and the presence of gold, but it could not *explain* mountains in general or where gold is likely to be found. Myths could not be made universal unless the behavior of the gods was predictable. Greek religion presented gods whose behavior was interesting but frequently irrational. Given this, no Greek could have suggested that all mountains were shaped by battles between gods or that all gold was formed from their blood.

Rational reasons can be applied in more than one circumstance. They are simple and comprehensive. Thales wanted just this sort of explanation. He decided that the fundamental unity of the cosmos was a common basic material: water. Everything was made of water or came from water. Simple observation may have suggested to Thales that of the four

Greek elements (fire, water, earth and air), water is one of the most widespread and is associated with life and the generation of life. Living things are moist; dead things are dry.

How did water, an inanimate object, create order? A universe made of water by itself might not show any order whatsoever. Thales' answer to this problem is implicit in the second fact we know about his philosophy: he also believed everything was full of gods. At first this solution does not seem to be much of an improvement over simple mythology and Homer. Thales, however, "tamed" his gods and made them part of the cosmic order. He naturalized them, costing them their personality but also making them a predictable part of the cosmos. He did this by associating the gods with the idea of *soul*.

By filling the cosmos with divine soul, Thales associated the gods with the source of motion, hinted at in Homer and other early Greek literature. In these works the living human was composed of two parts: a body and a shadowy substance called soul. The soul was the source of motion for the human, and its departure made a dead human body still and without breath. Very early on, Greek writers suggested that soul was the source of all motion in the cosmos. The existence of magnetic rocks, which move toward each other of their own accord, suggested that motion is not confined only to living things. Thales may have noticed all these ideas and incorporated them into his cosmology. Since the cosmos seemed to endure, this soul had to be divine. It was the closest thing to immortality a naturalistic system could support. The notion that motion was divine also hinted at an intelligence or rationality undergirding all the changes that occur in the universe.

By filling the world with this naturalized divinity, Thales was able to explain how order could exist. The cosmos had a radical unity because all substance came from water and all motion came from soul. There was no need to worry about chaos in such a system. Soul would drive water through the unspecified changes necessary to produce all the individual pieces of the cosmos. There is no way to know if Thales fully worked out these concepts himself, but later Greek philosophers did.

So there were two options regarding the order of the universe. The first option was the one accepted by traditional Homeric religion: order is an illusion; at bottom it is all chaos, and every action is the product of chance. The second option is the path of Thales: order is real, and the universe is knowable because there is a rational cause for everything.

Most of the pre-Socratics, Thales included, wanted the cosmos itself to contain the divine intelligence needed to sustain order. Thales provided for this with his gods, the divine soul that was found in everything. Such a naturalized god was incapable of doing harm but also incapable of doing certain good things. The gods for Thales were not outside the system; humans, rocks, ships, plants—all contained divinity. How could a person differentiate between a rock and a woman? According to Thales, both elements were merely forms of water containing the divine. How could one of those god-infested bits of water reason about the rest? How could one become self-aware? How could one have more value than the other?

Thales protected thought from chaos at the expense of the self-identity of the thinker. Thales's very act of examining the cosmos placed him in the position of standing outside the cosmos, but he provided no place in his system for getting outside and looking at the whole.

ANAXIMANDER: ADVANCING THE SYSTEM

Thales set the pattern other Ionian philosophers would follow. First was the search for the basic substance, the *archē,* which provided unity of substance to the world. Second was the need for a rational cause of motion. Where did change come from? Thales had hinted at a rational source of motion with his gods that were part of everything. Anaximander, possibly a student of Thales, built on the work of his master. He gave answers where Thales had given only hints.

Anaximander believed that the unifying material of the cosmos was a strange substance called the *indefinite*. No one can be sure what Anaximander meant by this term. Was this *indefinite* simply another term for the *spatially infinite,* as Aristotle believed? Was it a substance without internal distinctions, a sort of protomatter? The only thing certain about this substance was that it was necessary to the system Anaximander created. He believed that the reason things worked the way they did depended on it.

Anaximander was not content, like Thales had been, with one unifying substance and source of motion. He wanted to provide a mechanism to get from the original substance to everything that currently existed, and he found this principle in the early Greek idea of opposition. The four basic Greek elements could easily be divided into two pairs of opposites: earth and water, fire and air. By associating each element with a particular attribute (hot—fire, cold—air, wet—water, dry—earth), Anaximander devised an appealing account of why things happen the way they do.

Change involved one of the elements "encroaching" on the domain of its opposite. If there was more dry earth, then there must be less wet water. If there was more cold air, then there must be less hot fire. These sensible observations formed the basis for his law of opposites: the universe is composed of substances with opposite properties that exist in inverse proportions.

Anaximander believed the encroachment of one substance on the other was "unjust." He developed the law of retribution to handle this injustice. A wet, cold stage of history would be followed by a stage that was equally dry and hot. Practically speaking, he predicted that unusually hot summers would be followed by very cold winters. Like Thales, Anaximander gave his cosmology a religious flavor. The indefinite—the base for the interchange of the opposites—was "divine."

We commonly picture the early philosophers as lacking a scientific method. It is true that they did not engage in all the research practices of a modern laboratory. Anaximander was, however, very interested in observation. He introduced the gnomon, which perfected the sundial for the Greeks. Anaximander also made one of the first important maps of the world based on the available knowledge of his day.

THE BIRTH OF SCIENCE:
NATURAL AND TELEOLOGICAL EXPLANATIONS

The pre-Socratics were fumbling to discover new ways of thinking about the world. They did not simply sit under a tree and speculate about the nature of the cosmos; rather they tried to develop theories to "cover" the observations collected by Greek citizens. Why do seasons change? Why does the coastline crumble here and advance there? The ideas of men like

Anaximander fit the data available at the time. As the coastline near one city advances, the water retreats. Further down the coast, the water might be washing away the walls of a different city. The law of opposites "covers" this observed phenomenon, but the pre-Socratics were open to changing their theories in light of further evidence.

A less productive development was the rise of naturalism and a preference for naturalistic explanations. Naturalism, the belief that there is no "supernatural," must have seemed an improvement on the chaotic religion of the Homeric sagas. Why did a thing happen? More and more the pre-Socratics shifted from personal or theological explanations to naturalistic ones. A god or hero did not do a thing; some basic force of nature did it. If everything that happens in the natural world is given a natural explanation, then the gods and the dangers of their unpredictable personalities have been removed.

The difficulty is that this methodology might be very fruitful in one area but less helpful in another. Humans have personality, and it is not always possible to reduce their actions to naturalistic explanations. Anyone familiar with children knows how impossible it is to predict exactly which ice cream a child will choose when confronted with fifty flavors.

The world has two kinds of change: personal and impersonal. The change of seasons seems regular without being personal. Naturalistic science can develop laws to explain such events. Other types of phenomena seem to resist naturalistic explanations. A person with a free will cannot be explained by natural laws because part of the explanation must take into account his or her freedom from constraint.

Greek religion was so irrational that it made early Greek philosophers resist any but naturalistic gods. Gods that were no better than humans could not explain or provide a basis for the cosmic order one observed when looking at the stars. Anaximander, like Thales before him, reduced the divine to a source of motion.

The lack of a personal god or an intelligent mind designing the cosmos made it impossible for pre-Socratics like Anaximander to explain regular phenomena in nature that resisted naturalistic explanations. Living things, even through the observations available at the time, seemed too elegantly constructed for crude mechanisms like Anaximander's. Anaximander believed humans came from fishlike ancestors living in a primordial slime. How could such a complex set of changes occur? Could the law of opposites explain this seemingly magical development? Later Greek philosophers, including Plato and Aristotle, would recognize this difficulty.

The problem of the origin of complex living things was coupled with the problem of *teleology* in nature. Many things look like they are made for a purpose. This purpose is the *telos* of the thing. Eyes are for seeing and seem to be made for seeing. Most living things, and many nonliving things, seem to be part of a pattern or plan. It is nearly impossible *not* to think that the sun is the way it is to produce energy so life can exist. Fully naturalistic systems cannot speak meaningfully to these problems. Things cannot have a reason for what they are, beyond mere accident.

To the Greek, this seemed dangerously close to a return to the chaos and meaninglessness of traditional religion. Each of the pre-Socratics, like Anaximander, brought the divine back into the cosmic scene. The "god" principle was reduced to some part of nature, but it never disappeared. To remove it entirely would be to lose the possibility of meaning or explanation of apparent purposefulness in natural things.

This created a fundamental tension in Greek pre-Socratic thought. A physical *archē* was substituted for the gods as the basic reason for existence. However, some "divine" claim was reintroduced to allow for purpose and meaning. Eventually the Greeks would split into two camps. The atomists would carry reductionism to its logical extreme and banish the divine entirely. The last great pre-Socratic, Anaxagoras, would postulate a divine mind apart from the cosmos.

ANAXIMENES

In the meantime, the quest for a better theory continued with Anaximander's associate, Anaximenes, who was the first to suggest that the cosmos was a rational animal. He made another, more sophisticated attempt to find a means to have both the rational and the natural exist in the same theory. The cosmos in which humans live makes sense because it is a reasonable being.

Anaximenes rejected both water and the indefinite as the first substance. Instead he suggested that air was the *archē,* of the universe. Air was often connected to the soul in early Greek writing. Air was the breath, or soul, of Anaximenes' cosmic animal, while also forming the body. Anaximenes had simplified his cosmology to the maximum extent possible.

The desire for the simplification of a theory became a trait of science. Done correctly, it prevents ad hoc theories and over-elaborate explanations. I once spent the afternoon cleaning the kitchen for my wife, Hope. I used bottles and bottles of cleaning products, some pulled from the very back of the cupboard. When Hope returned, she made it quite clear that the whole job could have been done with one basic cleaner. She reminded me pointedly of the lesson the pre-Socratics learned: it is inefficient to use four substances to do a job that can be done by one.

Taken too far, the tendency to simplify does not allow a philosopher or scientist to acknowledge data pointing toward a more complex answer. Information is ignored to save the gloriously simple and elegant theory. Having learned my lesson with the kitchen cleaners, I later attempted to use a single spray cleaner to take care of all the problems in the bathroom. Even if the brass did not polish up well, that still did not detract from my fierce joy in my efficiency. But Hope did not share my sanguine acceptance of dingy fixtures. She wanted clean brass, and this time she claimed I needed another cleaner. In the same way science may discover that natural explanations are good in one area but do not work well in another.

How could Anaximenes' "divine" air actually become every other substance in the world? He believed that the essential factor was the amount of air. He postulated that there was a process of condensation as air accumulated, which allowed for the creation of other elements. The air could also be "rarefied" to move from the denser elements back to pure air. Small amounts of air would remain pure as the "rational" air of the world soul. In humans when breath or air is passing in and out of the body, reason is possible; but when air stops, reason stops.

Condensation follows an orderly process. Thick air becomes fire. If more air is gathered together, then wind, clouds, water, earth and finally hard stones are created. The motion of condensation and rarefaction is constant. Though this system was wrong, it was the most highly developed one up to that point.

Anaximenes developed an elaborate picture of the cosmos to go with his physical theory. A dome of fixed stars moved around a flat earth. The sun was an earthlike planet ignited by its motion in the air of the heavens. Anaximenes attempted to develop a worldview that would explain everything. He may have been wrong, but it was a glorious attempt.

Anaximenes developed an open philosophy of science. His science was not limited to personality acting in the cosmos. He did not reduce thought to matter or matter to thought, but he took both the personal cause and the material cause seriously through a combination of personal agency (cosmic soul) and material causes (rarefaction and condensation). These were wrong explanations, but wrong explanations that are *falsifiable*.

Anaximenes was in this way more sophisticated philosophically than many of today's scientists. This is to be expected, though, since specialization has led far too many people to become philosophically illiterate. Moderns have forgotten the philosophy of science that makes their work possible.

XENOPHANES AND HERACLITUS:
A BETTER RELIGION FOR THE INTELLIGENT

Any philosopher who buries himself in dung to prove a point commands attention. There exists a story that Heraclitus of Ephesus took his philosophy to such extremes. How did he end up in such an absurd position?

In his search for the universal constant, the *archē,* Heraclitus settled on fire. He applied this to every element of his thought, including biology. Heraclitus reasoned that fire was the source of life because fire is warm. Dead bodies are cold, and living bodies are warm. Heraclitus was not just content with this simple confirmation. If life was fire, or warmth, then he had a key to health. As he began to feel the pangs of death, he decided that his body needed more warmth. What was a philosopher to do? He could not simply leap into a fire. Observation came to the rescue. On a cold day Heraclitus had seen piles of bovine excrement steaming in a field. Since this substance produced controlled heat, Heraclitus had himself buried in it. Sadly, too much of this good thing proved to be the philosopher's undoing. Anaximenes had been correct about one thing: air is good for living creatures. So Heraclitus died as the first martyr to a radical commitment to his scientific beliefs. Scientists and philosophers have been buried in their own zeal ever since.

Heraclitus was the first scientist-philosopher to cultivate the inscrutable image of a crank. He spoke in short, pithy, seemingly contradictory phrases. He was fond of saying things like "The way up is the way down." Biographers report that he refused to help his city with practical political questions. He would not play the expected part of the "wise man," and his attacks on traditional religion did not endear him to his fellow citizens. He left no actual writings, and the complete collection of his known sayings is very small indeed.

Despite all of this, no pre-Socratic philosopher has exercised a greater influence on the history of ideas. Hundreds of years later the Stoics would adopt him as their ideological father. Martin Heidegger wrote a book motivated by Heraclitus's thought. Heraclitus's cryptic style turned him into a sort of intellectual Rorschach test: philosophers can see in Heraclitus what they want to see.

Heraclitus used his predecessors' methods to develop his own cosmology. In this he was not particularly original or important, but he also was able to kick away the final traces of traditional Greek religion. That move was of critical importance. Since the concept of soul now explained personal agency, there was no need for the Greek gods. Physical events received physical explanations. Events produced by agents received personal (soul) explanations. Greek religion, which always had been hard to defend on ethical grounds, now had no cosmological job left.

It would have been possible to save Greek religion if Zeus would do things only in those cases where contemporary cosmology or understanding was limited. This was a losing strategy, however. Increasingly sophisticated cosmologies explained more and more natural events without recourse to divine intervention. In addition, the notion of soul fully explained all the intelligently produced actions of the universe without the invocation of the Greek pantheon.

Unlike certain contemporary religious thinkers, Heraclitus was not willing to save Greek religion simply because he had grown up with it. Heraclitus had the integrity not to appeal merely to the possible but to allow what was probable to be his guide. His cosmology and religious views could find no meaningful place or function for the bloody sacrifices of Greek pantheism, so he rejected them. A true iconoclast, Heraclitus reportedly rejected his family role as one of the rulers of the city. He demanded rationality from his religion, and Homer and Hesiod were incapable of meeting such demands.

Heraclitus was looking for unity. The ability of any situation to fragment was all too familiar to the ancient Greeks. What could provide unbreakable unity for the cosmos? The previous philosophers had provided two principles: soul and matter. Heraclitus gave a revised concept of soul—*cosmic intelligence*—priority and linked material and intelligent causation.

Fire unified matter, but fire was coextensive with a divine *Logos*. What was Logos? Heraclitus was the first to use this common Greek term for "word" in a technical manner. Eventually so many ideas became associated with Logos that today its definition in *Liddell and Scott's Greek-English Lexicon* takes up more than five single-spaced columns.

Heraclitus's Logos is hard to understand for just that reason. The philosopher took a common word and gave it a technical use. Later thinkers were all tempted to find their use of the term in Heraclitus. It is safest to say simply that Logos was the divine idea that held the universe together. In a cosmos of change, Logos gave order, pattern and form to nature.

This divine unity manifested itself in the traditional opposites, such as hot and cold, dry and wet. These opposites were stages of a process of change that is constant and under the supervision of the divine Logos. Heraclitus said, "You can never step into the same river twice."

Imagine Cleopatra standing on the banks of the mysterious Nile River. She steps into the water, and it swirls around her legs. More than two thousand years later, another young woman steps into the Nile. Her experience is both similar and different. She does not feel the *very* water that touched the queen of Egypt. The water in the river is constantly changing, but the river itself endures. The change and constancy of the universe are both metaphorically present in this experience.

I once stood before a centuries-old baptismal font. When I dipped my hand into the water at the bottom of the old stone bowl, I felt a connection with hundreds of other Christians who had done the same thing in times past. The water was always changing, but the font was the same.

More important, the idea behind my action was also the same. Put in terms of the philosophy of Heraclitus, it looks like this: the idea of baptism is the Logos of the universe, the font is the material expression of Logos, and the water of *this* baptism is the rapidly changing element. As a result, every baptism is unrepeatable and unique. Years later as I stood in church watching my daughter's baptism, I knew there would never be another baptism just like that of Jane Victoria Anastasia, but there would be other baptisms. There is constancy in the change of the world.

XENOPHANES

About the same time that Heraclitus was breaking free of the old Greek religion in Asia Minor, Xenophanes was doing the same thing in southern Italy and Sicily. By the close of the fifth century, Sicily and southern Italy began to assume an important position in Greek culture. The city of Syracuse was one of the largest and most important Greek cities in the ancient world. Xenophanes, who was born in Ionia, took philosophy to these urban centers.

The Greek colonies of Italy and Sicily would take philosophy in a more religious direction. If the thinkers of Ionia emphasized the naturalistic elements of cosmology, then these western Greeks focused more on the divine or "personal" parts. This sort of mystical philosophy had its first expression in the teachings of the semi-mythical Greek philosopher Pythagoras.

Pythagoras associated number and musical form with the order and complexity of the cosmos. His disciples made many advances in geometry, including the development of the theorem that is named after Pythagoras. They believed that the "certain" truths of geometry and mathematics would lead to certain knowledge about every other area. They influenced the writings of Plato, who at one point in his career visited Syracuse, but they had limited staying power on their own. Their primary work was negative. Like Heraclitus, they made it next to impossible for a thoughtful Greek or Roman to embrace traditional paganism. When intellectuals of latter-day Greek and Rome spoke of the gods, they usually did so metaphorically or to preserve the traditions of the state.

When Xenophanes came to the region, he brought Ionian methods with him. He was influenced by the intellectual atmosphere of Italy and began to attack traditional Greek theology. He believed that the gods were immoral and viewed their existence as suspect because they were created in the image of humans. After all, to paraphrase Xenophanes, "If cows had gods, they would paint them with horns."[2]

Xenophanes also developed a positive theology. He believed in one god who was "totally other." This god was unmoving and shook the world with his mind. Aristotle said that Xenophanes believed the "world simply to be equal to god," but this is hard to square with other comments that Xenophanes makes. He is vague about the nature of his god, but he does seem to need a separate god in his cosmology to secure a special place for humans and animals.

Xenophanes believed that humans and animals came from the sea. He was the first to explain the origin of living (and fossilized) creatures in a purely naturalistic manner, but this ran the risk of reducing humans and animals to machines. The god of Xenophanes' system would provide a rational basis for the unique properties of life.

Xenophanes did not need design in order to justify the existence of a god. Believers like Xenophanes used a designed cosmos to ground the assumption that their scientific theorizing was reasonable. The role of a god in science was epistemological and not a matter of "proof" for the god's existence. Such proofs would assume, as no Greek would have dared, that a rational person is surer of the truth of natural experiences than religious experiences. This is not good reasoning, and to their credit the Greeks made no such assumptions.

The existence of God shows that human thoughts have a chance of being sensible. Xenophanes' philosophy was alive to the possibilities of both divine and natural agency. This is a point that both Plato and Aristotle would exploit in their own more interesting theorizing. Being open to divine action did not lead Xenophanes to explain everything in divine terms. He believed the sun to be ignited daily from a nightly collection of fire in the heavens, giving a natural cause for what had been explained

---

[2]"But if cattle or lions had hands, so as to paint with their hands and produce works of art as men do, they would paint their gods and give them bodies in form like their own—horses like horses, cattle like cattle" (Xenophanes, frag. 6, in *The First Philosophers of Greece,* ed. and trans. Arthur Fairbanks [London: K. Paul Trench, Trubner, 1898], p. 67).

supernaturally in traditional Greek religion. On the other hand, he was willing to allow a divine mind to "shake" the cosmos.

Xenophanes had a healthy skepticism about the ability of human beings to find the truth. He believed they could at best come only to ideas that resemble truth, not truth itself. Without a divine agent, this skepticism could have easily led to the destruction of the cosmological enterprise. Radical skepticism did this very thing to some Greek philosophers after Xenophanes. It destroyed a scientifically useful academy. Why study when thoughts are not likely to be anything close to the truth? A divine mind provided the guarantee that such skepticism would not get out of hand. This mind allowed for the benefits of skepticism without the dangers.

Skepticism is a valuable tool in the hands of philosophers and scientists, bringing the epistemological humility needed for advancement. If there is a mind behind the cosmos, skepticism need not be feared. Human minds reflect the divine mind—if not perfectly, at least to some extent. The principles of like being drawn to like and the lesser imitating the greater are basic to Greek philosophy. In Xenophanes' view, the lesser human mind is drawn to imitate the divine mind.

In Xenophanes and Heraclitus, Greek philosophy came close to a full solution to the problems that stood in the way of developing true science. Then Greek thought was faced with a seemingly insurmountable logical puzzle that delayed its progress.

PARMENIDES AND ZENO: THE PUZZLE OF CHANGE

Few individuals can change the course of the world with a single idea, but Parmenides did. He was the first philosopher to use an argument to tease out the full implications of his views. This careful thinking exposed a deep flaw in earlier cosmological work.

Parmenides was from the Greek colony of Elea (in Ionia). He flourished in the early to mid-fifth century. His only work, *On Nature,* or *The Way of Truth,* was written in poetic form. It is obscure, and almost everything about it can be debated, but the fragments that remain suggest a work of profound literary and philosophic merit.

Parmenides was the start of the great tradition of philosophers whose literary style was as important as their argument. One enforces the other.

Both Plato and Dante did philosophy this way, and it has only been in recent times that academic philosophy abandoned storytelling. The older tradition did retain some practitioners: both Sartre and C. S. Lewis used fiction to good effect in making philosophic arguments.

Parmenides was the first, or one of the first, to explore the connection between words and the world. Parmenides' predecessors had begun with the phenomenal world and a few standard Greek ideas, and tried to shape a cosmology. Parmenides would have nothing to do with such haste. What did the words mean that were being used in such cosmological innovations?

Parmenides also took the problem of change and order very seriously. Parmenides believed that in linguistic analysis he had found a certain truth. In the epic style Parmenides presented his readers with the story of a young man who meets a goddess. She demonstrates to him the folly of most of humanity. Humanity should realize that in seeking truth one can only speak of what "is" and "is not." However, one cannot speak of what "is not" since it does not exist. How can a person attribute properties to a nonexistent object? If a thing is, then the thing must be. Existence can have nothing to do with nonexistence.

This idea has odd implications, but it is not so easy to see what is wrong with it. A simple thought experiment shows the problem. I am now thinking about Gandalf, yet I believe Gandalf does not exist. How can I think about nothing? I cannot think about nothing. This means that Gandalf must exist, or I am not thinking about him. It seems certain, however, that I am now thinking about Gandalf. Any reader of *The Lord of the Rings* is now thinking about him too. Gandalf must exist therefore. If he did not, then I could not think about him. But it is not that my thoughts create Gandalf. Gandalf must have already existed for me to think about him. "Is" and "is not" can have no relationship with each other.

If this is true, then there can be no birth or death. There can be no movement from "is not" to "is." Where would the stuff come from in a state of "is not" to get to the state that "is"? If there "is," then it *is* and is *not* "is not." There cannot be a passing away because something can never become nothing. It always *was,* so it always *is.* Change itself is impossible.

Of course, as former president Bill Clinton once pointed out, it all depends on what the meaning of *is* is. There are three meanings, as Plato would conclude in his famous dialogue called *Parmenides*. *Is* can be used to express identity. Bob Hope is Leslie Townes. The two persons are identical. *Is* can be used to predicate something. Bob Hope is my favorite comedian. Bob Hope is very witty. In these cases I gain more information about Bob Hope, but he is not identical to "witty." Finally, *is* can be used in an existential sense. Bob Hope *is*. He exists, as anyone can see by watching any of the fabulous *Road* movies. Parmenides used "is" in the last two senses. He would be committed to the fact that if Bob Hope can be thought of by me, he always existed, he exists, and he always will.

The most common temptation at this point is to scratch one's head and respond, "Philosophers say the most amazingly silly things. This is just a word game!" Of course, the person who says this has the advantage of thousands of years of reflection on what word games can and cannot tell him or her about the world. Most people base their rejection of Parmenides on the seeming paradox of their experience and his argument. We *know* that things come into being and pass away. Many bald men have experienced this reality with their hairline. If Parmenides is correct, then no man who had hair could ever become bald. There are bald men, so Parmenides must be wrong.

However tempting this response may be, it must be rejected. Parmenides recognizes that things *appear* to change. The question is, are the appearances trustworthy? Humans know that some experiences are not trustworthy. My fish net appears to be crooked when I place it in the goldfish bowl, but this is just an illusion. Appearances can be deceptive. To make this point, Parmenides divides his poem between the "Way of Truth" and the "Way of Seeming."

Parmenides knows most humans will keep speaking of "is" and "is not" in a confused way. The philosopher and the scientist must do better. Sensible people will think rationally despite the initial uncomfortable consequences. What conclusions did Parmenides draw? First, that in the cosmos there is no real coming to be. Second, there is no real passing away. Third, there exists only one complete, unchanging, spherical cosmos.

Parmenides develops a cosmology in the remainder of his poem. Why would Parmenides develop a cosmology? First, to demonstrate to other philosophers that he could do so. He was not a skeptic about cosmology out of any intellectual inability He just chose to be skeptical about it because of the truth. Second, Parmenides supplies his reader with an immediate cosmological example that can be refuted using his own earlier arguments. "Look," he might say, "the minute I draw distinctions, I am guilty of denying the truth. Distinctions depend on *is not,* and *is not* cannot be. If I who know the truth cannot do it, how could philosophers succeed who do not?"

The Eleatics were Parmenides' disciples, and they continued to argue for the futility of sense experience. In the short run this move was harmful to the development of science. Though Parmenides had attempted a cosmology, his followers had no such interest. They became more interested in demonstrating that what *appears* to be true cannot be true. Zeno is the most famous practitioner of the art of creating philosophical puzzles that demonstrate the truth of Eleatic doctrine.

The most famous of Zeno's puzzles involved the impossibility of motion. Everyone knows that Achilles, the great Greek warrior, is faster than a turtle. If a turtle tried to run away from him, Achilles would eventually catch him. Things are not so simple, according to Zeno. Everyone also agrees that if Achilles and the turtle were twenty yards apart, Achilles would have to move one-half the distance before he could reach the turtle. Having run half the distance, Achilles would then be forced to run another half. He would then run another. The line between Achilles and the turtle is infinitely divisible, and Achilles cannot run an infinite number of "halves" no matter how much time he is given. Achilles will never catch the turtle. The fact that in life people like Achilles seem to catch turtles means only that what seems to be is mistaken. After all, which seems more certain—the belief that a line contains infinite points, or the human experience of a person catching this animal? Surely humans are more certain about geometry than their changing experience! Motion is therefore likely just a "seeming" and not a reality. Zeno developed many more puzzles about motion, some much more complex than this one. All pointed to the Eleatic conclusion that motion is impossible.

Pre-Socratic philosophy tried very hard to answer Parmenides and

Zeno. This had a healthy and not-so-healthy impact on the history of philosophy. Word puzzles like those of Zeno were fascinating, but they distracted philosophy from empirical study. Greek life was organized around public outdoor activities because of factors like geography and weather. Greece has a dry and temperate climate, so people met and conducted their business outdoors. Athens had much grander public buildings than private ones. The development of grand private houses was seen by the Athenians as a sign of their own decline. Though public dialogue is a necessary feature of science, so is private research. The hours Aristotle spent examining natural objects were viewed as unseemly by his contemporaries. This is attested to by Aristotle's defense of his research as a fit task for a gentleman.

Parmenides and Zeno had the unfortunate effect of strengthening this prejudice against empirical research. Their followers tended to view the chief problems of humanity as being best resolved in the head or with logic. This marked the beginning of the split between the use of "head" and the use of "hands" that still scars academics to this day.

The Pythagorean school of philosophy in southern Italy was strongly impacted by this division. They already had a strong mystical tradition. The problems of Zeno and others strengthened this tendency. If their mysticism and the Eleatic tradition encouraged their obscurity, there was an important counterbalance. Their belief in the interconnection of music and mathematics helped draw them back from totally intellectualizing philosophy.

Math seems like the most Parmenidean of subjects—totally cut off from reality. The number *one* seemingly exists apart from the actual world. If there are n number of objects in the world, there exists a number $n + 1$. That number exists, though it has nothing to count. But the world does seem to interact with mathematics. Strings can be stretched to make sound; if cut in half, the strings make a sound proportional to the cut. If the length is doubled, then again the sound becomes lower in proportion to the lengthening. The case of strings and music seemed to show that reality somehow relates to mathematics.

What did this mean to the Pythagorean Greeks? Parmenides was shaking human confidence in appearance. The Pythagorean school suggested that reality was ultimately mathematical. The real world just might be the world of numbers. Numerology became an ongoing fascination to the intelligent Greek. Geometry and music were not just arcane subject areas for specialists. Music was the language that mediated between pure number and the appearances of the cosmos.

Humans were surrounded by music. The very spheres of the circular heavens gave off constant harmonic sound. Why couldn't humans hear this music? It was around so constantly, like the hum of an air conditioner in an office, that humans ceased to notice it. If the sound itself ceased, the cosmos would cease. Such talk quickly led to a split in the Pythagorean movement. One major Pythagorean group focused only on mystical and religious aspects. Others focused more on cosmological, musical and mathematical elements of the system. The split had some important consequences for the development of science and philosophy.

Progress seemed to come more easily in mathematics than it did in the investigation of the natural world. The challenges of Parmenides and Zeno seemed unanswerable. If science was to continue, someone had to deal with these challenges.

EMPEDOCLES, ANAXAGORAS AND DEMOCRITUS: THE ATTEMPT TO RESPOND

Empedocles lived from around 495 to 435 B.C. He adopted the poetic style of Parmenides and attempted to modify his predecessor's devastating conclusions. Empedocles thought he could find some wiggle room in the argument. He accepted that the Eleatic arguments had shown that "being" could not begin or end. Empedocles also conceded that the cosmos was a sphere and was perfect. He would not concede that motion or change was impossible.

How did he do this? Empedocles cleverly conceded that the cosmic order as a whole did not change. But change *within* that whole was possible. If I take the wedding ring off my finger and spin it on my desk, then I can grasp what Empedocles was after in his cosmology. If I spin the ring correctly, it will go round and round without moving about the desk. It is stable on what appears to be an axis: one unchanging system. The ring is changing relative to itself because it is moving. Imagine a ring that has always been doing this very thing. It eternally moves in itself, but it does not change relative to the outside world.

Empedocles saw the cosmos in a similar way. There exists a great sphere that has been, is and always will be. Its existence is fixed and immutable. Parmenides was right about the cosmos taken as a whole, but there exist four roots to the sphere. These roots are the four traditional Greek elements, which are constantly combining and coming apart.

What drives this motion? *Cosmic love* brings them together, and *cosmic strife* tears apart whatever love builds. These opposite forces are in overall balance, which makes the universe changeless. Love is not "good," and strife "bad"; both are necessary to the whole. Within this great balance either love or strife can become temporarily dominant. This temporary dominance itself occurs in an unchanging, cyclical pattern.

This is a brilliant synthesis of the cosmologies of the Ionian Greeks and the concerns of the Eleatics. It does not really deal with the thought experiments of Zeno, but those could be dismissed as mere puzzles. The four roots combine and separate. At times this creates living creatures, including some very odd creatures. The creatures that can survive do so. The "monsters" die out. Put crudely, the fittest survive. In some ways Empedocles anticipates Darwinism by centuries. Of course, for Empedocles the fit only survive *longer*. Nothing can survive the homogenous period of strife when the four roots are perfectly separated from each other.

Empedocles was no naturalist, however. He was deeply religious about this cosmic pattern. He saw a spiritual cycle of purification that existed at both the human and the cosmic level. Like all Greeks, he tended to see humanity as a microcosm of the great macrocosm. A person's soul survived cycle after cycle; everyone's goal was to purify themselves so that they could live rationally in that cycle.

This brilliant cosmology was rife with problems. What are love and strife? Where do they come from? These terms make sense as an analogy, but what is their cosmic equivalent? An inadequate theology seems to have prevented Empedocles from attributing them to a divine agent. If he makes them simply naturalistic forces, then the connection between his views of the soul and his cosmology vanish.

Naturalistic combinations could explain some details (e.g., why this "monster" was a hopeless design but this animal might make it). They could not explain the overall order and structure of the cosmos. Empedocles invoked personal agency since only an agent can love and hate. Who was the agent? Empedocles had nothing more to offer.

Anaxagoras, a contemporary of Empedocles, did have the boldness to identify this agent. He was the first great philosopher to spend most of his professional life in Athens. He marked the start of the dominance of that city on the thinking of the world. He did not accept the details of Empedocles' cosmology, but like him he accepted the notion of change only within a changeless order. This change was directed by Mind *(nous)*. As Plato would later note, Anaxagoras had found the solution to the problem of purpose-filled change. Sadly, Anaxagoras did not develop that solution, so it was Plato who would carry this idea to its logical conclusion.

Anaxagoras believed that "everything contained everything." The "all" could be divided into many parts. No matter how small the parts, each basic substance, each piece, contained the innumerable seeds that would allow for the reconstitution of the whole. These seeds formed the foundation for substance. Any one seed could produce, by itself, any basic substance. Anaxagoras could have great confidence in the order of the universe. No matter how many worlds came into being, the basic substance would survive: the seeds would see to that.

Anaxagoras's cosmos is a great vortex set in motion by Mind. The heavy earth is at the center, surrounded by the stars and the distant ether. The vortex could produce and destroy many things, but substance itself would continue. Mind saw to that.

Of course, there was another way to solve the problem of change. One could argue that change was purposeless, despite appearances. The ancient atomists tried this secularist explanation millennia before Darwin, so contemporary philosophers frequently consider the atomists the greatest of the ancient scientific philosophers. Their uncanny ability to anticipate modern naturalistic dogma is made much less remarkable when one recalls that Greek society was simply developing a school of thought that covered each sensible cosmological option.

How to answer Parmenides? Like the fly in the soup, the Eleatic philosophy was the unbidden guest at any philosophical dinner party. Leucippus, Democritus and other atomists thought they had a new strategy. They decided that the world was composed of solid, homogeneous, unchanging particles called atoms. (These are not the atoms of modern physics. Scientists are able to split these atoms, so they cannot be atoms in the ancient sense.) These atoms are all the same in terms of substance, but they are different in their qualitative characteristics. There are an infinite number of them in different shapes, sizes and configurations.

These atoms exist in a void. They have inherent motion. Why? Moving is what atoms do. They are solid little cosmic building blocks that eventually collide. These collisions gradually form worlds as atoms stick to other atoms. Other collisions break up collections of atoms. Objects in the world can come and go, but the atoms themselves never change. If Empedocles found stability in the superstructure of the universe, the atomists found it at the bottom.

Why do atoms collide? The later atomist Epicurus postulated a "swerve" in atomic motion. If atoms swerve ever so slightly, they will collide. Like tiny indestructible building blocks, they make up the world that humans see. Atomists were consistent naturalists. Democritus reduced the soul to merely a fast atom. All agent terms found in Empedocles were removed by the atomists. They even had an answer to the puzzles about infinite divisibility. Atomists could turn to Zeno and say, "Look, things cannot be divided forever. The atom is at the bottom of it all."

The problems with atomism were obvious to Plato and Aristotle. How could humans know anything in this random universe? Randomness could not produce order but only the appearance of order. The universe could not be a cosmos—an ordered thing—but only *appear* to be so. This meant that no system could ever capture the big picture. Humans could know all there was to know about the tiny atoms. Nothing else had any pattern to know. Sadly, all there was to know about atoms did not turn out to be very much—and not very interesting at that. All the things humans wanted to know, the cosmic questions, turned out to be unknowable.

Atomists explain what a thing is by looking at its parts. This is absurd because most things, such as persons, cannot be known just by looking at a pile of the parts that make them up. The person is found in the whole.

To know a thing, one must see the order of the whole as well as the functioning of the parts that make up the whole. What is the good of knowing about a person's parts if you never know the person?

Humans think. How can thought be explained in a universe made only of atoms, intellectual building blocks? Building blocks, no matter how intricately stacked, cannot produce thought. Thoughts and atoms are not the same sort of thing. Atomists were not trying to get thought and reason from *nothing,* just from the wrong sort of *something.* Materialist attempts to explain thought are category errors.

Materialism developed a following but was never dominant in the ancient world. As Plato points out in *Laws* book ten, the evidence for design is too overwhelming. There was also the concern that materialism would undercut morals and political stability.

SOPHISTRY: REASON FOR HIRE

Philosophers were and still are sensitive to the charge that all this discussion doesn't do anyone any good. What good is one hundred years' worth of new philosophical systems? Was progress possible? One Greek thinker, Gorgias, decided to demonstrate the futility of cosmological speculation by compiling a list of contradictory opinions from the philosophers. He is an example of a movement within Greek philosophy. The philosophers in this movement are most often called Sophists. The term *Sophist* is a rough way of describing a group of people who were not a school but had a certain style and set of ideas in common.

It is hard to talk about the Sophists because most information about them comes from Plato, and Plato hated the Sophists. He disliked them so much that he has ruined the word forever. For Plato, Sophists were pompous blowhards who pretended to know things they did not and then charged a fee for it. To call oneself a Sophist was to describe oneself as a wise person. This self-referential praise was one of things that irritated Plato the most. Plato described himself merely as a lover of wisdom. The Sophists thought they knew, and so they charged for their teachings, but they actually knew nothing.

The Sophists were for the most part professional teachers of rhetoric, the art of speaking well. In the beginning such teaching also included the art of reasoning well. If modern American political candidates cannot make it without good television skills, no ancient Athenian citizen could prosper without rhetorical skills. The ability to make a persuasive argument was highly prized. It could lead to prosperity in business, victory in the courts and political influence in the life of the city. It was a virtue that Athens ranked above almost all other skills in importance.

At first Sophists sought right living as a part of their teaching of rhetoric. After all, it seems obvious that the just person armed with good speaking skills will be the one most likely to prevail. Isn't truth the best defense? Doubt began to creep into the culture when clever speakers began to win ruthlessly, regardless of the truth. The Sophists began to teach more how to persuade and less how to find the truth.

Many Sophists embraced ethical relativism. The Sophist Protagoras put it best when he said, "Man is the measure of all things."[3] Some things are true for you but are not true for me. Other things are true for me but are not true for you. Protagoras fell into both epistemological and moral relativism.

Gorgias is an excellent example of a Sophist and a skeptic about knowledge. He believed that it was impossible to know anything and that it was impossible to communicate. Misunderstanding is always possible, so language was his chief concern. Truth was elusive at best. Even if the truth were out there, no one would be likely to find it, and if they did find it, they would not know they had found it. Since truth is so hard to find, the speaker might as well settle for winning.

Gorgias was sure that nothing actually existed. He believed he could demonstrate this by argument. Strictly speaking, this means Gorgias could not really be a skeptic or a relativist since he was sure about so many things. Gorgias also liked to worry the crowd by praising Helen of Troy, the villainess of the *Iliad*. He did this in his aptly named thumb in the eye, *In Praise of Helen*.

One other Sophist is worth mentioning. Thrasymachus claimed, in true Sophist fashion, that humans are by nature beasts. Society exists only to protect the strong; laws and social customs exist only to serve the rich and powerful. The important thing is not to be just but to appear to

---

[3]Quoted by Sextus Empiricus in *Outlines of Pyrrhonism* 1.216.

be just. This will lead to a happy life; whether it will lead to a good life is simply irrelevant.

Athenians tolerated the Sophists, even paid them for their services. But they killed Socrates. Why the difference? The Sophists seemed to challenge the gods and the morals of the city, and Socrates was the one killed for this crime. The truth is that Sophist patronage at the hand of the city undercut the seriousness of their beliefs. The college professor who rails against capitalism and then drives home in his Lexus is irritating but co-opted. Sophists were the paid "bad boys" of the ancient Greek world.

Socrates on the other hand lived his philosophy not of bogus relativism but real skeptical inquiry. He wanted to *know,* not just seem to know. He demonstrated that others made hollow claims and that those were the real threat to the establishment of the city. He challenged the easy orthodoxy of his day and lived as if the city were wrong. His whole life was an indictment of Athens.

The Sophists were content with verbal games. They attacked Athens with words, and Athens was mostly apathetic. To the extent that the Sophists taught real rhetorical skills, people were even happy to learn from them. A culture will tolerate criticism of its idols only when the criticism is made by those who worship the idols.

In the late fifth century, Greek culture was in turmoil. Greece had defeated Persia to retain its freedom, and Athens had established a great trading empire in the wake of that victory. By 404 B.C., however, Athens was in trouble as its trade empire gave it fits. It was constantly at war with the neighboring city of Sparta, and was losing. It experienced political turmoil as tyrants ruled with brutal force. The intervals of democratic government were not much better. Within two men's lifetimes the freedom of Athens would be lost forever.

Every intellectual option had been tried during the two hundred years since Thales "invented" philosophy. Ethical confusion and moral decay were frequently cited by writers. The culture seemed splendid, but it was sick. Like the flush of fever that gives the appearance of good health, Athens was in trouble despite its plays, great buildings and busy port. Into this atmosphere stepped one man who would search for the truth. He would fail. He would be a martyr to philosophy, killed by his beloved

Athens. But his "failure" transformed the city. Though Athens could not recover from political mistakes, the followers of Socrates transformed Athens from a political, to an educational, center.

2

THE DEATH OF A GOOD MAN

HE WAS NOT MUCH TO LOOK AT. He had a snub nose and a bald head, and he usually did not dress very well. When he showed up at a party, he was more interested in looking for truth than he was in flute girls, young men or drinking. In a city that admired getting along, he did not. His pupils, mostly drawn from the young wealthy men with time on their hands, never forgot their time with him. In the end, Athens killed him for his boldness in asking questions that the establishment could not answer. He was the closest thing to a Christ figure in the pagan world. His name was Socrates.

Socrates lived from 470 to 399 B.C. His life embraced both the high point of Athenian culture and the beginning of its end. By the end of his life, the city he had loved was also dying. He could not bear to see what he knew was coming. When Athens betrayed him, he chose death over exile.

Socrates was born at a time when the Greeks had established their ability to defend themselves against the Persians. The heroic victories of Salamis on the sea and Plataia on the land occurred about ten years before his birth. Athens was the center of a group of Greek city-states known as the Delian League (founded in 478). The league assaulted Persia and acted to spread Greek culture throughout the Mediterranean. This alliance rapidly evolved into an Athenian empire under the direction of the brilliant Pericles (462–429).

Athens moved closer and closer to democracy, though democracy for citizens and men only. Women were kept closely confined at home, and citizenship was limited to about one-sixth of the population. The relative freedom of these citizens to participate in the life of the city was based on the labor of a large class of slaves. Great public works were built with the money from the Athenian empire, and a golden age of culture ensued. Pericles himself was trained by the philosopher Anaxagoras.

The good times were not to last for long. Sparta and other Greek cities were jealous of Athenian prosperity, and many cities in the league rightly resented being dominated by Athens. Athens fought continuing wars with its neighbors (the Peloponnesian Wars), which are brilliantly chronicled by one of the first historians, Thucydides. These wars dragged on from 431 to 404 B.C. At one point Sparta placed Athens under siege, and many, including Pericles, died of the plague. Nothing came of this suffering except more suffering. Athenian naval power was balanced by Spartan land power. No one was able to win a decisive victory. Truces were frequently broken as one city after another tried to establish itself as the dominant Greek city-state.

By 420 Athens had fallen under the spell of the brilliant demagogue Alcibiades. He led Athens into another miserable war with Sparta. Sparta won major land victories, but Athens used its sea power to gain its own conquests. While this endless war was going on, Alcibiades convinced Athens to intervene in the troubled affairs of Greek-speaking Sicily. During preparations for the invasion of Sicily, Alcibiades decided to profane the city gods of Athens. The rich aristocrat escaped punishment for the time being, and the fleet sailed for Sicily. Alcibiades was later recalled to stand trial for his impiety, but instead he sold out Athens to Sparta.

Alcibiades would go on to switch sides again. After he was pardoned by the city of Athens, Alcibiades led a campaign against a combined Spartan and Persian threat. At first he was successful, but eventually his armies met disaster, which was not all his fault. Instead of returning to face certain censure, Alcibiades again abandoned Athens. As a result, Alcibiades became the archetype of the rich, spoiled young man who cares nothing for morality or patriotism. Sadly, he was also a sometime student of Socrates, but the teacher received the blame for the infidelity of the pupil.

By 406, Athens was finished—her fleet gone, her walls destroyed and, most humiliatingly, a Spartan garrison in the city helping a group of sympathetic Athenian aristocrats hold power. The days of democracy seemed to be over. The aristocrats, called the Thirty, instituted a reign of terror over the city, persecuting leaders of the democracy who had deprived them of the power they viewed as a birthright. One leader of the Thirty included Critias, another former pupil of Socrates.

From 404 to 401, the leaders of the exiled Athenian democracy fought back and gradually regained control of the city. Sparta accepted the new democracy, and Athens entered a period of reaction against the upper classes. In the midst of all this Socrates had acted as a loyal citizen of the city, not as a friend to the aristocrats or to the excesses of the democracy. This did not save him from the wrath of the democrats, and he was condemned to death in 399. The restoration of full democracy was marked with a human sacrifice to mediocrity and the popular mood.

Athens would eventually recover some part of its greatness, and for a short period it would again act as an imperial power. But the rise of the Macedonian kingdom of Philip and Alexander brought an end to full Athenian independence by 337. Athenian freedom was gone forever, and other powers dominated the city of Socrates until modern times.

A MAN OF HIS TIME

The idea of the "just" or "good" life consumed Socrates. He wanted to know *how* to be good. Athens was in a time of crisis. Who was he to sit on the sidelines? Socrates had been a brave solider in the Athenian army, and now he had to face the fact that the city for which he had risked his life might be changing. Athens seemed to be changing in ways that alienated Socrates from it.

The oracle of Delphi, in a typical enigmatic pronouncement, declared Socrates to be the wisest of the Athenians. How could this be? Socrates knew how little he knew. He wanted to know the meaning of terms that seemed important to the good life, such as piety, courage and justice. He searched endlessly for the wise person who could teach him these things. The Sophists he met were no help, and none of the Athenian leaders cared to examine the platitudes they proclaimed.

Socrates' very methods betray an interest in *how* to learn and *what* it is that can be taught. Socrates did not play academic games. He was not interested in virtue for the sake of solving intellectual jigsaw puzzles but for the sake of living a better life. In a world where intellectual questions had become a game, he brought earnestness to the table. Unlike the stereotype of the useless philosopher, Socrates saw philosophy as the most pragmatic of disciplines. Philosophy existed to teach a person how to live.

THE SOCRATIC EDUCATION

Socrates wrote no books. Like Jesus, the only record he left was in the lives of those impressed by his life. Aristophanes, the great comic poet, made fun of Socrates in the *Clouds*. The prizewinning playwright made his Athenian audience laugh at learning, but the *Clouds* derives its chief modern interest from his assault on Socrates.

Xenophan, a conservative student of Socrates', left us a collection of fond memories of his master. In it Socrates resembles a glorified version of Xenophan. Socrates is the wise and conventional popular sage. It is impossible from Xenophan's account to understand why Athens would have bothered to kill Socrates.

Socrates survived beyond his execution because Plato made him immortal. No teacher has ever had a better pupil. Plato, especially in his earliest dialogues, captured the essential Socrates. To read the *Apology*, the defense of Socrates at his trial, is to understand the man. Were these the very words used by Socrates? It does not matter. Plato uses his memories of the trial to make Socrates live again. But even this worshipful student began to outgrow his pain. The Socrates of Plato's dialogues gains his own voice, and that voice matures. Plato's own voice in the *Laws*, where Socrates does not appear as a character, is not that of Socrates.

Though the Platonic dialogues are not historical documents, they are valuable in revealing the real Socrates. In fact, if the goal of reading them is to know Socrates, they are better than modern histories. Plato uses every tool in his unsurpassed intellectual arsenal to present a picture of the *living* Socrates. It is not Plato's concern to get every historical detail right. He invents conversations between other people and Socrates, conversations that never could have happened in actuality. The famous drinking party in the *Symposium* is a prime example of Plato's willingness to take liberties with history, but he does want to defend his master against the charges brought against him. To do so, he presents a plausible picture to the public. How could Plato hope to swing intelligent opinion to Socrates if the Socrates he described did not resemble the man Athens had known?

Socrates did not claim to have knowledge. In fact, Socrates frequently claimed that he did not know anything—except that he did not know anything. By this he meant that he did not know anything he had come to think worth knowing. Socrates had served as a loyal citizen of Athens in the government and the army. He was a craftsman—a stonecutter, which was a highly skilled trade. Socrates saw, however, that these external "goods" were not enough since they did not teach him how to live the good life. This integrity came at a price because Socrates did not charge fees for his teaching or mentoring.

Socrates believed the best way to learn was to examine the opinions of those who claimed to know. At the very least an exposure of their ignorance would eliminate one way of going wrong. The person who debunks the inflated claims of a healing evangelist does not show that healing does not happen, but rather provides the useful service of showing that healing has not happened *here* and *in this way*. It is a negative path to a limited sort of knowledge. Socrates hoped in the process to meet a person who knows, and then become like him. It may also have occurred to Socrates that the communal quest for the truth, like that pictured in the *Symposium,* would bring answers. Perhaps no one person could teach, but many persons together could find the right questions.

Socrates became skilled in the art of asking questions. Plato formalized his method, called the *elenchus,* in his early writings. Socrates would approach a man esteemed wise in Athenian culture and engage him in conversation. At some point the wise man would claim to know something important to the life of a good citizen. This might be the nature of courage or of justice. Socrates would then ask, "What is *it?*"

The sophisticate was always ready with an answer. Socrates, however, would quickly demonstrate that the answer was confused or no answer at all. The expert in justice could not state the nature of justice. This is surprising and disconcerting; if the man everyone agrees is the expert does not know the field, it is doubtful anyone does.

After this period of confusion, the interlocutor usually turns to traditional answers. Using a quotation from Homer, Hesiod or one of the canonical "wise men," he attempts to slip the problem. Socrates is not so easily put off, however. While recognizing the importance of tradition in the life of the city, he wishes to know if the tradition is *true*. This, of course, is a very difficult question for a person who is intellectually stagnant, as were most Sophists. Ask a conventional person for an answer, and you are likely to get it; ask for a reason for his answer, and you are likely to get a punch in the mouth.

The Sophist has rarely thought about the truth of the tradition and so is unready to meet the Socratic challenge. Socrates then presses for better and better definitions. Frequently the Sophist is left in bewilderment (aporia). Socrates has shown that the professional "teacher" or "model citizen" is a windbag. An excellent example of this sort of intellectual dissection is found in the early portions of *Meno*. This dialogue is one of the first in which Plato goes beyond Socrates to express his own views, but in the beginning it is a model of the Socratic method in action.

Meno is a conventional and self-satisfied Athenian citizen. He is the Athenian dream incarnate. He is a good citizen, well liked by his friends and has few enemies. Socrates asks him if he knows the nature of virtue. What is it to be excellent at the art of living? Socrates is looking for a universal definition for the "good." Meno responds by giving a list of virtues. Men have one "good"; women have another. Soldiers are "good" if they fulfill their duties. Instead of defining the term, Meno simply gives a list of examples, but Socrates is after bigger game. He wants to know what, if anything, these individual virtues have in common. What exactly, universally, is a virtue?

Some fifth graders learn to hate looking up words, whether online or in a dictionary. "What is *frabulate?*" they might ask. Turning to the dictionary, they find the definition is "the act of frabbing." In frustration they look up *frab;* the dictionary says "one who frabulates." At this point a poor fifth grader wishes to curse the gods and die. Of course, a dictionary like this would be useless. If a person does not know what *frab* is in the first place, then circular definitions will not help. Yet much of what Meno offers Socrates is circular definitions of virtue. Telling Socrates to live virtuously does not help him to know the nature of virtue.

"Wait!" the reader of these Socratic dialogues is tempted to cry. "What difference does it make if the person can define what *it* is? After all, typical folk are not interested in definitions but in the ability to use the word sensibly. I can talk about cabbages and kings with some degree of authority, though I might be hard-pressed to define them exactly."[1]

Such an objection misses Socrates' point. The problem is not that a person has to know what a thing *is* to do it. It would be better, however, to have this knowledge. If a person knows exactly what courage is, then he or she is never going to mistake mere bravado for the real article. It is not that one has to have exhaustive knowledge of love to live, but it would be much better if one had it. In fact, human experience seems to indicate that people are easily led astray due to their imprecision. People frequently think someone just who simply seems to be just. This can have horrific consequences for the life of the city, as the career of Alcibiades shows.

The Sophists claimed to be able to improve a citizen's ability to know these essential concepts. Socrates challenged their claim to knowledge. Did they know enough to survive questioning from a citizen who professed ignorance? If not, then they were not what they claimed to be: teachers of virtue. For Socrates believed that virtue was a matter of knowledge. No person would *knowingly* do evil.

If Socrates believed anything, it was this. But it also seems obviously false. People kill other people, and many who kill know it is wrong. At this point, however, Socrates would shake his head. The murderer *seems* to know that murder is wrong. It is the seeming that provides room for Socrates to maneuver.

Would a sane man knowingly do evil to himself? Socrates thought the answer to this question was plainly no. People act in their own best inter-

---

[1]The belief that a person must be able to define a word in order to use it well is often called the Socratic fallacy.

est. Real evil does harm, at least to the soul of the person doing it. Socrates believed this was true by definition. People who do evil must not realize they are harming their souls.

Evil people may be ignorant of the outcome of their actions. Smoking has always been harmful, but in the 1950s many people did not realize this was true. People harmed themselves without realizing it. They did not do evil to themselves knowingly; in fact, many believed smoking helped them avoid harmful weight gain. Such people confused a bad action with a good. Even the case of people who smoke today, though they know it to be harmful, is not a good argument against Socrates. The average smoker simply *believes* that smoking is bad but cannot picture the actual outcome. If they *knew* the harm, they would stop. Socrates makes a distinction between opinion and certain knowledge. No one with certain knowledge acts to his or her harm.

High school athletes may dream of playing professional basketball even if they are fairly rotten at it. If asked, most would say they *know* the odds are against them. They frequently admit they do not *seem* talented enough to play professional basketball. Yet many of these same students pour all their time into basketball and little or none into study. In their hearts they believe none of what they claim to believe, but they are afraid to admit that their plans are foolish dreams based on sports movies they have seen. They do not harm themselves knowingly because they don't really believe what they say they believe.

People could also do evil to themselves by failing to understand the actual degree of evil they commit. Wicked people sometimes believe that the evil they commit is a mere trespass and "not so bad." After all, a speeding ticket isn't going to send anyone to hell, and they classify their thuggery as a moral speeding ticket. "Borrowing" some concrete from the building site cannot be that bad since the city has so much of it, and besides, everybody does it. If not caught, such sinners believe that their wicked actions were not bad. They incorrectly classify their behavior and so harm themselves in their ignorance.

Suicide seems to be the obvious exception to the rule. How can one kill oneself? Isn't it obvious to everyone that dying is harmful? On serious reflection, however, this is not at all certain. First, there is no reason to think that Greeks would have viewed taking one's own life in every circumstance as bad. Even Christians think that killing oneself can be virtuous under special circumstances.[2] Second, a person who commits suicide in bad circumstances is frequently confused. The question of the ethical competence of many who commit suicide is a real one. Finally, those considering suicide may not really believe in their own death. Many such people imagine their own funeral and the sorrow their death will cause as if they will be there to see it. It is hard to contemplate not being able to contemplate. In short, in any particular case of suicide it is possible that the person *knew* what he or she was doing, but it is also perfectly plausible to assume that he or she did not. If one had independent reasons for assuming that no one does evil knowingly, then the issue of suicide need not hinder that belief.

Socrates' beliefs about knowledge and virtue assumed a high view of each human being. People are not taught but *helped* to see. People need tutors or guides, not paid Sophists. Why is this so? With proper guidance, humans can be brought to see the good life. At least for some humans, knowledge is possible. Socrates shows no signs of despair, even at the end of his life. He continues in dialogue with his friends to the last moment of his life.

Socrates equated virtue with knowledge. Ethics was merely epistemological. This put a premium on education. Ignorance was not just unwise or imprudent, but wicked. If the Sophists had reduced education to an interesting trade, Socrates elevated it to a religion.

The Socratic epistemology, however interesting, is inadequate. There is more to ethics than epistemology. Aristotle will make the compelling argument that weakness of the will can prevent humans from doing what they know they should do. Drunks know a swig of the old "alkie" can kill them, but their thirst is too great to stop. Knowing the good is not enough to do the good if the will is too weak. Knowledge plays a central role, but not always the decisive role.

In any case Socrates elevated the seriousness of education. He connected virtue with a good education. In a society that prized politics

---

[2]See Eusebius *History of the Church* 8.12.3.

above all else, he made education necessary to being a good citizen. He also made the practice of asking the right questions the central character-istic of a sound academic order. One need not know all the right answers to do well in the Socratic school. A well-educated man would be a gen-tleman. American popular culture has not yet succeeded in utterly re-moving these ideas from the academic community.

THE DEATH OF SOCRATES

Socrates' death separates him from the Sophists. Some Sophists were relatively serious about philosophy. A few took cosmology and ethics se-riously and tried to escape the dead end of cynical relativism. A few were not just in it for the money, but it is difficult to imagine any Sophists dy-ing for their beliefs.

Socrates had so few positive beliefs that it is not quite fair to say that he died for them. It is better to say that he died for a way of life. Socrates famously believed that the unexamined life is not worth living. The ex-amined life produces excellence. This excellence is often in conflict with the values of a democratic society.

I. F. Stone, an influential twentieth-century journalist and critic, ac-cused Socrates of being an enemy of the open society of Athens. Though he does not justify his execution, Stone accuses Socrates of bringing it on himself with his attitude. It is certain that Socrates was no particular friend of Athenian democracy. Though he served the city faithfully, in-cluding in times of war, Socrates drew his best friends from the aristo-cratic class. This is not surprising.

The twenty-first century is the great age of equality. It is also an era that prizes freedom, believing that equality and freedom are usually found together. There is another tradition deeply rooted in Western cul-ture that says freedom cannot exist in an egalitarian society. Socrates' life demonstrated that philosophy could not long survive in a truly egali-tarian culture.

For the Athenian citizen the time of Socrates gave the most radical expression to majority power in the history of the world. The majority of Athenian citizens could do anything. Nothing checked their will, not even theoretically, in the days of the full-blown democracy. The voice of the majority of citizens was as the voice of a god. All major decisions in peacetime were made by the direct vote of the citizens assembled together. Most of the political jobs in the city were chosen by lot. This was the ultimate expression of democratic belief. Any Athenian was thought worthy of any task. People were equal in the most radical sense of the term. Eventually, practical problems removed the government of the army from this egalitarian philosophy, but most of the city was still governed by pure equality. Any citizen could, in principle if not in fact, stand in the assembly and speak his mind. Of course, the leisure to do so was built on the backs of slaves, the industry of foreigners *(metics)* and the household management of women. Yet none of these productive elements of society had many rights in this democratic state.

Most of history has since deemed the Athenian experiment in (relative) egalitarianism a failure. America's founders lived in horror of such a state. They set up a representative republic that looked more to Rome than to Greece. It was no accident they called their new country a republic and not a democracy. The Founders, along with most traditional Christians, believed that all people were created equal, in terms of being human beings. Such ontological equality did not mean functional equality. People were not equal in their abilities and so must have different functions. Freedom to pursue one's own happiness would inevitably lead to a natural aristocracy. The cream would rise to the top. Freedom would lead to a hierarchy in which everyone finds their place.

Socrates saw that freedom to excel was not possible in a pure democracy. The existence of virtue, or excellence, of any sort is a positive danger in such a state. Excellence must be stamped out to avoid the formation of a hierarchy based on merit. The many must soon take away freedom in order to survive. Radical equality is therefore hostile to freedom or liberty.

Athens provided the perfect example of the tyranny of the majority when its citizens degenerated into a voting mob. Eloquent speakers could manipulate them into committing horrific crimes. They were not limited by effective religious restraints, a constitution or a strong tradition. For example, during one stage of their many wars the Athenian democracy was convinced to butcher every resident, including women and children, of a city that dared resist their empire. Any form of government can commit such crimes, but in a pure democracy it is impossible to assign blame, so usually nobody is punished.

Socrates worried that the very idea of excellence was a threat to democratic values. If one person rose above the rest, it was a living rebuke to the notion that all are created equal in abilities. Pericles was the exception that proved the rule. It is true that he was a brilliant man who was able to rule with great authority. He was able, for a long time, to flatter the majority into doing what he wanted. He did so, however, by pursuing an imperial policy that was popular in the short term but disastrous in the long term. Even Pericles was rebuked by the city. Even successful leaders were exiled or executed when their actions did not meet the expectations of a fickle Athenian public.

As practiced by Socrates, philosophy is a problem for a state that bases itself on the dubious notion that people are the same in talents. Not all people are interested in the examined life, and not everyone who is interested is equally able to pursue it. If knowledge of such things leads to virtue, then not only will certain people be wiser, they will be better.

The death of Socrates is so noble that it raises a disturbing question. Why not love the Greeks and dispense with Christianity altogether? Perhaps what is best and truest about historic Western Christian culture was gained from the Greeks through the Romans. Victor Davis Hanson has implied as much in some of his recent books lauding classical education. The contemporary world might be able to dispense with Christianity—and the dangers of religion—and adopt a broader, intellectual classicism.

If Christianity is true, then it is important—but most classicists forget to ask if it is true. In fact, devotees of the West and Greek and Roman culture should *hope* Christianity is true. Most people entertain some reasonable doubts about things they believe. These same people reasonably maintain these beliefs if they can muster some counterarguments to the doubts. Of course, an idea might become indefensible, but it is self-evident that at least some forms of orthodox Christianity are not at that stage. It is rational to be very slow to abandon a helpful or useful belief. Christianity is a useful completion to Greek science. It is also a helpful completion to Socratic living. The disciple of Socrates should hope for the truth of Christianity and accept reasonable arguments from the apologists.

First, the aristocratic impulse of philosophy is good, but it is also dangerous. The critics of Socrates were happy to point this out at his trial. No culture has easily maintained the ontological equality of all human beings. Inequality of persons in terms of ability is easy to see, but their equality is much more difficult to grasp. Believing that all humans are created in the image of God, as traditional Christianity has always taught, is a helpful balancing fact. It is a fact that is easy to communicate to all members of the community, whether philosophically inclined or not.

Christianity is a popular religion capable of rational defense. This was not something that the Greeks or the Romans succeeded in creating. They had plenty of religions. Some of them, such as the cult of Mithras, may have been as popular as Christianity. The religious Neo-Platonism of late antiquity was intellectually interesting. However, only Christianity could move both the scholar and the simple with the same story. As Augustine points out in *Confessions,* the Bible is simple enough to communicate to those not at all interested in philosophy, but it is so deep that it has taxed the intellect of the world's greatest thinkers.

A Christian religious proposition such as "In the image of God, he created them" is understood by every member of the church. Christianity is uniquely able to communicate to a whole culture. This includes protecting the intellectuals from the recurrent tendencies toward anti-intellectualism among the masses. It can also protect the masses from the great ambition and hubris of the intellectuals.

Christianity also helped transmit the riches of Judaism to the rest of the West. These riches have been of critical importance to the development of the West. For example, Moses and his writings deeply impressed on the non-Jewish West the idea that divine law trumps any human consideration. The ends do not justify the means. Persons can be judged as bad who acted in their own best interest or in the interests of their particular place and time. When we judge Southern slave owners of the antebellum South to have done badly, then we are applying this concept well. Without it such judgments are merely anachronistic.

Finally, Socratic investigation in a cosmos without a *lawgiver* runs the risk of futility. There may be no truth to seek. If the universe were fundamentally chaotic, then the investigator would have no promise of eventual success. The examined life would still be preferable to the unexamined life. One should not abandon reason simply because reason is deemed unlikely to meet with ultimate success. But still it would be pleasant, very pleasant, if humans had reason to hope that the truth was out there and knowable. Christianity provides grounds for such hope. It lessens the amount of moral courage—rare enough in humanity—needed to pursue philosophy. That is a good thing.

FINAL CONSIDERATIONS

Socrates left behind a great life. Everyone can agree he was dedicated to good living at any cost to self. He was a good citizen of his city. He also left a cadre of disciples willing and able to memorialize his work. However, the exact content of his work was so ambiguous that Plato and Xenophon came to two different pictures of the man and his message. Is the truth out there? What would happen when the disciples continued to pursue the examined life?

Socrates' greatest student, Plato, provided one model. Plato believed that he found some answers to the great questions of life. In so doing, did he betray the master? If Socrates was a skeptic, merely a debunker of other people's answers, then Plato did betray this heritage. The other possibility is that Socrates wanted to know the truth and that Plato, using both Socrates' methods and some of his own, attempted to find it. The answers Plato found were so powerful that, if false, they were the greatest, most powerful deception in the history of human thought. If true, they were the greatest single contribution to philosophy by any human being. Plato changed philosophy forever, but it was the example of the snub-nosed man from Athens who provoked this revolution. What he would have made of it, we shall never know.

3

THE IDEAL PHILOSOPHER

Plato and His Teachings

PHILOSOPHY WITHOUT A GOOD STORY tends to be sterile. The pre-Socratics suffered from a message increasingly unappealing to the average Greek. Philosophers despised practical people who had their revenge by mocking and marginalizing the philosophers.

The Sophists had higher ambitions. They wanted to rule, but they reeked of arrogance and feelings of superiority while having few practical things to say. Even Socrates, a good man, was lampooned in the *Clouds,* by Aristophanes, as a useless windbag. In that play Socrates was pictured as floating above the heads of the multitude, running his school on hot air.

Socrates was rescued from oblivion by a better storyteller. This genius recognized that philosophy must not only concern itself with the good and the true but also the beautiful. It needed a good story. What does philosophy look like if it is lived? What is it to be a good follower of Socrates?

Plato was the first writer to wrap his beliefs in a compelling, even beautiful, story. Others, such as Dante and Shakespeare, would do it as well, but Plato did it first. He did not write treatises on nature as did the pre-Socratics or drift about in conversation with young aristocrats. He illustrated how philosophy is born in *dialogue* between passionate people about the biggest issues facing humanity. He did so in a way that invites argument and dissent. To read a dialogue carefully is to live in a virtual reality.

Plato used myths to make his ideas gripping. He invented the legend of Atlantis, which is so compelling that people have wasted centuries looking for it. His writing is not merely dramatic but many-layered. The first words of the *Republic* are, "I went down . . . ," and the rest of the dialogue focuses on numerous trips *down*. One can read the dialogues quickly and gain a great deal from them. It is impossible to study them with too much attention. Plato's text always has deeper depths and hidden meanings.

If Plato wrote it, then it still exists, which is a rare thing for an ancient author. The young Plato mourned the death of Socrates in the *Apology*. The aging and dying Plato lost any vision of his old master in the *Laws*. In between is seen the growth of a great mind that reaches its full power in the masterful *Republic*.

Plato wants his reader to argue with his conclusions. His Socrates in *Republic* leans forward repeatedly and urges his students to think for themselves. This is not a hopeless journey, because it ends in goodness, truth and beauty. Plato's philosophy is bewitchingly optimistic.

Plato is no Christian; the great Dante puts him in hell,[1] but Plato is the best teacher for a culture wandering from biblical faith. Imagine a rebel living far from his father's house. The prodigal does not want to go home because he has twisted memories from a rebellious childhood. He wanders to strange lands, eventually coming to a place that is like his home. He loves it for that likeness, but he does not realize this because he cannot remember what home is really like. His memory is corrupted. This strange land that is not home but is so much like it enables him to see with new eyes the thing he once had. So the strange place is truer to the reality of home than his memory is. He settles in this city and journeys further and further into its streets. One day he looks up as he drifts into a new area of the city. He is shocked to discover that he has journeyed to a place just around the corner from his father's house. The rebel is not yet home, but he is almost there. Plato is near enough to truth to be helpful,

---

[1]Dante *Divine Comedy* 6.134.

but novel enough to give a rebel a fresh perspective. He has brought many a rebel close enough to home to really see it for the first time.

Of course, being near is not being *there*. The prodigal must walk the rest of the way to his father's house. Plato is often suggestive of the Christian faith even when he seems furthest from it. At least this is the way it was for me. Even when he was wrong, Plato suggested to me the truths of my childhood. His glimmers of the truth were often easier for a prodigal to swallow than the truth itself. Plato does not let his reader enjoy a mere academic exercise, and to a lapsed Christian, such a pagan can be a powerful prophet.

It is no shock that Plato has this impact on even a simple seeker. Plato wrote for the seeker of truth in Athens, a city in cultural crisis nearing its death. Plato's disciple, Aristotle, would witness the destruction of the Athenian city-state. For Plato the best evidence of the decline of his city was that it had killed Socrates. How could the city take the life of the best man in it? It was one thing to ponder the abuse of power in the abstract, but Plato saw evil done by his beloved Athens.

Plato was the effortless master of many different types of literature. *Menexenus* parodies the best speaking style of the time. Plato did better science than any pre-Socratic investigator. His style ranges from the simple to the obscure, sometimes in the same work. Just try moving from the biographical portions of the *Phaedo* to the arguments for the existence of the soul!

He wrote some things so that they were obvious: "The unexamined life is not worth living."[2] Other things he couched in obscure numerology and wordplay. Plato may never have written down some of his deepest teachings. These were reserved for lectures at his school, the Academy. Careful readers may be able to discern traces of these hidden doctrines in the later dialogues.

PLATONIC DEVELOPMENT AND DOCTRINES

Plato's work remained in the shadow of the death of Socrates for many years. It would be decades before he found his own voice. Scholars usu-

---

[2]Socrates *Apology of Socrates* 38a.

ally divide his work into three periods, based partly on the role of Socrates in them. Early in his career Plato focused on transmitting a sympathetic picture of his teacher. These Socratic dialogues contain little that is doctrinal. Works like *Laches* and *Euthyphro* fit this category. Later Plato began to find his own voice. His masterwork, *Republic,* is the model for this period. The Socratic method is still there, but it has been joined with more Platonic ways of doing philosophy. Finally Plato moves beyond Socrates altogether in *Laws,* his last, unfinished work.

Socrates was not the only influence in Plato's development. Parmenides' puzzle about reality served to stimulate Plato's view of what is. Heraclitus's vision of a world of constant change also had an impact on Plato's cosmology. The Greek school of thought in southern Italy founded by Pythagoras contributed an interest in numbers and geometry. Plato is critical of Homer and the surrounding Greek culture, but he cannot help being influenced by them.

It is possible that Plato was also influenced by cultures beyond Greece. He almost certainly visited Egypt, which was part of the Persian Empire that also controlled Ionian Greece. The borders of the Persian Empire stretched to India, possibly allowing far Eastern ideas to be transmitted to Plato. His dialogue *Timaeus* was enough like Genesis that some church fathers thought he may have met Jeremiah or some Jews in Egypt. Many connections like these are possible though not provable, and ultimately unimportant.

Plato took ideas from many sources and developed a whole that has changed the West. All of the pieces were not original, but his synthesis and presentation of the material was. Plato took scattered ideas, made them into a coherent worldview and presented them all in an argument.

The ideal way to understand Plato is to simply read his dialogues, but this can be confusing to the first-time reader. The confusion is not because Plato is hard to read. The difficulty is that Plato anticipates his reader having a broader background in Athenian and Greek culture than what is actually the case for most students. This unintentional obscurity creates difficulties when combined with Plato's *intentional* obscurity about ideas he views as dangerous to the reader or to himself.

It is not so weird that Plato would be a careful writer. After all, Athens had executed Socrates for ideas that made the state uncomfortable, and Plato was not eager for a hemlock nightcap. The good news was that Athens was not normally an intolerant culture and did not spend much effort on censorship. With a little bit of verbal trickery, a thoughtful critic could say whatever he pleased. Socrates had been directly confrontational, but Plato was more careful.

This careful and indirect political criticism was not an invention of Plato. The theater was a prime place where criticism of contemporary Athenian life was disguised in more acceptable forms. Classical theater would use traditional, even Homeric, themes to make contemporary points. Plays like Euripides' *Bacchae* attacked Homeric religion but did so in the conventional setting of Greek myth. Traditionalists could swallow revolutionary ideas presented in traditional settings.

Like the Bible, Plato's writings do not give a list of doctrines but allow readers to find them as they explore the text for themselves. Of course, anyone can read the Bible and get most of the story. That is also true of Plato. Anyone with patience can read a dialogue like *Symposium* and understand the plot, but there are also deeper levels to the dialogue. If these ideas are critical enough, it can be useful to have a knowledgeable guide to help move the learning process along.

First, read Plato's dialogues in light of some of the traditional Platonic doctrines. Following this first reading, go back to the text again. Does Plato really believe these doctrines? If so, how do they develop? This project works well with three big Platonic ideas: the theory of recollection, the theory of forms and the idea of the soul.

THE FIRST BIG IDEA: THE THEORY OF RECOLLECTION

Socrates claimed that no one does evil knowingly. The death of Socrates must have presented the young Plato with a horrible problem. How could Athens have done such a wicked thing? Good people had allowed the rabble of the city to execute Socrates. Where were the virtuous citizens? If there were any, why hadn't they taught more people to be virtuous?

One natural conclusion is that there were no virtuous citizens. Another is that there were good people, but virtue could not be taught and so was not widespread. The Athenians had skills, which is all Homer meant by virtue, but this was not enough to save Socrates. Socrates needed a just jury, but either the just did not exist or they were a minority unable to teach the majority.

How does a human learn? How does one teach? Fundamental things that humans believe they understand turn out to be very tricky to describe. Plato wrestled with educational problems all his life, but he maintained several core beliefs.

But isn't Plato engaged in the very process he is urging his students to examine? It seems absurd for a teacher to ask a group of learners to examine whether teaching and learning are possible. Something is happening when learning takes place, but perhaps it is not what it seems. Plato does not challenge the experience itself but simply what humans believe the experience to be. Most people have had the experience of misinterpreting something that happens to them. *Something* did happen to them, just not what they believe happened.

Plato questions the "commonsense" intuition that the learner is like an empty word-processing screen waiting for input from the wise teacher. Humans are not blank slates on which ideas are written. Something is happening when humans feel like they are learning, just not the teacher giving new ideas to the learner. Plato has two basic reasons for rejecting this interpretation of the mysterious process of teaching and learning.

First, Plato was puzzled by the failure of great citizens to teach their children to be good citizens. A good person would want to make other people good if possible. However, most good leaders, such as Pericles, failed in their efforts to pass on their virtues to their own children. Of course, goodness may be unteachable without implying that no subjects are teachable. Perhaps one can teach facts, such as the height of the Empire State Building, but not virtues.

This is an important limitation to the kind of education Plato is discussing. He is *not* discussing the memorization of facts or details about the physical world. He wants to know how to educate students in deeper truths. Mathematics, moral virtue, the nature of language— Plato was concerned about these educational topics on which schools were abject failures.

Plato's second worry with education was how one would recognize a basic truth he or she did not know. If learners are blank slates with no previous experience of the thing they are learning, how do they know when they have learned it? If the learner does know it already, then there is nothing to learn. If the student does not know it, then he or she cannot know it when presented with it. If an excited explorer claims to have found the first "birxot," then the world can only accept the explorer's definition of this new word. Nobody can say, "Ah, yes, a birxot." If the explorer says that a birxot is a monster in Loch Ness, then people will know what he means but will not know that it is so.

The same thing applies to anything a teacher suggests. If not already known, the learner would only be able to take it on faith or on the authority of the teacher that the thing is so. But this does not fit human experience when learning first principles. Humans seem to get it, not just be given it.

Learning the height of the Empire State Building from a teacher is a matter of faith on the part of the student. The student does not have any *personal* experience of the Empire State Building after reading an article on it. She takes it on faith that the source knows the subject. However, if she were to experience the Empire State Building herself by measuring it, she could confirm or disconfirm her experience, though she would never be *sure* of the height of the skyscraper. Doubt and discovery are always possible.

Facts are memorized, but there is an "aha" experience in the life of a student that a teacher can stimulate but never simulate. Plato wants to grasp this kind of learning. Most people know from experience the difference between the two types. I distinctly remember sitting in primary school at a desk with a bundle of Popsicle sticks that was supposed to help me understand the idea that ten plus five equals fifteen. I knew the answer to the problem was fifteen; I could work it out with perfect accuracy. But one day while staring at the red and purple stains on the ends of the sticks, I got it. I knew that ten plus five was fifteen. I got the concept behind addition. No one ever had to help me with adding again. I got it.

Watch children play a game using dice. Young children will count the individual dots on the die. They get the idea of one, but six escapes them.

They build six out of a set of ones. Then one magical day they no longer need to count. They can simply glance at the die and see the total of the dots. They understand the higher numbers in themselves. This is not just a matter of recognizing patterns. One can quickly show this by putting three dots on a paper in any order. If the dots are close enough together, most ten-year-olds will simply say there are three dots on the paper; they will not count. The child experiences "threeness."

Humans can *appear* to learn because they already *know* the important things. Learning is remembering. Human infants are born with all the "big ideas" planted within their thick little heads. The travails of birth and life cause them to forget what they know. The good teacher reminds them of those forgotten truths. Learning is recollection.

Plato would say this explains the "aha" experience. As a gradeschooler I was hard-wired with the concepts of addition and numbers. Staring at the Popsicle sticks and hearing the leading words of the teacher triggered the memories within my soul. This is why the concept seemed so familiar to me when I finally got it. It is why it is so hard to doubt it once it is remembered.

Recollection is not merely bringing to mind an intellectual concept once forgotten. For Plato the idea is far more powerful. As humans are helped to recall, they pass through stages of thought and experience. They cannot rationally justify to their satisfaction every step on the way. The would-be philosopher may make use of likely stories (myths such as Atlantis[3]), dialectic and hypothesis to stimulate his memory. Once the memory is triggered, it seizes his mind, and he is changed. He can no longer doubt the truth of what he has remembered. He also understands the reasons for each step in the rational journey that led him to recollection. Further memories of goodness, truth and beauty are now more likely. In fact, correctly used, this one truth can be the key to unlocking every important idea he has forgotten.

This recollection is the most real experience humans can have. It will seize every part of their being. Love for goodness drives the true philosopher to this recollection of truth. Once he finds it, this addiction to the

---

[3]Plato *Timaeus* 25a.

overwhelming beauty of truth and goodness will keep him pursuing it. He will feel it emotionally and physically. Plato compares this experience to sex, to being dazzled by a great light and to the most beautiful music that can be imagined. The true philosopher is the person who has had the mental, emotional and gut-level experience of *truth*. There is no need to encourage such a philosopher to continue his studies; the difficulty will be in getting him to do anything else.

Each human has incredible potential locked inside. Some humans seem unable to learn, but this is due to a complex set of bad choices and bad education. In theory every student could see the mysteries of the universe if properly trained. The role of the teacher is to not write over what is already on the slate. The good teacher tries to pull out of the student what is placed within the mind of every human being. For Plato the role of the teacher is the role of a guide and fellow traveler. The role of guru is not possible in pure Platonism since student and guide know the same things. The student may remember less but is ontologically equal to the teacher.

What kinds of things are humans born knowing? Scholars disagree about what Plato thought, but common suggestions include basic mathematical concepts, laws of logic and a linguistic framework. Ultimately Plato would see humans as coming "prepackaged" with *at least* the idea of the good. Goodness manifests itself in many different ways in the chaotic world. What is an *idea?* That question leads the reader to Plato's doctrine of forms, or ideas.

THE SECOND BIG IDEA:
THE DOCTRINE OF FORMS

Plato believes that humans are born *knowing* ideas, or forms. An idea does not just exist in the human mind, it exists apart from human thought. Ideas are only things that have real existence. They give form to all of the cosmos. Plato's ontology, his theory of being, is very simple: only the forms exist.

Why *form?* The things humans see are made up of two parts. First, there is the stuff that makes up the object. If one imagines a LEGO car, this stuff would be the LEGOs that make up the car. However, a LEGO is pretty much a LEGO. Blue, red, yellow or green: a pile of LEGO blocks is not much to look at. For things one would need a pattern or form. In the case of the LEGO car the form would be "car-ness."

Plato would have believed that the interesting part of a LEGO car was the "car-ness." All the LEGO blocks could pass away, but the idea of "car" would endure. Before humans put the first two square pieces together, this idea existed. Long after the last human has snapped the last plastic blocks together, the idea will still be there.

Ideas are eternal. They cannot be destroyed because they are not the kind of thing that can come apart. As Plato points out in *Phaedo,* ideas simply have no parts. For most Greeks, including Plato, a person or force could destroy a thing only if it had parts. One can see this in the atomists, who postulated indestructible little balls of matter as the basis for all things. Since these pieces are eternal, they can form the basis for knowledge and for continuity within the created order. Instead of atoms at the physical level, Plato had forms at the metaphysical level.

Plato had Parmenides' argument before him. How can things come into being and pass out of being? The argument seems foolproof. No change is possible, yet change is all around. Plato postulated that the only things that exist are changeless forms. What humans see are simply shadows of those forms reflected in substance. The forms are so *ideal* that the material cosmos (endowed with a rational soul) desires to emulate them. It becomes as much like the forms as it can, but since it is *becoming* like the forms, it never can have full *being.* It does not *exist;* it is about to exist.

Perhaps the best analogy Plato could use is biological. The forms are. They birth the material world. The material world is always being born. It never completes the process of becoming because it is always shifting. It can possess a likeness of goodness, truth or beauty, but it cannot have those forms themselves. A material object cannot be the good itself because the good itself has only one property—goodness. A material object cannot have only one property.

Sesame Street had an amusing song that said, "One of these things is not like the others." The trick was to look at four objects and discern which one did not fit. Bob, the genial host, would show the watcher the objects, and "before he finished his song" most children would be able to tell which object did not fit. In one episode Bob showed three different types of shoes—a cowboy boot, a ballerina slipper and a loafer—with an aardvark. Even a child who has never seen a ballerina slipper before could recognize the three types of shoes. Long before Bob got to the end of his song, most children were shouting that the aardvark was the wrong object. It was not like the others.

What is a shoe? Probably none of the children watching could have given a very good definition, but they still *knew* a shoe when they saw one. Aardvarks are just not shoes. What is *it* that those three very different shoes had in common? What binds them together? For Plato it would be "shoe-ness," the form of shoe.

One might think the children did have a crude definition in mind. They were not recollecting "shoe" as much as applying some rough and ready concept such as "shoes are things that go on people's feet." However, if Bob were to replace the aardvark with a toe ring, most children would still get the game right. Almost no child would identify the toe ring as a shoe. Toe rings go on people's feet, but the correct intuition would have been nearly immediate that the idea of shoe does not reach that far. Children grasp differences without adequate definitions. They make elaborate and almost universal distinctions all the time. This sounds very simple, but in practice computer specialists have had a hard time "teaching" computers to differentiate objects. Plato explained this ability through the recollection of unchanging and basic forms.

The theory of forms also helps explain the ability of humans to develop mathematics. Like the Pythagoreans, Plato was fascinated by the fact that math worked in the real world. The ideal world of the geometers could be useful in the imperfect world of the natural philosopher or engineer! No one sees a true square in nature, but humans soon started thinking about perfect squares. How could imperfect experiences in nature generate the thought of perfection? Does imperfect nature generate the perfect idea, or does the perfect idea degenerate into nature? Plato's intuition was that it was more plausible that the perfect came before the imperfect.

Of course, Plato's doctrine of forms or ideas is not quite so simple.

Plato often uses examples that make it seem as if he believes there really are forms of trees, roses and human beings. Humans know about each object because they recollect the form and notice the participation of a given object in the form.

In the dialogue *Parmenides,* Plato brings this simple view under withering fire. Plato refuses to hide from criticism even in his own writings. Plato developed what became the standard attack on Platonism. Ever since, readers have wondered if Plato saved the doctrine from his own assault.

A disturbing problem with the doctrine of forms is aesthetic. Plato must believe in forms for certain unworthy items. It is quite romantic to think of the form of the rose. It is not quite so beautiful to imagine the form of the gnat intestine. Plato could accept that such forms exist. However, his aesthetic sensibility had helped motivate the creation of the doctrine in the first place, and Plato was not eager to embrace ugly forms.

The doctrine also seems to postulate an infinite number of forms. It is difficult to imagine a limit to the number of theoretical objects. Does a form exist for any *imaginable* object? Is there a form of the unicorn? If numbers count as things, then the disaster is compounded. Is there a form for the number 7? Plato seems to say so. Then there must also be a form for the number 777 and 7,777 and 77,777 and so on.

A more serious problem for the doctrine of forms is the "problem of the third man." This problem asserts that the doctrine solves nothing epistemologically. In fact, belief in the forms leads directly to an ugly tangle.

To use another *Sesame Street* illustration, according to the theory of forms, humans can tell that both Bert and Ernie are "human" because Bert and Ernie have the form of human in common. An observer can recollect the form of man and correctly recognize that Bert and Ernie are both participating in it.

If left alone, Plato's proposal seems nice and tidy. However, this "third man" (the form of man) creates a difficulty. Don't the form of man and men have something in common? Suppose that the observer were to look at this new set of manlike objects. What do Bert, Ernie and the form of man have in common? Applying Plato's doctrine, the common element must be the form of the form of man. Like a four-year-old who cannot stop asking why, the observer can press the problem again. What do the form of the form of man, the form of man, Bert and Ernie have in common? To say "the form of the form of the form of man" is to face the jeers of the skeptics. An infinite regress has arrived in all its ugly glory.

If the "third man" problem has a solution, that solution would have required a logical apparatus not available to Plato. Modern analytic philosophy has spent countless hours discussing the third man. Some philosophers think a solution is possible. Others do not. Plato seems to have proposed the problem but then moved on without considering an answer. What can one make of that?

Plato retained a belief in the theory of forms to the end of his career. But he proposed a problem for his theory to which he had no solution. Did Plato fail in his pursuit of wisdom? Did he become dogmatic at the end of his life? The mere fact that Plato developed the problem suggests that the answer is no. Plato was aware that he had finally proposed a question he could not yet answer. On the other hand, it was not as bad a problem as existed for any competing idea.

Plato adopted the theory as the only way to sustain both his observations of the world and reason. He observed change, but reason demanded stability. The theory also could account for human learning and knowledge. He knew of no other theory that could even begin to fulfill either task. The "third man" argument does not say that forms *cannot* exist, just that their existence seems to presuppose an infinite number of forms. Either the existence of an actual infinite did not disturb Plato, or he believed that a pruning problem was preferable to the philosophical crisis that would ensue without his theory.

Plato dealt with some of the difficulties relating to the forms by trimming away many candidates for forms. In the end he may have believed only in the actual existence of the form of the good. Every other "form" was simply a manifestation of the good in a particular substance, place and time. For example, there is no actual form of a rose. "Rose" is just the form of the good when the good is imitated by just this sort of material, in this sort of way, in this place, at this time.

This reduction in the number of forms removed the danger of infinite forms produced from the infinite number of conceivable objects. It also eliminated having to discuss the form of rat dung. This move does not solve the "third man" argument, but it does limit the scope of the problem.

Early Jewish and Christian scholars such as Philo and Boethius did something new with the forms. They postulated that the forms (or the form) were ideas in the mind of an almighty personal God. The advantage of this religious Platonism was that it brought *personality* more directly into the Platonic cosmology. The form of the good is not a fit object for a relationship. One can participate in the form of the good, but one cannot worship it. It may also help solve the "third man" argument since God has no reason to keep thinking about things about which he does not need to think.

Ethics would be greatly simplified if the gods would speak to humans in a way that could be recognized. Plato consistently suggested this possibility. However, Homeric religion simply was not ethically acceptable. The gods of the Greek pantheon were moral degenerates.

Plato sometimes wrote as if the form of the good was God, but he could not really have meant it. The form of the good can have only one attribute: goodness. His own religious experience of the Greek gods made the idea of an all-powerful and good God inconceivable. A childhood spent hearing the stories of the Trojan War and the wanderings of Odysseus left Plato with an inadequate religious imagination.

Plato wanted to explain why the cosmos was a cosmos (an ordered thing). His explanations for objects were teleological. How could he give purposeful cosmic explanations? This could be done only through the introduction of a controlling Mind to the universe. Mind would create and sustain a rational universe. This is why his Socrates praises Anaxagoras, the pre-Socratic who used Mind as an explanation. Plato had to postulate a third type of substance in order to provide for Mind.

THE THIRD BIG IDEA: THE SOUL

The forms and matter are not very similar. forms are eternal and unchanging. Matter is ephemeral and mutable. It is easy to explain the motion of the cosmos with the use of some physical principles. Plato adopted common Greek concepts such as "like is attracted to like." Earth moves toward earth not because of any plan, divine or otherwise, but because it is the nature of earth to move toward earth.

Plato did not think such naturalistic principles were sufficient explanations for the orderly motion he observed. This was particularly true about the motion of heavenly bodies. Why do the stars and planets keep such regular and beautiful motions that humans can set their calendars by? One also has to explain the actions of humans and animals.

Plato borrowed the old Greek idea of soul and gave it new meaning and importance. For Homer, soul had been "wind" that filled living beings. A stray breeze revived a dying warrior in the *Iliad*. Plato transformed soul to act as the seat of mind and reason. This move was anticipated in the pre-Socratics, but Plato took it much further. Plato made soul into the form for living things. Soul was eternal, unchanging and simple. It gave a living being (stars, humans, animals) its rational shape and energy. Since it was simple and unchanging, it was most like the forms (or form) of true being. As a result, soul could act as a bridge between the human world of becoming and the ideal world of being.

Soul for Plato was the source of endless rational motion. In the *Timaeus,* he would describe this motion as circular. Why pick circular motion? Circular motion can continue endlessly without going anywhere. This means the motion can go on forever no matter how limited the space. Unlike other closed shapes no point on a circle is different from any other point. In a square there are corner points, which are distinct from side points. On a circular track any given point is just like any other given point. Each cycle of motion is exactly like the last cycle. Each segment of motion, from any given point to any other, is exactly like any other segment. If an object must move, the best motion is one that goes on forever around the same point. It is eternal, ceaseless, unchanging motion. Since it is most like the eternal and divine forms, such motion is the most rational. It best imitates the state of the world of the forms (the world of being). Natural motions (such as "like being attracted to like") have an end. If the universe followed only such laws, any given motion would be accidental. There would be no life or reason.

At this point, moderns may roll their eyes in frustration. How can

Plato make such large leaps in reasoning? Plato believed the best way for a philosopher to proceed was to develop a hypothesis based on what seemed most sensible. If humans live in a rational universe, the best possible universe, then philosophy and science should be able to make progress. Mathematical models controlled by reason and the search for purpose would produce useful ideas. The working scientist would take these ideal models and compare them to observations. Looking at the cosmos, one could modify the ideal in light of observation. The result would be likely stories to explain what one saw. These stories would improve with time and further experience. In a changing world there would never be a final theory of everything. Theories would be useful approximations that would allow for fruitful speculation. In fact, such Platonists and early scientists, including Copernicus and Kepler, made use of this very sort of Platonic thinking in developing their models of the cosmos.

The great advantage of Plato's way of thinking was that it kept science closely tied to mathematics and reason. A Platonic scientist does not approach a great big pile of facts and try to blindly turn them into a system. No one can do this anyway, but the illusion that one can leads to bad results. People can pick worse guides than mathematics and teleology.

Plato saw the motion of the stars as the great fact that needed philosophical explanation. Unlike the earth, the heavens seemed rational and orderly. It was impossible to predict the weather, but one could count on the stars. The sun rises and sets in an orderly manner. Compared to the hellish chaos of the earth, the astral area seemed like heaven. This fundamental rationality of the great sphere enclosing the earth made Plato sure that the cosmos itself was rational. If the principle of rational motion in animals on earth was soul, then it was simplest to assume that the entire cosmos itself had a soul. The cosmos is a great rational animal—spherical, of course.

The cosmic soul provides the orderly motions of the astral realm. There is not a great deal of matter in the astral realm. Most matter in the astral realm was fire, and so lightweight. As a result, the soul could easily control the motions of the astral bodies. This is why their movements are so orderly and precise. The higher the concentration of matter, the more physical laws come into play.

Like most ancients Plato made the spherical earth the center of his universe. He did not do so to elevate human status. Matter attracted to other matter often fell down to the center of the great cosmic animal. The earth is the septic tank of the cosmos. The extra "stuff" (particularly earth and water) that might distract from the perfect motion of the heavens came here, where it least bothered the cosmic animal. (The cosmos is complete, so there is no space outside it in which to expel waste.)

The Platonic earth is a tough place for reason. It is filled with matter flying about based only on physical laws instead of behaving according to reason. Matter does not move as it should but as it must. It is difficult for the soul to control this motion. However, one does see orderly motion on the earth. This can only be understood as the partial success of the cosmic soul in bringing discipline to the frontier area of the cosmos.

Animals, including human beings, move independently and sometimes rationally. This rational motion is not obviously linked to any of the great cosmic movements that can be observed in the night sky. Plato decided that animals must possess a secondary type of soul. This soul is not part of the cosmic soul but like it. It is the bridge between the heavens and the earth, just as the cosmic soul is the bridge between the forms and matter.

If the cosmic soul in the world of becoming is the thing most like the forms, then the animal soul on the earth is the thing most like the cosmic soul. Humans are forced to live in the thick, dense atmosphere of earth with all of its confused motions. This is tough for the ordered life. Fortunately, they have been provided with rational, immortal souls. These souls are hard-wired with the knowledge of the forms.

Plato believes all animals possess one type of soul. Souls simply migrate from animal type to animal type in a series of incarnations. Good souls are allowed to live in higher animals. Bad souls end up in dull animals like fish. These incarnations are chosen for a soul based on the state of the soul at the time of death. Human souls are immortal because souls are not the sort of thing that dies. This immortal, rational soul enables humans to pursue the good, the true and the beautiful.

Human souls seem to be divided. Sometimes the inner nature of a person seems torn. In Star Wars, young Anakin wishes to marry the princess, but the rule of the Jedi Order forbids it. As in any great romance, this is not mere physical passion. Young Skywalker's soul is torn in two. One part desires to behave rationally and the other passionately.

To explain this psychological problem, Plato hypothesized that the human soul has two major parts. The first part is the immortal part, which allows for reason. This sits in the head. The other part of the human soul is mortal. This part also has two parts and can pass away at death. It acts as a buffer between the immortal, rational soul and the world. It allows the rational soul to communicate with the body without being overwhelmed by it. It also provides the energy or passion needed to pursue the good in a confusing world. Sadly, this mortal soul can itself be confused. The duality of the soul allows for psychological conflict.

The mortal soul is divided between parts found in the chest and the belly. The chest area, the heart, contains the passions, which are higher. This is the spirited nature of humans. Traditional Greek virtues like courage are the function of this soul. The soul in the belly is concerned with the erotic nature of human beings. This erotic nature is not limited to sexual drives but to all the passions necessary to sustain the body. Taken together, these two parts of the mortal soul would ideally allow the rational soul to safely control the body. However, if one of the two parts gets out of order, the result is irrational (hence wicked) behavior.

Overall, the human (or animal) soul has three parts: one immortal and two mortal. Plato frequently uses the word *soul* in his dialogues in a confusing way. He uses it to refer to any one of the parts or to the whole soul system or to the mortal or immortal divisions of the soul. Keep this in mind while reading Plato. One should try to use the context to help determine which sense of soul is being referred to in a dialogue. For example, the *Phaedo* only discusses the immortal, rational soul. The *Republic* uses soul in all its senses, and in a confusing manner. The *Timaeus* uses all the terms in a more precise manner.

Plato's division of the human soul into three parts endured in Western thought. Dante assumed it. Theologians such as John of Damascus utilized it as well. The nonphysical soul remains the only viable alternative to modern reductionism that reduces mind to matter.

TIIE QUEST FOR GOODNESS, TRUTH AND BEAUTY

Homer told wise stories. The pre-Socratics gave disjointed rational answers to certain problems. Plato gave a total package, as richly mythical as Homer but as keenly analytic as Parmenides.

His worldview was rational, defensible and open-ended. Platonism could account for the world. It was optimistic about knowledge but hardheaded enough to account for failures. It did not try to explain evil away but provided for failure without destroying a chance for goodness. Humans live in a shadow world but might be able to catch glimpses of the real. At the same time, Plato incorporated compelling verbal pictures and stories into most of his philosophy. No one can read the *Republic* and forget the story of the cave. His Atlantis myth was so realistic that countless generations have foolishly gone looking for the lost continent. He *sold* his philosophy to every part of the human being. He cajoled and he seduced.

Plato was the first author with whom one could argue, fall in love and learn at the same time. He invited dialogue through his style. He demanded that humans follow reason wherever it led. He believed he had discovered broad truths about the world and human nature. He was the first great system maker of Western philosophy whose work survived to influence all future generations.

Plato believed that the pursuit of philosophy was powered by love. The erotic and spirited soul would provide a passion for finding the good, the true and the beautiful. How could it help it? A beautiful human cannot compare to the beautiful itself. A good cause cannot be as fulfilling as the good itself. Some truth cannot satisfy as much truth itself. In this way Plato tied his worldview into the most basic passions of the human experience. He believed that by writing for a popular audience he could seduce it into following reason. Once the soul was carefully and slowly exposed to the forms, there would be no going back. Plato's philosophy is intellectually rich and emotionally addictive. As Socrates might say, these are dangerous waters, and a Christian must pray that God himself will protect him or her.

4

FOLLOW THE LOGOS
WHEREVER IT LEADS

What Is a Dialogue?

PROFOUND BOOKS MIGHT BE EASY TO READ but are always hard to exhaust. A great book gives back more to the reader than any effort made to understand it. But modern readers of Plato have a problem: Plato wrote in dialogues, and few people read or write dialogues anymore. Dialogues are not hard to understand—people do more difficult things every day—but they do have a few simple rules. Learn the rules, and Plato will unlock intellectual treasures for a lifetime. Of course, nobody is likely to understand everything. The goal is not to master Plato but to learn enough to be taught by him.

Plato's dialogues are not a list of important ideas to memorize. Dialogues are interactive stories about conversations and speeches. The reader should *argue* with the characters of the dialogue. If Socrates makes a bad argument, then call him on it. If a character gives up too quickly in the face of Socrates' withering irony, then try to construct a better case. Doing so often reveals that Plato has anticipated and assumed this participation in the rest of the book!

In the *Symposium* the first thing a careful reader notices is the long setting of the scene before the dialogue really starts. It can seem like extra padding to be skipped, but assuming that this background has a purpose will help make sense of the entire book. In the prelude Plato pictures the absence of love in each of the speakers who are about to give speeches praising divine love. Eunuchs are giving advice on lovemaking.

This example screams danger to a good student. For many readers the first experience with a serious book is reading a textbook. They learn, or are even taught, to skim to get to the main idea. Whatever the merits of this strategy for reading books written by committees of corporate educators, it is absolutely the wrong way to read Plato. These dialogues have no filler, no fluff. They are the unique, sometimes eccentric but always brilliant fictional inventions of a first-rate mind.

Why take Plato so seriously? Intellectual fads may come and go, but Plato has endured centuries of scrutiny. Not many writers could simultaneously inspire a medieval philosopher like Thomas Aquinas and a modern political theorist like Leo Strauss. A well-worn copy of *Symposium* left to a grandchild will be relevant if it is read.

His works are profound but also beautiful. The death scene of Socrates in *Phaedo* is touching without being too sweet. Plato created stories, such as the Atlantis myth, that still inspire every genre of the arts. He wrote in the voice of a comic poet, tragic poet, philosopher, child, wise woman, foolish old man and poor man so well that it is easy to forget he is not transcribing real conversations.

Close examination of Plato brings more and more insights, which do not come from the reader but from the text. The bleak *Laws,* Plato's last, great, unfinished work, has an unnamed Athenian stranger as its central character. Where is Socrates? Is his disappearance an accident? Not any more of an accident than Shakespeare giving a character the name of Painter in *Timon of Athens* because the playwright ran out of names. In *Laws* Socrates cannot appear because at the very core of the conversation there is a deep alienation from Athens.

A Platonic dialogue must be read as a whole before it is closely studied. The first reading is best done in one sitting, quickly enough to read the entire dialogue. After a break of a few days to allow for reflection, the student should reread the dialogue. This process should be repeated at least once more. Then the student should spend as much time in *commu-*

nity discussion as was spent in close reading of the book. Ultimately dialogues were not meant to be read alone but in the midst of conversation. They are conversations to stimulate conversations. Careful readers will be eager to share their opinions in a group and just as eager to allow the text and the discussion to change their minds.

Sitting with good friends, a wise mentor and Plato's dialogues has provided me with some of the richest times in my life. It deepens my understanding, reveals my folly and, with practice, produces great pleasure. Plato taught me the joy of inquiring for myself, full of hope and not fear, leading me by a long road to God. Nothing I write can be a substitute for this conversation, but merely a guide to some tasty intellectual feasts and some help in appreciating their unusual flavors.

EUTHYPHRO (EARLY PERIOD)

What if a character in a movie or novel is correct, but repulsive or clueless? Stealing and crime are bad, but who wants to fall into the hands of a Javert? Many Americans did not like what Bill Clinton did with a young intern, but they disliked Ken Starr even more. As my grandfather used to say, some people are just so straight they lean a bit.

The *Euthyphro* is named after such a man. Euthyphro is a wealthy, highly religious, middle-aged man about to prosecute his father for murder. A slave on the family estate had killed another slave, and Euthyphro's father carelessly allowed the murderer to die while deciding what to do with him. In ancient Greece such murder was believed to pollute the land with bloodguilt. Since the gods are offended by unpunished murder, Euthyphro has decided to have his father tried before the Athenian religious court. His father has behaved impiously, and now he will be forced to pay. As one might expect, the family is horrified, but Euthyphro is unmoved by their pleas.

Euthyphro's disinterested pursuit of justice is good, but the man himself comes across as insufferable. He has no sympathy for the bonds of family duty, which were particularly important to ancient Greeks. He is intellectually self-satisfied, demonstrates almost no imagination, believes he is an expert on religion, but cannot begin to defend his views.

Ironically, Euthyphro's name means "right-minded."[1] He chooses abstract justice over family duty, and this presents an ethical dilemma.

The tension in the dialogue is not as obvious to modern readers as it would have been in Athens when it was written. Aristophanes, the great author of comic plays, had given Socrates a good roasting in his *Clouds*. In the play Socrates teaches a son to justify beating his father by teaching him "wrong logic" that enables the son to make the bad look good.[2] The father eventually sets fire to the "think tank" where Socrates is based. The father says, "For with what aim did ye insult the Gods, and pry around the dwellings of the Moon? Strike, smite them, spare them not, for many reasons, but most because they have blasphemed the Gods!"[3]

Aristophanes accuses Socrates of loving abstract ideas of justice more than people, which leads to monstrous injustice. This is a tension some still feel. Sometimes people will not turn in a friend who commits a crime, even when the friend is doing serious harm to others and self. Some crimes are kept in the family regardless of the harm done. I once served on a jury with another juror who would not vote to convict a member of her ethnic group. It is important to understand this tendency to get the full force of this dialogue.

Plato increases the tension by setting the discussion immediately before Socrates' trial for impiety. Justice will soon miscarry, and Socrates will die. Euthyphro is to try his father for impiety, and we know the father is guilty. What is Plato implying by this parallel? At the least, the setting suggests that not all impiety should be subject to the courts. Perhaps not all things that are legally impious are actually impious.

The *Euthyphro* contains all the elements of the Socratic method discussed in chapter two. Euthyphro, an "expert" who claims knowledge about what it is for a man to be pious, meets Socrates. Socrates asks him what piety is. Euthyphro gives conventional answers that are destroyed by further questions from Socrates. Euthyphro attempts to fix his an-

---

[1] It is often useful to track the meaning of the names of the characters in Plato's dialogues. These are fictional works. Plato is so convincing as a writer it is easy to forget that he could have used any name, or invented a totally new one, like Timaeus, in order to further his meaning.

[2] Aristophanes *Clouds* 889-1112.

[3] Aristophanes *Clouds* 1505.

swers, does very badly and eventually gives up. As often happens in Socratic dialogues, Euthyphro gives up just after making his most interesting observations.

Falling into the pattern Plato sets for his Socratic dialogues, the question "What is piety and impiety?" is asked by Socrates. Euthyphro's first
answer appears to be the worst but is deceptive.[4] Euthyphro says, "To be
pious is to do what I am doing now, to prosecute the wrongdoer . . .
whether the wrongdoer is your father or your mother or anyone else."[5]
This may not be a *definition* of piety, but it is a defensible ethical position.
It is the indefensible example that Euthyphro uses to support his position that is his undoing. Euthyphro compares himself to the greatest
god, Zeus himself, who punished his divine father for impiety.

Socrates will not accept divine impiety, and he rejects the traditional
mythology of Homer as an inadequate theology. This is a major theme in
the *Euthyphro* and Plato's later writings. Gods who fight and act badly are
not gods at all. Plato does not have Socrates argue for this position so
much as rely on the intuition that gods should be better than humans.

Initially Socrates makes little impression on Euthyphro's Homeric
fundamentalism. He does seem to move on without accepting Homer. At
6e Socrates presses Euthyphro to give him not just an example of a pious
act, like punishing murder, but the form of piety so that Socrates can use
it as a model to guide his own behavior. If all pious actions have piety in
common, then what is this element that they have in common?

Euthyphro accepts this task because he believes he knows what piety is.
He also accepts that knowing what it is will help him live. But despite his
pompous claims, he knows neither. Whatever the merits of his court case,
he should receive no credit for any good that comes of it. Euthyphro is acting without reason. "Right-minded" is exactly what Euthyphro is not!
Many of the later dialogues will search for a uniting form or idea not just in
order to understand what a thing is, but as a way to know how to live.

Euthyphro then defines piety this way: what is "dear to the gods is pious and what is not is impious."[6] Socrates quickly points out that this

---

[4]Plato *Euthyphro* 5d.
[5]Plato *Euthyphro* 5d-e.
[6]Plato *Euthyphro* 7a.

definition would fall to pieces in the Homeric world. Gods disagree all the time on what actions they love or hate. People might be both pious and impious at the same time. Euthyphro claims he knows the gods agree with his actions. Socrates asks to be shown Euthyphro's proof, but he can only stutter, "This is perhaps no light task, Socrates, though I could show you very clearly."[7]

Plato is intent on destroying the Homeric religion, whose power structure reached from its center in Delphi across much of the Mediterranean world. It had a tight grip on the Athenian imagination and represented a dark power against which even the love of wisdom seemed scarcely enough protection.

Delphi, the center of Greek mysticism, sat between heaven and sea, wrapped protectively in mountains. The great oracle of Delphi was based there, making prophetic utterances in the name of Apollo. Blind acceptance of oracular utterances stood in the way of human progress, but Socrates and Plato were not given to thoughtless submission.

The oracle once told Socrates that he was the wisest of all men. Socrates took this statement seriously but thought it to be false. He tried to understand what the oracle meant, and in doing so he began to dialogue with the gods. Socrates in the writings of Plato claimed that this was praise for his knowledge of his own ignorance. The Delphic oracle famously commanded the seeker to "know thyself." This command for humans to know their limits and their place under the god of the oracle was reinterpreted by Plato as a command for self-examination and philosophic reflection.

Plato was not opposed to all religion, but to religion without reason, like that of Homer and the oracle. Plato pictured Socrates saying to his students, "You inquire for yourself." Euthyphro cannot follow the argument (the divine Logos) wherever it leads, because the Homeric religion gives him no basis for the just, the beautiful and the good.[8] Conventionally religious Greeks can only make speeches or gape at Socrates; they cannot dialogue.

---

[7]Plato *Euthyphro* 9b.
[8]Plato *Euthyphro* 7d.

The unexamined life is not worth living, and Euthyphro is living an unexamined life. Plato shows that even in a good person such a life is devoid of meaning. Just acting, doing, is not enough for a meaningful human life; people also have to know what they are doing and why. For Plato Euthyphro's actions have little meaning because he is not thoughtful. Euthyphro is ethically dead.

The problem Socrates poses to Euthyphro is difficult for any ethic based on divine will. Is an action good because the gods love it, or do the gods love it because it is good? Is there something in common among the things the gods love that *causes* their love? The goodness of an action, not some powerful god loving it (by itself), should commend the action to humanity.

Some Islamic and Christian scholars disagree with Socrates' intuition. They are hesitant to limit God's sovereignty by any standard external to his will, and so they argue that a thing is good just because God wills it. If God created a universe in which abortion was good, then abortion would be good. All right and wrong are based ultimately on divine command.

Why then should humans praise God for his goodness? There does not seem to be a great deal of purpose in praising a being for doing whatever he wants. There is something wrong with an idea that would make God less worthy of praise and honor.

Worse still is the fear that divine command theory undermines trust in God. According to divine command theory, if God were to lie, that would be good. How do we know God will not lie? Because he said so. But according to divine command theory, if he changed his mind and lied, then that would be good too. God might have the power to do this, but power does not make a thing good.

Given the Euthyphro dilemma, some Christians accept the Platonic notion that there exists a good independent of God, but this runs the risk of making the good greater than God. Some Christians try to escape this by asserting that God *is* the good, and the good *is* God. Others suggest that the good is an idea in the mind of God.

There are serious problems with this response, however. Plato argued that things that last cannot have parts. If they have parts, then they are subject to change, and change leads to decay. No decay means immortality. Things without parts are called simple, and simple things are immortal. Since God is immortal, he must be simple and so changeless. This doctrine is called divine simplicity.

Both divine changelessness and simplicity are controversial, but divine simplicity has proven the most difficult to defend. God is a person, and it is hard to imagine a simple person. Are God's will, emotions and thoughts all one? This would be a very odd sort of person if a person at all. If God is simple, then his love must be the same thing as his justice. Is this even coherent? Most contemporary Christian philosophers have abandoned the idea of divine simplicity, though a few continue to defend it.

Recently there have been attacks on divine changelessness. Some argue that the Bible says God changes and that it is not possible to be a person and never change. These arguments are less impressive than those against divine simplicity. First, biblical language about divine action is bound to be metaphorical at some level given the chasm between the nature of God and humanity. Second, divine changelessness does theological and not just philosophical work. It makes God trustworthy and worthy of worship. Third, divine changelessness is much easier to defend than divine simplicity, and many philosophers do so. In any case, while both divine simplicity and changelessness may have disadvantages, both protect God's ethical independence ("He is the good, answering to nothing else"), his praiseworthiness ("His very essence is the good itself") and his sovereignty.

Often overlooked in this discussion of divine commands and their relationship to ethics is the argument that provoked it in *Euthyphro*. Euthyphro agrees that a thing is led, carried or loved because something leads, carries or loves it. Euthyphro could have asked if being loved is really the same sort of change as being carried or led, but he did not. Accepting this philosophic intuition carries huge consequences.

Plato believes that anything that changes a person is motivated by an external agent. Most controversially, this includes the changes that occur when one sees a beautiful object or is ethically transformed. Humans see beauty because it is there, not merely in their own minds, and are led to beautiful thoughts by it. Humans become better because the good confronts them and draws them to the good. Ethical change is not merely within, but is based on transforming contact with an external good.[9]

MENO (MIDDLE PERIOD)

How do we know what we know? In a culture where Hesiod pictured the world beginning in chaos and skeptics attacked even the possibility of knowledge, knowledge was not a sure bet. But Plato longed for reason and secure knowledge. In the dialogue *Meno* Plato seeks an epistemology in which to ground that desire.

In *Meno* Socrates is still the main character, and the Socratic method is still very much on display. Socrates asks Meno, "What is virtue?"[10] Having asked the usual opening question, Socrates destroys the conventional answers of the easily bewildered rich man, but then the *Meno* takes a new turn. Socrates proposes a solution to the problems that Meno is facing. Socrates begins to propose Platonic doctrines, in this case the theory of recollection. Plato is beginning to find his own voice, making the *Meno* an excellent example of a transition dialogue from the early to the middle period of his writings.

While *Meno* may be the clearest statement of Plato's epistemology, Plato does not come at it directly.[11] His epistemology is *not* found in a dialogue where the Socratic question is, What is knowledge? Like the *Euthyphro,* the dialogue begins in mid-discussion, and Meno asks the first recorded question. Meno was well known to Plato's readers as the boyishly handsome commander of a disastrous Greek expedition against Persia. He was eventually tortured and killed for his lack of virtue. He wanted money and power and would evidently say or do whatever it took to gain both. Meno was a clever speaker and had no rhetorical scruples.

In the dialogue Meno is presented as a student of Gorgias, the great rhetorician of his age. Gorgias's vanity was so great that he presented a golden statue of himself to Delphi. He was famous for teaching people to argue without concern for the justice of their case. Plato's dialogue that

---

[9]C. S. Lewis's *Abolition of Man,* the most important essay of the twentieth century, builds on this argument.

[10]Plato *Meno* 71d.

[11]*Alcibiades* is more pointed, but most scholars don't think it was written by Plato.

is named after Gorgias presents him as a pompous windbag and an ass. Here Meno has become like his teacher.

The first question of the *Meno,* therefore, is asked by a man trained out of any virtue. Meno asks if virtue can be taught, and Socrates asks what virtue is. Not surprisingly, Meno is not a very helpful companion for that discussion. Socrates, a good man, also claims not to know what virtue is, and this frustrates Meno greatly. In his frustration Meno asks Socrates how they can learn or know anything.[12] Surprisingly, Socrates has an answer: recollection.

Knowledge must occur with virtue. In his lifetime Socrates had taught that the person who knows the good is virtuous. Plato agrees but makes the relationship a two-way street. Only the virtuous can know the good. As a bad man Meno cannot be a knowing man.

With his glib tongue Meno seizes control of the conversation. He tries to out-Socrates Socrates. With any other Athenian this might work, but Socrates is a good man who knows only one thing: he does not know anything. Knowledge of his ignorance has produced virtue in Socrates. When confronted with this virtue, Meno is shown to be helpless. He blames Socrates for his confusion, but in reality he has confused himself by trying to seek virtue without knowledge.

Socrates believes that cynicism and confusion are byproducts of attempting to learn without virtue. Doesn't this create a hopeless situation though? If humans have to be good to learn, and learning is what makes them good, then what are they to do? Plato's answer is that students who are *almost* virtuous can *remember* things implanted in their soul from before their birth. This does not require teaching, since even accidental images can remind a student of a truth he has known from birth. In the hands of a good teacher who chooses proper images and activities the student can remember even more readily. The student cannot learn new things yet because he has not attained virtue. If the student is hopeful, not vice ridden, then he might be able to remember enough to produce sufficient virtue in his soul so that learning can begin.

Socrates laughingly refuses to be drawn into any trap Meno sets. He

---

[12]Plato *Meno* 80d.

cannot define virtue and does not know if it can be taught in a formal education program of the sort Meno has in mind. Meno believes he knows what virtue is and that he can define it easily. Socrates mainly presses Meno for a definition of virtue so that Meno can see his own ignorance. Knowledge of one's own ignorance is both the easiest thing for any human to learn and the hardest thing to acknowledge. Meno will have to let go of his pretended wisdom in order to gain true wisdom.

Meno defines virtue for each individual citizen in terms of roles assigned to them by tradition.[13] Men, women, children, slaves and the elderly all have their roles and hence their assigned virtues. Meno is following the old Homeric idea of virtue, that it is simply excellence at a task. A virtuous slave is one who is good at being a slave.

Socrates does not accept this and asks what each of these persons has in common. He is not asking Meno for a list of the virtuous, but what virtue is. When each citizen is being virtuous, what is the idea that they all have in common? What is virtue itself?

Meno tries again. He defines virtue as "ruling." However, a tyrant cannot be virtuous; so Meno patches up the definition by saying the virtuous person is one who rules justly. This traps Meno in a circular argument because justice is a virtue, and he has used a single virtue to define the category. Meno must try again.

At this point the reader is apt to be frustrated with Socrates and with his method. Meno is plainly a fool. Why can't Socrates just help him? Isn't Socrates the great teacher? Why is he tormenting his student as a cat might torment a particularly dull mouse? But Meno is no dullard; he is simply following the techniques of his famous teacher, Gorgias. Gorgias sought favor with the crowd, and Meno gives answers in the manner of Gorgias. He gives conventional answers that will bring electoral victory in the Athenian democracy, where truth is often determined by vote. On the other hand, Socrates seeks truth rather than victory in debate. Socrates says, "If my questioner was one of those clever and disputatious debaters, I would say to him, 'I have given my

---

[13]Plato *Meno* 71e.

answer, if it is wrong, you must refute it.'"[14]

Meno cannot be quickly refuted or taught because he is not yet in a position to learn. Socrates hopes to persuade Meno to gain philosophic wisdom. To do so Socrates is not willing to become a clever though less pompous version of Meno. Gorgias has given Meno answers to all the important questions, but Socrates wants an intellectual friend instead of an intellectual servant.

Meno has reached the second stage of following the Logos, or argument. Instead of participating in the present discussion with his own ideas, Meno falls back on the authority and splendor of the poets. Quoting one, Meno says that virtue is "desiring beautiful things and having the power to acquire them."[15] Meno misuses poetry to make rhetorical points. Poetry may be beautiful, but poetry is *true* in exactly the same way any other statement is true. Beauty is no guarantee of truth. False poetic statements can persuade because they sound beautiful, so Socrates frequently has to place himself in opposition to the traditional poets. He has to do so because their beauty can dull people's minds to the truth or falsity of their message. To break free to follow philosophy, he must break the power of traditional Greek poetry to dictate every aspect of life.

"Desiring" and "having power" are the dangerous ideas in Meno's definition. Since even the wicked desire beautiful things, the definition is also not very useful. This notion, that virtue is the power to get good things, greatly disturbs Socrates. He calls Meno the close friend of the enemy of Greek liberty—the Persian king.[16] Greeks who worked with the Persians were not widely admired. The comment had the same sting for Meno that an American might feel if someone called him or her an intimate of Osama bin Laden. The Athenian reader is reminded that Meno was happy to sell his services to the enemies of his people. However, even Meno would not admit that he was willing to get gold and silver unjustly, so he was quickly reduced to adding "justly" and "piously" to any good exercise of power. As Socrates immediately notes, Meno has again defined virtue by tacking one or two

---

[14]Plato *Meno* 75d.
[15]Plato *Meno* 77b.
[16]Plato *Meno* 78d.

virtues onto an unsatisfactory definition.

By 80, Meno can pontificate no longer, so he turns on Socrates. He compares him to a torpedo fish that numbs its prey; he archly warns Socrates not to leave Athens because other cities might not be so tolerant of his behavior. Meno still does not question his own wisdom, but like a sick patient he blames the doctor for revealing his illness. Socrates is not daunted. He has gotten Meno to admit that he does not know the answer. He proposes seeking the nature of virtue together in a community.[17]

This marks a critical shift from Plato's early dialogues, which are frequently adversarial in tone and end, as we saw in the *Euthyphro,* with little progress made. But here in the *Meno,* bewilderment is not the end but a new beginning. In the later dialogues, especially in *Republic* and *Timaeus,* Socrates is actually helped by his students.

Meno is a hopeless student and a bad man, but he asks a profound question: "How will you look for it Socrates, when you do not know at all what it is? How will you aim to search for something you do not know at all? If you should meet with it, how will you know that this is the thing that you did not know?"[18] Meno is not inspired by any greater goal than stumping Socrates, but in trying to answer Meno's questions, Socrates will progress.

Socrates accepts Meno's challenge and agrees that learning seems impossible. You cannot learn a thing you already know. If you don't know it, then you cannot know you have found it. Therefore learning is impossible.

Socrates is stuck and claims that only a divine revelation can save him. He transforms a quotation from the poet Pindar to argue for the immortality of the human soul and the justice of the gods:

> As the soul is immortal, has been born often and has seen all things here
> and in the underworld, there is nothing which it has not learned, so it is
> in no way surprising that it can recollect the things it knew before, both
> about virtue and other things. As the whole of nature is akin, and the
> soul has learned everything, nothing prevents a man, after recalling one

---

[17]Plato *Meno* 80d.
[18]Plato *Meno* 80d.

thing only—a process men call learning—discovering everything else for himself, if he is brave and does not tire of the search, for searching and learning are, as a whole recollection.[19]

Socrates rallies Meno's courage and invites him to join in a search for truth.

Socrates shows Meno how the process of recollection works by calling in a slave boy and teaching him geometry. The real target of this demonstration is Gorgias. Gorgias taught his followers to speak confidently and worry about the truth later. The ignorant slave has mistaken ideas about geometry that he is willing to express loudly. Socrates uses simple questions to help the boy recollect and find the truth. Along the way the slave boy makes many mistakes and at one point becomes bewildered, allowing Meno to see bewilderment as part of progress.[20] When the boy solves the problem, Meno is forced to concede that it is likely the boy has recollected the truth.

Most readers find this demonstration unpersuasive, believing Socrates led the slave boy to the truth by introducing to him concepts he did not know. Socrates' questions are more like statements. As one reader once said in frustration, "Socrates is giving a geometry lesson with question marks."

It would be quite possible to defend Socrates, but let us assume that Socrates has not demonstrated recollection to *our* satisfaction. That is rather beside the point, because he has demonstrated it to Meno's satisfaction. In my experience with many classes, it is possible to modify Socrates' questions so that a particular group is persuaded. Plato is writing a conversation not so that it will persuade us, but in the hope that we will try to duplicate the experiment. In this way he can provoke us to *actively participate* in philosophy. A child who watches enough *Superman* episodes wants to fly and wear a cape. A student who reads the slave boy example wants to be Socrates. No given set of questions could possibly work for everyone. Instead, Plato composes an argument that tempts us to try dialogue for ourselves.

It is not that Plato has written an intentionally bad argument to pro-

---

[19]Plato *Meno* 81c-d.
[20]Plato *Meno* 84d.

voke the reader. Nor can every bad thing Plato wrote be excused on the grounds that he wanted his reader to do better. But in the case of the slave boy, the demonstration is a decent one. It is good enough to allow readers to see pretty clearly what a good demonstration, from their point of view, would look like. They are easily able to propose changes to the textual example that would make it work for them.

In a hopeful moment in the dialogue Meno accepts the theory of recollection. Socrates wishes to press forward and find out the nature of virtue, but Meno turns back. He asks his original question: "Can virtue be taught?"[21] Recollection combined with Socratic questioning produced change in an ignorant slave boy, but in handsome and successful Meno it cannot. Meno does not really want to become truly virtuous, because true virtue can lead to execution in Athens, as Plato points out twice in the dialogue. People say they love righteousness, but frequently wickedness is safer.

Socrates rebukes Meno for his error, but he must follow his partner, demonstrating the dark side of learning in community. When it works, it is wonderful. When the community is rotten, then no progress is possible. Only a miracle can provide those who love wisdom with a community that will aid them and not hold them back. This miracle does occur in Plato: in *Republic* Socrates will gain better, bolder partners. But in *Meno* his partner does not love following the Logos.

Can virtue be taught? Recollection gives a basis for knowledge, and knowledge might lead to virtue, but it is *not* virtue. No one is good by nature since good people would be treasures to be guarded and Athens does not have any such people to guard or cultivate. People do not appear to be able to learn virtue since there are no teachers of virtue in Athens. Surely if virtue could be taught, then intellectual Athens, the schoolroom of the world, would contain such teachers. Meno and Socrates are at a dead end.

At 90, Socrates brings Anytus into the conversation since he can get no further with the exhausted Meno. Anytus is the prototypical Athenian gentleman and one of the chief accusers of Socrates. Meno is one type of bad man, and now Plato brings in another. Athens generally rec-

---

[21]Plato *Meno* 87c.

ognizes the error of Meno, but Athens will agree with Anytus and condemn Socrates. Socrates is unlucky in his students.

Anytus believes that any good citizen can teach virtue, but Socrates points out an obvious problem with this happy idea: some of the best Athenians have raised rotten sons. The best men should want all the best for their own sons, yet many of their sons are the worst in the city. If virtue can be taught, why don't the virtuous teach it to their sons or find someone who can?

Anytus hates the Sophists, but he hates them as innovators and foreigners. He would purge the city of their influence if he could. Anytus is a complacent bigot, and Socrates cannot dialogue with him. If Meno wanted to make speeches and take control of the conversation, Anytus wants Athenian norms to be accepted without any challenge. He is angry that the civil order is being attacked and warns Socrates that his words could prove dangerous.

Anytus represents one of the greatest dangers Plato sees for Athens. Plato is deeply conservative, despising mob rule. A stable and prosperous city provides the means and the time for the pursuit of higher things, including philosophy, but complacency is always a danger. Athens was the most open city of the ancient world, but this freedom had been won by great men. Plato believed such men were no more.

Anytus confused the virtues of his city with the virtue of the individuals in it. Plato sees that Athens is in decline, with the average decadent Athenian being carried along by good laws. At an early point in the development of a community, the sum is not as great as the parts. Plato sees that in his own day Athens has become greater than the sum of her parts. A residual corporate righteousness covered up for individual decay, but it could not last. Private vice would undermine public virtue.

Plato is not interested in philosophy that is detached from a discussion about the city because philosophy can only take place in a well-ordered soul; such a soul needs a well-ordered community to flourish. Socrates would be condemned by the city for "corrupting the youth,"[22] but Socrates did not corrupt Meno and Anytus.

---

[22]Plato *Apology* 23d.

Meno and Anytus represent two intellectual types in Athens. Meno is the attractive, superficially well-educated cynic who is interested in appearing wise but in reality loves power and cold hard cash. Education like that given by Gorgias created Meno. He was taught to get his way but not what way is good.

Anytus is the opposite type. He loves Athens but is disinterested in knowing why his city is good, refusing to consider his own assumptions personally. He looks at the yammer of philosophers as destructive to the social order that has enriched him.

Compared to later dialogues, the *Meno* is a disappointment. Progress has been made from the early dialogues, but bewilderment still does not lead to understanding. Merely getting the right doctrine does no good if the students who hear it are interested only in money, convention and power. Socrates ends the conversation with this:

> If we were right in the way in which we spoke and investigated in this whole discussion, virtue would neither be an inborn quality or taught, but comes to those who possess it as a gift from the gods which is not accompanied by understanding, unless there is someone among our statesman who can make another into a statesman.[23]

The theory of recollection teaches that human knowledge was implanted by the gods. True piety is remembering what the gods have taught, which provides a way to produce just humans without an infinite regress of just humans existing in Athens.

If humans know all the important ideas at birth, then surely some of these ideas are the virtues. If a person were to remember the idea of justice, for example, then he or she would become just. Knowledge of ideas like the just itself is built into human souls. This memory *leads* to justice when activated but is not by itself just. Knowledge of a virtue is a catalyst to virtue, but it is not virtue itself. If this is true, then no teachers teach justice or any other virtue; they just help their students to recollect an idea. It is the built-in memory, not the lesson, that leads inevitably to virtue in the student. There are many possible ways to recollect justice, but there is only one virtue of justice. With luck even bad teachers could

---

[23]Plato *Meno* 99e-100b.

create virtuous students, or some people might come to virtue on their own by chance if stimulated correctly. The oracle of Delphi may have done this for Socrates, if it intended merely to flatter him when it called him the wisest man but instead provoked him to question himself, which led to the recollection of some virtue. This is hopeful, but it is a hope that depends on the nature of the human soul.

PHAEDO OR *ON THE SOUL* (EARLY MIDDLE PERIOD)

The *Phaedo* comes in two parts: the seemingly endless and complicated set of arguments for the eternality of the soul, and the moving story of the last moments of Socrates. Socrates' death hangs over the whole of the dialogue like a dental appointment looming at the end of a Saturday afternoon, casting a pall on everything else. To give the English translation of *Phaedo* the punchier title *The Death of Socrates* misses the point, which is not the death of Socrates but rather his continued life. The arguments of *Phaedo* point to the triumph of the dialectical life over death itself.

SCENE SETTING IN A PLATONIC DIALOGUE

Phaedo presents a good example of the scene setting that often occurs in Platonic dialogues. Viewed as mere philosophical exercises, these are often skipped, which is unfortunate. The literary prologue provides important clues to the meaning of the more philosophical sections.

In some dialogues, such as *Timaeus* or *Republic,* prologues are quite lengthy and full of interesting details. Since these are works of literary as much as philosophical art, the reader should ponder their connection to the rest of the work. The prologue of *Phaedo* (57-59d) is not very long, but it does set the scene for the rest of the discussion.

In the *Euthyphro* Plato began the discussion between Socrates and Euthyphro immediately; in *Phaedo* Plato begins with the character Echecrates, who is not from Athens, asking Phaedo for details regarding the death of Socrates. Why this literary device? There are several possible reasons, but at the very least it appears that Plato is taking pains to remove himself from the scene. Phaedo actually mentions that Plato was ill and not present at the death of Socrates. This is highly significant because the only other time Plato mentions himself by name in the dialogues is in the *Apology.* Most scholars think this is Plato's way of signaling that the dialogue is not authentic history.

This explanation is inadequate because to gain this minor point, Plato excuses himself from one of the critical moments in the life of his master. His brothers are present in *Republic*, but there he does not feel the need to mention his absence. None of the dialogues, with the probable exception of the *Apology,* has much historical content. Why exclude himself by name in *Phaedo* just to gain the obvious?

Plato believed an important doctrinal truth, the immortality of the soul, that utterly changed his view of the death of Socrates. The historic Socrates may not have believed in the immortality of the soul, but by the time Plato wrote *Phaedo,* the student had gone beyond his teacher. Plato's illness is symbolic of the fact that he is not yet well enough to see what death means. Later in life he can hear the life-changing, death-defeating arguments. *Phaedo* is the way Plato *would* have experienced the death of Socrates if the young Plato had the wisdom of the mature Plato.

Plato connects the death of Socrates to the Theseus myth. On Crete the Minotaur, a fierce bull-man, was fed virginal victims from Athens. Theseus sailed with the virgins one year, and "he saved them and was himself saved."[24] Theseus saved the Athenian virgins only when he slew the Minotaur in the middle of his den, the Labyrinth. The Athenians promised Apollo of Delos a ship every year in honor of this event.

Young Plato was lost in despair at his master's death, but he did not sink into impotence or conventional religious answers. He followed the dark maze of argument, arguments for the immortality of the soul, into the heart of his own pain, where death was transformed into life, dying into healing.

The execution of Socrates was delayed while a ship was sent to Delos to fulfill the Athenian vow. Apollo, the great god honored in Delos and Delphi, is mentioned by name in *Phaedo.*[25] Apollo, the god of the arts, light and plague, represents both the best and the worst of the old religious order. As a god who cultivated the arts, great works of beauty were

---

[24]Plato *Phaedo* 58b.
[25]Plato *Phaedo* 57b.

created in his name, but he destroyed countless innocent Greeks just to revenge the shaming of one of his priests.[26]

While the ship went to Delos, the Athenians kept their city pure in imitation of the island. Delos was sacred and kept pure, so much so that eventually no burials were allowed there. Only priests could come to the island. Athens made itself a "little Delos" by delaying executions during the time of the voyage, but Socrates would still die. Dramatic irony was not just the domain of Socrates.

Plato uses many Pythagorean ideas in *Phaedo*. Plato was interested in life and rebirth and had questions regarding both. The Pythagoreans had answers, though not always good ones. Their skill in mathematics commanded respect from any earnest thinker, but Pythagorean philosophy had degenerated in Plato's time to mysterious religious ritual without adequate intellectual content. Plato picks up on Pythagorean themes of music, harmony, numbers and the soul.

In death Socrates is pictured as calm because of his justified belief that life continues after death. Socrates also believed in better gods than those of Homer and Hesiod. A court, no matter how it is constructed, can only be as just as its judge. If the gods of Homer were seated at the bench, there was no hope for justice in the obscure revelations from Delphi. *Phaedo*'s Socrates has no such fears. He has come to believe in immortality, new gods and the justice of their divine order.

At the start of the dialogue Socrates is casting the fables of Aesop into poetry and writing a hymn to Apollo. His dreams have been telling him to "practice and cultivate the arts."[27] Socrates recognizes that philosophy needs morally instructive storytelling. Plato renews Greek moral and religious instruction through a discussion regarding the immortality of the soul.

THE PLEASURE TO COME: WISDOM

Socrates stresses that the true philosopher will do nothing to prevent his own death, for the true philosopher longs to die.[28] So fierce is this desire

---

[26]Homer *Iliad* 1.8-21.

[27]Plato *Phaedo* 60e.

[28]Plato *Phaedo* 60d.

to get to the "undiscovered country" that Socrates has to caution against suicide. Humans are possessions of the gods; they placed people here. Humans have no right to shirk their duty or flee this prison before the gods call time.

Socrates is to be executed, so he knows his time of travail in this life is almost over. It is highly significant that Socrates begins with a religious argument. Some of his arguments for immortality will depend on the existence of the forms or on the theory of recollection, but for Plato his newly purified divine realm is always there to explain why everything rationally works together for good. Plato insists that if things make sense, then there must be a reason. This inevitably points to a creator and a divine order.

Socrates does not want merely to live but to be in a better place. He is convinced that he will go from this life into the company of reasonable gods and good people. In that rational place he will see the truth and not just talk about it.[29] Socrates wants paradise, not just survival.

Death is separation of the soul from the body.[30] People have at least two basic parts: a soul and a body. The body and its needs prevent the philosopher from pursuing spiritual things. Often when pursuing truth, "the spirit is willing, but the flesh is weak" (Mt 26:41). If this life is the time for the body, surely the next life will be the time for the soul. *If* there is immortality, then it will be philosophical, making the afterlife heaven for the philosopher but hell for the hedonist.

Does Plato hate the body? The language in *Phaedo* compares the body to a prison; the joys of the life to come are described in purely intellectual terms. Our materialistic, sex-obsessed age cannot stand anyone suspected of denigrating the flesh. Yet on balance, in all his works Plato is guilty only of preferring one thing over another.

Plato's Socrates is no prude or killjoy. In fact, he is condemned for being too attractive to the young men of Athens! Socrates is familiar with the ways of the world, and he does not go out of his way to condemn them. Plato himself came from a wealthy and powerful family. He presents a Socrates who enjoys sexually attractive people and loves a good

---

[29]Plato *Phaedo* 63c.
[30]Plato *Phaedo* 65c.

meal, but who has found something better. Compared to this better thing—spiritual and intellectual growth—everything else is small and unworthy.

It is no condemnation to say that Plato has a Victorian attitude toward the pleasure of the body. These joys are delightful, but there are better things about. The danger in sensual pleasure is that such experiences are initially so attractive and addictive. Philosophy hides its pleasures, but material things do not. Fleshly delights mean pleasure now. It is no surprise that when facing death, Socrates reaches out for the better thing at the cost of the lesser.

Plato does not deny the importance of the body to the human. In *Timaeus* Plato asserts that human beings are always in bodies. Sometimes we are in the fallen bodies of this world. Plato believes humanity's natural home is embodied in the stars, so for him this fallenness is literal. After death humans return to these better bodies if they have lived virtuous lives. Plato is not opposed to the flesh in some neurotic way since having some kind of flesh is part of what it means to be human. He simply does not want people to get stuck on this plane of existence, as they often do. Plato is no ascetic; he is a hedonist, but a hedonist who believes that the only real pleasure is wisdom.[31]

Plato wants people to wisely trade the joys of this physical body for the better physical body that will come. This new physical body will not impede the soul, as a disordered material body does, but will help the soul reach its goal of seeing the good, the true and the beautiful. The *Phaedo,* the dialogue that deals with the death of Socrates, is the most world-denying of all the dialogues. It is written at the moment of transition, death, when all the proper attention of the soul is directed to the *other side.* Of course, a person cannot live at this point in the journey for long. It is too forward focused. This vision of the *present* body-soul relationship is only appropriate at the moment of death.

Plato shows amazing insight, even if seriously wrong in some details. Plato realizes there is something wrong with the world: it is ordered, but it also contains chaos. A starlit night reveals truth to a person who studies

---

[31]Plato *Phaedo* 69b.

it, but optical illusions are also common. Given the many errors into which one can fall, the rational person must hope for redemption found in soul-work motivated by a world beyond the physical. Redemption cannot be found in knowledge of the physical world or the pleasures of this life. Plato denies the world as it is only because he sees that it is not his home. The world, the real, physical cosmos, will be better in the life to come.

The biblical account is more intellectually satisfying than the details of the Platonic scheme. As the Eastern fathers of the church stress, this physical world can be fully redeemed, and even physical pleasures should be a foretaste of that redemption. In the *Symposium* Plato acknowledges that this role for the erotic pleasures, given his experiences with the hedonism of Athens, remains skeptical about the present value of some pleasures. They are good, but not beneficial for the type of people he knows.

FIRST ARGUMENT FOR IMMORTALITY: DEATH FROM LIFE, LIFE FROM DEATH

Socrates tries to comfort his friends with a pretty story about why it is sweet to die. However, one of them, Cebes, says:

> Socrates, everything else you said is excellent, I think, but men find it very hard to believe what you said about the soul. They think that after it has left the body it no longer exists anywhere, but that it is destroyed and dissolved on the day the man dies, as soon as it leaves the body; and that, on leaving it, it is dispersed like breath or smoke, has flown away and gone and is no longer anything anywhere. If indeed it gathered itself together and existed by itself and escaped those evils you were recently enumerating, there would then be much good hope, Socrates, that what you say is true; but *to believe this requires a good deal of faith and persuasive argument, to believe* that the soul still exists after a man has died and that it still possesses some capability and intelligence.[32]

Cebes is looking for persuasive argument. He is attracted to the tale but needs some reason for having faith in it. Socrates has helped Cebes develop a wish that Socrates' picture of death is true. Now Socrates must supply the reasons for thinking it is so to people already half inclined to

---

[32]Plato *Phaedo* 70b (italics added).

believe him. By telling a good story, Socrates has created a better living environment than one in which a student is determined at almost any cost to be hostile to immortality.

These arguments are for Cebes and his friends. These particular arguments are not for the reader. Plato would almost surely use different arguments, or frame these arguments differently, if addressing different people. After all, everyone following the Logos will think of different challenges or have different experiences that make their questions unique. The conversation in *Phaedo* serves as a signpost to point out directions where conversation might be fruitful.

In that light the first argument makes better sense. After some probing Cebes accepts that "opposites come from opposites."[33] Traditionally, Greek thought had relied heavily on categories of opposites: wet and dry, hot and cold, and others like them. To these Socrates adds opposites such as large and small, just and unjust, fast and slow. Cebes admits that for a thing to become faster, it must first have been slower. A horse must be slow before it can be fast, and the reverse is also true. It must be fast before it can be slow.

Death and life are opposites. If Cebes accepts that opposites come from opposites, then death must come from life. Nothing can die unless it first lives. Yet if that is so, then surely nothing can live unless it first dies. Life must come from death.

As Socrates points out, living things keep dying, and if none come to life, then soon all will be dead: "Even if living came from some other source, and all that lived died, how could all things avoid being absorbed in death?"[34] If death is the end, then all the raw material to make living things will eventually be used up. Death would bring the process to an end, but cosmic processes are cyclical and sustainable. Plato does not mention the age of the cosmos, but if the cosmos is eternal, then no matter how large the original stock of life stuff in the cosmos, it would have been used up by now. Everything would be dead. Whatever the age of the cosmos, if there is no cycle of life from death, then everything will

---

[33]Plato *Phaedo* 71a.
[34]Plato *Phaedo* 72d.

be dead eventually, so it seems easier to accept a cycle.

This argument relies on psychological dualism. Platonic souls cannot be created out of matter. If Cebes rejected dualism, he could claim that life does come from nonlife: matter. This matter can be used and reused. When the body dies, the person dies, and death comes from life. Generally, some other life takes the dead matter and uses it to create new life.

Actually even a dualist could object to Socrates' argument, since the soul of a dead person might disintegrate back into soul stuff upon death. In this way the supply of soul-making material in the cosmos would be renewed; out of death would come new life. Sadly, this would not mean the resurrection of the dead person—Socrates, for example. The dead Socrates would contribute his worn-out soul to the supply of soul components just as his body would contribute its matter to the earth.

This objection is addressed later in the dialogue, but Cebes is not the one who raises it. Cebes, good Pythagorean that he is, cannot imagine that soul could break up and agrees too easily with Socrates. Fortunately, he is not the only person in the room.

There may be cycles of birth and death, but the cycles do not help secure personal immortality. The individual soul would have to be an indestructible unit in that cycle. But the argument does help Cebes. He and his friends follow the argument from generation of souls to recollection and onward to the nature of the forms. Socrates turns the attention of his mourning friends from his death to the world of forms.

This is the best comfort Socrates could have provided. Why? The world of the forms is eternal and good. If life has meaning, then it must come from the world beyond. It turns out that the world beyond is worthy of human hopes.

SECOND ARGUMENT FOR IMMORTALITY: RECOLLECTION

Cebes, no longer merely led by Socrates but now a full participant in the discussion, generates the second argument for the immortality of the human soul. It is rare but wonderful when one of the participants in a Socratic dialogue makes enough progress to participate with Socrates in directing the conversation. What is it about Cebes that allows this to happen?

Cebes and his friend Simmias demonstrate purity in their pursuit of wisdom.[35] Both want to believe what Socrates is saying, and they find Socrates' arguments somewhat persuasive, but they still object to the arguments. This is a rarity in the dialogues, and perhaps even more rare in life. Cebes is a young man, and while there is no inherent virtue in being young, it is still true that the young are often more open to new ideas. They have less invested in the old order and so can tolerate even radical changes. Socrates, an older man, has the ability to follow the argument (Logos) wherever it leads, and so do a few young men in the dialogues. One can only advance in wisdom if one is willing to argue against one's deepest desires. Cebes has this rare ability.

Cebes argues that if souls learn by remembering, then it is likely that the soul is immortal. Why? The soul existed without a body before death and could exist without a body after death. Of course, death could destroy the soul, but there is no reason to assume this is so. Recollection suggests that the soul can survive without a body.

Simmias says, "It is not that I doubt . . . but I want to experience the very thing we are discussing, recollection, and from what Cebes undertook to say, I am now remembering and am pretty nearly convinced. Nevertheless, I should like to hear now the way you were intending to explain it."[36] Socrates enters into a long discussion with Simmias, who experiences recollection. If the sole goal of the *Phaedo* were to argue for the immortality of the soul, then this section is a diversion. When will Socrates get on with it?

This diversion points to the deeper purpose of *Phaedo*. Arguments cannot be read but must be experienced in the soul. Socrates causes Simmias to recollect the forms, and this puts eternity into the soul of Simmias. This seeming diversion from the argument for immortality brings Simmias to a personal experience of an immortal idea. This orders his soul, and if his soul is in right order, then truth will be naturally appealing. Ideas that the average, disordered soul would find appealing will be rejected quickly by a well-ordered soul. A major goal of the *Phaedo* is to make the reader argue with the text and so order his or her soul.

---

[35] Plato *Phaedo* 84c.
[36] Plato *Phaedo* 73b.

Simmias and Cebes fear that the soul simply blows away at death, but a strange thing has happened because of their pursuit of the Logos. They are able to laugh with Socrates about their fear. The love of wisdom is beginning to set them free from the fear of death. In this harmonious fellowship Socrates, Cebes and Simmias can agree that only half of the argument has been given. Recollection proves preexistence but can only suggest immortality. Socrates then suggests the third argument for immortality, which is really a companion to the second.

THIRD ARGUMENT FOR IMMORTALITY: SIMILARITY TO THE FORMS

In *Phaedo* 78b, Socrates completes the argument by comparing the forms to the material world. The world of forms is invisible and unchanging, as Parmenides said it must be. Each form is simple, having only one attribute. The other world, the world of Heraclitus, roils with change. This world has a secondary existence trapped between the full being of the forms and nothingness. It is visible and complex, changing endlessly. Because it changes and has parts, things in it are made and destroyed. Here is the realm of the body, which grows and decays. This is the world of birth and death, of life and of destruction.

The soul is a very odd thing. It is in a body, and so it is part of the world of becoming. The soul makes the body move. So in two respects, location and motion, the soul seems more like the body than the forms. The body can be destroyed, so perhaps the soul can be as well.

However, as we shall see in the *Timaeus,* the natural motion of the soul is circular. Circular motion goes nowhere. Each moment of motion is exactly like the moment before, since circular motion has no discrete points. Therefore, the motion of the pure soul is as much like being still as it can be. While moving, it is at rest.

The soul, like the forms, is invisible. The soul rules the body just as the forms rule the world of becoming. Both soul and form are called divine. Furthermore, when a soul reasons well, it contemplates the forms, something impossible for the body to do. It is also simple, having no parts. The soul is the thing in the material world that is most like the forms.

The soul acts as the bridge between the two worlds. The Greeks believed it necessary to have a third thing to connect two things that were not alike. Form and matter seem as different as they can be, but the soul brings them together, acting as the glue in Plato's cosmology.

Can something in the bodily world be immortal? Greeks believed things were destroyed by being broken apart. A body decays when it breaks down into the parts that make it up. How could a thing without parts be destroyed? If a thing has no parts, then it cannot be destroyed. The soul is invisible and has no parts, suggesting that it is immortal.

Plato has asked his reader to buy a great deal into his worldview in order to accept a tentative argument for the immortality of the soul, but *Phaedo* does not exist in isolation. Plato writes persuasive arguments in each area where assent is needed. One cannot get the full force of Plato without reading all of Plato. No dialogue is a rhetorical island but is part of an exhaustive worldview. To receive the full force of the *Phaedo,* one must follow the Logos through the *Euthyphro* and *Meno* and on to the *Republic* and *Timaeus.*

THE CENTRAL SECTION OF *PHAEDO:*
THE VALUE OF THE DIALECTIC

Repeatedly Plato signals that comfort is to be found only at the end of hard discussion. At the start of the conversation on suicide, when Cebes challenges Socrates, Phaedo says, "I thought that when Socrates heard this he was pleased by Cebes' argumentation. Glancing at us, he said: 'Cebes is always on the track of some arguments; he is certainly not willing to be at once convinced by what one says.'"[37] The way one gets to the answer is more important to Socrates than the answer. When facing the biggest problem of all, death, one needs confidence about the answers, which can only be won at the cost of long conversation. *Phaedo* is very practical because it is preparation for death.

Cebes and Simmias do not end in bewilderment, like Euthyphro, because they are willing to be bewildered openly. At the end of the third argument for immortality, Plato writes:

---

[37] Plato *Phaedo* 63a.

When Socrates finished speaking there was a long silence. He appeared to be concentrating on what had been said, and so were most of us. But Cebes and Simmias were whispering to each other. Socrates observed them and questioned them. "Come," he said, "do you think there is something lacking in my argument? There are still many doubtful points and many objections for anyone who wants a thorough discussion of these matters. If you are discussing some other subject, I have nothing to say, but if you have some difficulty about this one, do not hesitate to speak for yourselves and expound it if you think the argument could be improved, and if you think you will do better, take me along with you in the discussion."[38]

The city of Athens is about to kill Socrates, having accused him of many crimes. Plato wishes to condemn the city by vindicating his master and making his case. Socrates is no guru, for even at the moment of his death he urges his students to think for themselves. Socrates is willing to follow his students even now if they can take him further toward goodness, truth and beauty. Like the swan, which the Greeks believed sang most beautifully at the moment of death, Socrates hopes his swan song will be his most beautiful conversation.

Simmias is not so foolish as to demand certainty from Socrates, but he has a counterexample to Socrates' last argument. The harmony produced by a lyre is destroyed when a lyre is destroyed, even though the lyre is "most divine" while being played. If the soul is the harmony of the body, as Greek medicine taught, then it, too, might be destroyed with the death of the body that produced it. Simmias wonders if the soul is not simply a product of the body rather than a thing apart from the body.

Socrates listens carefully to Simmias and then calls on Cebes to present his objection. Socrates says, "When we have heard him [Cebes] we should either agree with them, if we think them *in tune with us* or, if not, defend our own argument."[39] Socrates wishes to produce harmony in his small group of friends before his death. He is open to producing harmony around the idea of a mortal soul, if Cebes and Simmias are correct. Socrates wishes the group to unite around truth, not the happiest answer.

---

[38]Plato *Phaedo* 84c.
[39]Plato *Phaedo* 86e (italics added).

Cebes thinks Socrates' arguments have shown that the soul is likely to endure for a very long time, but not that it is immortal. Like Simmias with the lyre, Cebes makes his point using an image: a cloak and a weaver. The weaver may wear out many cloaks, but in the end one of his cloaks will outlast him. In the same way the soul may wear out many bodies, but one day it too will perish. The soul is most like the forms through long endurance without immortality.

Simmias used the image of the lyre, and Cebes used the image of the cloak. Modern analytic philosophy is wary of images, but Plato loved them. The more striking the image, the more likely it is to provoke recollection. If the world itself is an image, then the carefully crafted image of the philosopher simply removes distracting elements. Of course, such images can be deceptive, but Plato felt that, properly used, they could spur recollection of the deeper truths.

SOCRATES RESPONDS TO OBJECTIONS

Phaedo says at 88c, "When we heard what they said we were all depressed, as we told each other afterwards. We had been quite convinced by the previous argument, and they seemed to confuse us gain, and to drive us to doubt not only what had already been said, but also what was going to be said, *lest we be worthless as critics or the subject itself admitted of no certainty.*"[40] These worthy students are as concerned about failing as critics as they are about proving the immortality of the soul. Echecrates says he can see no way out for the argument.

Socrates is not distressed at the state of his arguments, but "there is a certain experience we must be careful to avoid."[41] Socrates fears the difficulty of the problem might make the young men *misologues*—haters of the Logos. Misologues despise discussion because they only know who to criticize and so cannot make progress. Socrates knows that any discussion is potentially endless but that progress is possible in the harmony within the souls of those having the discussion.

Socrates reminds Cebes and Simmias that they have agreed to the the-

---

[40]Plato *Phaedo* 88c (italics added).
[41]Plato *Phaedo* 89c.

ory of recollection. If so, Simmias must abandon his belief that the soul is
a harmony. Since the lyre causes harmony, it must exist before harmony;
but for the soul to recollect, the soul must precede the body. Simmias
must abandon either the belief in recollection or the belief in the soul as
harmony. Simmias has picked up his ideas about the harmony of the soul
from Greek medical opinion. He has no reason for this belief, but he does
believe in recollection on the basis of compelling arguments.

There are several other problems with thinking of the soul as a harmony of the body's desires. First, Socrates believes that is difficult to
account for evil people if the soul is a harmony. Second, the soul would
not be able to rule the body if it were a smooth blending of physical desires. Often the soul must contradict the desires of the body and rule
over it, but this is not possible if the soul is a mere harmony.

Cebes and his image of the cloak calls for Socrates to prove that the
soul is not just long lasting but immortal. Socrates shares a bit of his bi-
ography to describe how he is going to go about answering Cebes' criticism. Early in his career Socrates was very interested in finding the natural causes for things, only to discover that natural causes were not fully
satisfying. They could explain what made a thing what it was, but they
could never tell the *purpose* of a thing. Each event also had a huge number
of possible natural causes. Like a detective with too many suspects and
too many clues, Socrates could make no progress.

To his delight Socrates heard that the philosopher Anaxagoras had postulated Mind as the cause of a rational creation. If a thing was, it was best that
this was so. This limited the field of investigation, since one need not consider all the possible explanations but only the best possible explanation.
Anaxagoras was on the verge of a method that might explain everything.

Sadly, like many more modern scientists, Anaxagoras practically ignored Mind as a cause, using only natural causation. Socrates was frustrated with this inconsistency. He points out that he is not sitting in jail
merely because his bones are there, but because other intelligences have
willed him there, and he assents to stay and not escape. His body's location is only part of the story. To Socrates it is obvious that the true reason
for his being there is his will. The story of Socrates cannot be told without reference to Mind.

Socrates moves from Mind as a cause to the intelligible forms. Cebes agrees that the forms exist. Socrates reminds Cebes that a form cannot contain properties contrary to its own. Three cannot be even but is necessarily odd. Four is necessarily even. Counting does not destroy three when moving forward to four. According to Plato, three exists as an odd number and four exists as an even number. One can count over them, but one cannot change one to another. Cebes accepts these ideas.

Socrates reminds Cebes that the soul brings life to the body. No body is alive without the soul, and no body is dead with it. Life cannot admit its opposite, death. The soul, which is life to the body, therefore must be deathless. If it is like the forms, then it must never admit opposite characteristics.

Of course, this seems to beg the question of whether the soul is like the forms *in this respect*. The soul is, after all, not a form. Granted that forms cannot admit opposites, how does one know this particular characteristic is true of the soul? If the soul does not have all characteristics of a form, there must be a reason for assuming it has a particular one. Socrates must make use of the principle of the creative Mind to close these final holes in his argument. The soul could be the sort of thing that does not admit opposites, so Mind would make it so since this would imitate the best things: the forms. On the other hand, the body cannot be like the forms because it is composite and so must sometimes admit opposites within its varied parts.

CONCLUDING MYTH: GODS ARE GOOD

Socrates comes to the end of his conversation, and his life, weaving a myth. Many Platonic dialogues contain stories, and often they end with them. Socrates knows his students are not just heads: they possess spiritedness and passion. Those who merely attend a seminar on courage will be better prepared for bed than for battle, but those who hear a good lecture on courage and then watch *Braveheart* will be better able to act.

In Socrates' final speech Plato completes the transformation of the Delphic religion. Socrates has proclaimed himself a servant of Apollo, but not Homer's Apollo. Socrates' gods do not compete with natural explanations; they complement them. No longer are the gods arbitrary and chaotic; these new gods cooperate with the demands of justice. The soul of the good person is released from the body easily. It flies free and is taken to the gods to be judged. The soul of the wicked person has a hard time being released from the world.[42]

If this is the best possible world, Plato can tell the best story he can imagine. Given the difficulty of the task, he is likely to get the big picture right and the details wrong at first. Plato accepts that he probably won't get it right in the first attempt.[43] As critics think of improvements, he can incorporate them, since the best conceivable answer is bound to be closer to the truth. This is what he did. Plato will return to his account of the afterlife again and again, notably in *Republic* and *Timaeus*. The broad picture will stay much the same, but he will refine the details of the myth right to the end of his life.

In the *Phaedo* version of his great story Plato notes the large size of the spherical earth and the small portion of it known by the Greeks. He states that there must be many unknown peoples and nations in the world.[44] It is a big world, and Greek thought must take that into account.

The cosmos in the myth of *Phaedo* is even bigger. Earth is surrounded by a vast heaven, which starts with the orbit of the moon. It is a good place, better than the world in which humans live. The stars move in an orderly procession, nothing disturbing their glory. Any night Plato could look up at a perfect heaven filled with beings higher than humanity. The great expanse of the heavens did not make Plato feel lonely and small, but hopeful. There is no empty, horrifying space above the cities of humans, only the splendid realm of light. Any Athenian is small compared to the world and to the cosmos, but this is comforting. The world of humanity is dangerous and chaotic, like the Olympus of the Homeric gods. The heavens proclaim the glories of greater gods.

Intelligence formed a world where some mechanisms are based on natural laws. The entire beautiful cosmic picture is one where Mind harmonizes nature into a realm where justice is rewarded and vice is punished. Ethics, religion, biology and cosmology are no longer distinct fields that

[42]Plato *Phaedo* 108a-c.
[43]Plato *Phaedo* 114d.
[44]Plato *Phaedo* 109b.

never touch; rather, they are one. In the great cosmic scheme, the body impacts the soul just as the actions of the soul affect the body. The gods assent to the natural consequences of virtue or vice. Souls that are wicked become unfit for the heavens, while good souls naturally fly there. Some souls are so wicked they must receive eternal punishment. The cosmic order vindicates the judgments of the gods because they are servants of an even deeper Mind. It is no wonder that early Christians read this dialogue with delight.

The new religion of *Phaedo* uses the language and ideas of Homer, but it is nothing like it. Plato postulates a rational cosmos; Homer had a chaotic one. Plato's universe is the product of Mind; Homer's universe was not a product at all, but an accident. Plato presents a world where even the gods are servants of virtue; Homer's gods were superhumans who could act as they willed without fear of punishment.

The Delphic oracle came from a woman possessed by a god and could not be challenged. Socrates, the Delphic oracle of the new gods, makes the single demand that people know themselves. Homer presented an *Odyssey* in which the best of men discovers he cannot live in heaven. Plato's new *Odyssey,* the *Phaedo,* pictures a better man who finds his true home in the heavens. For intellectuals paganism would never be the same, and for all Greeks *Phaedo* prepared the way for the sermon of Saint Paul on Mars Hill in Athens (Acts 17:16-34).

The *Phaedo* concludes with Plato's moving portrait of the death of Socrates. Plato is not just giving historical fact but includes important details to solidify Socrates' new status as oracle. Socrates bathes before his death, an image of the purification of his soul coming from the completed dialectical life. Socrates drinks the poison freely, not prolonging his life by waiting until the last minute, an image of the courage that comes from philosophy. He has already had his last meal in the feast of words enjoyed with his disciples. The death of Socrates is an icon of the philosopher's willingness to accept the pleasures of this life when appropriate but to move past them when their time is over.

Socrates' friends begin to weep after he drinks the poison, and he rebukes them. Their intellects but not their hearts are persuaded that he is going to a better world. His friends are still governed by their passions.

Even as he is dying, Socrates is still able to help them govern themselves correctly. They stop crying and become calm.

With his last words Socrates urges Crito not to forget. Forget what? Crito is to sacrifice a rooster to Asclepius, a sacrifice reserved for healing. By making Crito and his friends *recollect* his death as a healing, Socrates can continue to teach them even after he is gone. This teaching will not just be in recollecting his words, but in acting out his command to remember. In *Republic,* an old man will leave off following the Logos to sacrifice to the gods because he fears death and the afterlife. Socrates commands his friends to sacrifice so that they will remember to follow the Logos.

Plato showed in *Euthyphro* that people needed to know why their actions were just. In *Phaedo,* Plato went further and placed human ethical behavior in the context of immortality. Good people are on a journey to the gods. In *Symposium,* this journey is driven by love.

5

IN LOVE WITH THE GOOD

SYMPOSIUM (MIDDLE PERIOD): LOVE IS A GREAT GOD

Erotic love sends some to hell and drives others to heaven. The Homeric god Eros was not the playful cupid of Valentine's Day but a sly and dangerous foe. Though not physically powerful, every other god feared him. He could make Zeus himself lose control and act like a fool. Idiots courted him, but wise Greeks were glad when his power over their lives waned. He was praised as a great god and feared as a terrible demon. In *Symposium* Plato will wrestle with Eros's power, subdue it and put it in the service of virtue.

The setting is appropriate, as a symposium was a party with every possible pleasure. Greeks did not separate their physical and intellectual pleasures, so a good symposium might include food, wine, flute girls, crude jokes and the most demanding philosophy. It was common for some of the members of a drinking party to make long speeches in praise of something. A symposium with Socrates would be light on drinks and long on speeches. This was fine with his audience, since the ancient Greeks loved to talk.

Symposium is first ugly and then beautiful, base and then brilliant, but always dangerous. Why dangerous? Plato imagined a glittering array of Greek artists, thinkers, pretty boys and leaders—some of whom make speeches so seductive that they can snare the unwary soul in their errors. The worst of them, Aristophanes, wrote the most brilliant attack on Socrates ever produced, which led directly to his death.

In Greek thought *eros* did not just mean sexual passion but included any of the bodily desires such as hunger and thirst. However, the men at this party are consumed with sexual passion. The sexuality of most of the speakers in *Symposium* is extremely degenerate. The men at the party are not merely homosexuals but also celebrate pederasty. Athenian culture had developed a base social system that encouraged relations between younger and older men.

Women were held in contempt by upper-class men except as breeders. *Symposium* contains a group of such men who praise their own lusts. Plato is disgusted with them, but he is also trying to save the younger men if he can. Homeric Delphi destroyed the best Athenians with eros, and Plato tries to turn this desire in a new direction. Having created a new Apollo, he now tries to create a new eros.

Some contemporary philosophers have tried to use the *Symposium* to make Plato a defender of modern homosexual practice, but this is impossible. In his last book, *Laws,* Plato makes any such sex a crime. "Homosexual identity," the idea that some people are only attracted to members of their own sex, was not known in ancient times.

For the Greeks, the roles assigned to a person in sex defined much about them: some people were the "penetrated," and others were the "penetrators." The lower classes were the "penetrated," and the higher classes the "penetrators." Women, slaves and boys were the "penetrated," and so had low social status. To place a free-born boy in this demeaning, womanly role was always controversial in ancient Athens. To volunteer to be the "penetrated" for an entire lifetime was to volunteer to be a sexual slave. No male citizen would have wanted that role.

Even worse, the entire practice was connected to the educational system. Older men taught the younger men, sometimes trading their educational expertise for sexual favors. Younger men, usually described as "beardless," were treated like women. Since many Greeks viewed women as naturally irrational, young men were the most "feminine" thinkers available. Most men had wives, but women could not be equals or friends. Young men raised in this system would get married and grow up to perpetuate it themselves.

Plato condemns this horror in the most effective manner. He tells a story that changes the Athenian imagination. Instead of great lovers, he shows these men to be selfish brutes with nothing to teach. At the end of the *Symposium* he shows how false even their passion is by showing them to be intellectually barren. His realistic characters express the lusts of the day and dramatically reveal their wickedness. Plato transforms without preaching.

Symposium is a conversation within a conversation. The first dialogue begins in mid-conversation with an unknown man saying, "In fact, your question does not find me unprepared." The good reader asks, "What question? Who has asked a question? Who is answering the question?"

It is as if the reader is already intellectually drunk, coming awake immersed in a dialogue with no idea what is being said or who is saying it. Eventually the context informs the reader that a man named Apollodorus is relating the story of Socrates at a symposium. The person asking the initial question is never named, leaving the reader a role in the dialogue

Apollodorus is ready to speak to the unnamed friend because "just the other day" he had rehearsed the entire story with his friend Glaucon." Another Glaucon, Plato's brother, will be Socrates' chief interlocutor in the *Republic*. Here Glaucon loves Socrates' message if anyone does, but Glaucon was not at the party.

There is dramatic distance between the reader and the action. Plato is primarily speaking to the reader through the character Apollodorus, who is relating what Aristodemus told him. Aristodemus had been rehearsing speeches made by other men at the party when he told Apollodorus about Socrates' speech, which includes the teachings a wise woman had given to Socrates. By this time the reader is at least four confusing levels from the action.

Why would Plato, the master writer, invent such a confusing opening? It will not do to say that he is merely hiding something. After all, he did not have to write the dialogue. He is publishing it for the average middle-class Athenian. Why write a dialogue at all if you don't intend for people to get past the first few pages?

Plato has important things to say that some citizens of Athens needed to hear, but that not *all* should have heard. It is written for those who could be saved by his message, but it is cleverly constructed to bore the wicked and put off the fools who might otherwise be harmed by the appeal of the topic. The *Symposium* creates distance between Plato, the reader and the action.

Plato presents a series of speeches to trap the unwary before harm can be done. Each speech contains more truth than the one before it; for different personalities there are different speeches. The naive speeches come first, with the best last. Plato masterfully imitates the styles of some of the best writers of his day. Aristophanes and Agathon were prizewinning playwrights, and Plato does more than mimic them—he improves on them. The best Aristophanes one can read is in Plato's *Symposium*. In this way Plato can trap the unwary reader before revealing the sacred mystery of real eros, which Plato does not want to fall into unholy hands.

The average erotic man agrees with the first speech, and it colors the rest of his reading of *Symposium*. The slightly less vulgar man is captivated by the second speech, and so goes for each class of men through all seven speeches. The next to the last speech, the speech of Socrates, will entrance the pseudo-philosopher, potentially the most dangerous reader. It contains the most truth by far of the first six speeches. Socrates tells a story so philosophically engaging that the Sophist will never move past it.

Meanwhile, Plato buries the most explosive information in a short conversation at the center of the dialogue, the only example of dialectic in the *Symposium*. Most readers cannot even remember whether there is any Socratic questioning in the *Symposium*. Plato also has the drunken Alcibiades reinforce his hidden truth in a seemingly comic speech, the seventh and final one, which few readers take seriously. The last speech of the Symposium is the most important. The last speech is not given by Socrates but by Alcibiades.

At the start of the dialogue Socrates is going to a symposium to celebrate the victory of Agathon in an Athenian dramatic competition. Agathon wrote tragedies, none of which survive except as fragments in the works of other writers. Like his teacher Gorgias, he was addicted to flowery rhetoric. He gets credit for introducing the chorus, whose lines do nothing to advance the plot. Agathon loved ornamental speech, as

Plato shows in his imitation of Agathon in *Symposium.* He refused to change his bombastic style, despite widespread criticism.

The greatest comic writer of the ancient world, Aristophanes, is also at the party. Aristophanes was a conservative humorist who defended traditional Athenian values against any innovation. His greatest play, the *Frogs,* stages a duel between traditional theater, represented by Aeschylus, and the new Athenian theater, represented by Euripides. This contest was decided by the god of wine, Dionysus, who came down in favor of traditional theater. The central question used to judge between the two playwrights is, What do you think of Alcibiades?

At the time of the play's performance, Athens was losing a war with Sparta. It needed its most brilliant son, but Alcibiades had betrayed Athens twice. He was in exile for his own safety. Only Alcibiades had the talent to defeat Sparta, but he could not be trusted. In *Frogs* Dionysus described the popular feeling in Athens: "They love him. But then again they hate him. And then again, they want him back."[1] Aeschylus, the winner of the contest, argues for tolerating Alcibiades because he is a great man, "a lion's whelp."

The entrance of Alcibiades marks the conclusion of the *Symposium.* At 176 Agathon says, "Dionysus will soon enough be the judge of our claims to wisdom." This recalls the judgment scene in the *Frogs.* Alcibiades comes in his drunken folly. What is to be done with Alcibiades? In some ways this party is Plato's answer to the *Frogs,* to show how to judge that most erotic of men. Aristophanes in *Frogs* says of the bright young men:

They sit at the feet of Socrates
till they cannot distinguish the wood from the trees,
and tragedy goes to pot;
they don't care whether their plays are smart;
they waste our time with quibbles and quarrels,
destroying our patience as well as our morals
and making us all talk rot.[2]

Symposium vindicates Socrates.

---

[1] Aristophanes *Frogs* 1424-26.
[2] Aristophanes *Frogs* 1490-99.

Agathon and Aristophanes represent the traditional arts. They both appeal in different ways to the erotic nature. Socrates is the greatest critic of the old religion and of art being used to empower the intellect. The party has in attendance fans of all three men. The battle lines have been drawn. In the *Symposium* Plato allows the erotic arts to clash with philosophy in a fair fight. He also allows science a place at the table. Which discipline will win? Can they be harmonized?

On his way to the symposium Socrates meets Aristodemus, who has no invitation. Aristodemus is madly in love with Socrates and manages to get invited to the party. Socrates is behaving unusually. First, he is wearing shoes and is all dressed up. He also seems to be intensely engaged in meditation, scarcely able to get to the party without falling into a philosophical trance. He arrives at the party late because he stands meditating in a doorway. When he arrives he is seated at the end of the table.

The prologue warns the reader of the conflict to come. Socrates is drunk on philosophy. He comes dressed as he would for his trial to confront his critics. This "friendly" party takes place in a house where the door is wide open. Plato will later gather these same speakers in a house with a closed door (in *Protagoras*), but this confrontation has the appearance of being friendly and open to all. In reality it ends in tension and danger. Though Socrates brings a friend and witness with him, his philosophical reveries delay him, and he arrives alone. He will also leave alone. Socrates' mission creates separation between himself and his own disciples. Plato pictures the hostility of the traditional Athenian social and religious world toward Socrates.

THE FIRST SET OF SPEECHES:
PHAEDRUS, PAUSANIUS, ERYXIMACHUS

One guest, Phaedrus, proposes that they make speeches praising the god Eros. The group agrees and begins harmoniously. Phaedrus gives the shortest speech of this dialogue. In the dialogue named for him, Phaedrus is described as a handsome youth who studies rhetoric but does not have much to say. He worships Eros as "a great god." There is nothing complicated in his view of Eros, as Phaedrus is trapped in perpetual adolescence. Erotic pleasure feels good, so it must be good.

Phaedrus praises all love as good because the lover is ashamed to be foolish or wicked in front of his beloved. Love motivates virtue through shame, but this makes the beloved the standard of what is shameful. If one loves a coward, then one could get away with being a coward. It also means that one can behave badly if there is no chance the beloved will know of it. None of this even occurs to Phaedrus. Phaedrus's speech is flowery but inadequate.

The most unstinting praise of love uses shame as the motive for positive action! The lover is frequently in fear of shame; Phaedrus is correct about this. The lover is sensitive to every whim of the beloved. No priest or preacher could ever make someone fear the wrath of a god half as much as he or she fears the least frown from the beloved. To be put down would hurt more than death. Such is the power of eros. Unrestrained, it promises pleasure, but with pleasure comes shame.

Death creeps around the edges of Phaedrus's speech in a disturbing way. Leo Strauss notes that the examples of lovers in the speech are those who died for their beloved. One, Orpheus, who would not die for his woman, is damned. Why this obsession with death and damnation?

Sacrifice can be noble, and Phaedrus thinks he picks a good example: Alcestis. According to myth she went to Hades so her husband could live. If love could make a woman do such a thing for a man, what would an army composed of men in love with each other do? Each would behave heroically out of fear of shaming his lover, and would sacrifice himself for the city.

Phaedrus is wrong. Love does not cause the lover to *wish* to die for the beloved. The lover wishes to love but *will* die for the one he or she loves. Alcestis did not pray for a chance to die for her husband, though she was willing to do so. Her death was a tragedy, not something to try to replicate. No lover would demand that his beloved die for him or tolerate placing his lover in harm's way intentionally. In the same way, manipulating social structures so that self-sacrifice is forced on the lovers is monstrous. Every sacrificial death is courageous but also creates a corresponding tragedy. One applauds the brave men of the Titanic who went down with the ship so others could live. One does not praise the designers of the ship for giving humanity the opportunity to see such courageous love. Any who would intentionally build such a ship for such a purpose would be bad indeed. Yet when Phaedrus proposes a city and an army built on lovers motivated by self-sacrifice, he is proposing just such a thing.

In the end the good-looking young Phaedrus knows what it is to be admired, but he does not know much about being in love. The sick Athenian social customs have left him admired and used, but not beloved; it is a path that does lead to shame and death. Phaedrus likes big speeches and talking about sacrifice because in his pampered life he has never had to give up anything but real love for his great god Eros.

Sometimes the important things in Plato are the things that are not there. At 180c Plato writes, "That was more or less what Phaedrus said, according to Aristodemus. There followed several other speeches which he could not remember very well. So he skipped them and went directly to the speech of Pausanius." Most of the people at the party, and in the city, fall for the error of Phaedrus. There is no reason to hear any more speeches of that sort since Phaedrus's will do as a sample. Like beer commercials, they all sound alike.

The shortest speech is followed by one of the longest ones, from Pausanius, an older lover of young men. He has the opposite perspective of Phaedrus, who at this point in his short life has only known the benefits of erotica. Pausanius knows the folly and pain of eros. As an old man he is desperate for love.

Pausanius's speech makes an important distinction that Phaedrus overlooked in his passion for eros. Pausanius divides love into a heavenly love and an earthly love. In this manner he can account for the dark side of love. Bad love pursues beautiful bodies, while good love pursues the intellectual pleasures. Good eros loves the soul of the young man it pursues. It seeks to help the beloved and to educate him, and in return the lover receives the physical intimacy he craves.

Pausanius's speech is better, but still self-serving and wicked. "Low" eros enters the city in the Trojan horse of "high" love. Why doesn't the older man fall in love with other older men and not young men? After all, if he loves young men rather than women because men are more reasonable, it would seem even better to love older men. Older men might have more wisdom, but Pausanius is not attracted to them. His seemingly so-phisticated speech is nothing more than a way of justifying his lusts.

Pausanius recognizes the mixed feelings in Athens about his vice. It is legal for an older man to proclaim his attraction to a young man, but it is ridiculed. The old lover is frequently mocked. Fathers are not terribly eager to hand their sons over to older men since none of them want their citizen sons treated like women. Pausanius does not just want his vice to be legal, he wants it to be celebrated.

This explains his key ethical statement: "Considered in itself, no ac-tion is either good or bad, honorable or shameful."[3] Pausanius recognizes that love is not its own justification. He cannot say, as Phaedrus would, "I love that man, so whatever I do is acceptable." He knows too much of public opinion and the way of the world to try this sort of appeal.

Pausanius wants to change Athenians' minds, and he starts by point-ing to the different laws and customs of various Greek cities.[4] To the half educated such disagreement points to the arbitrary nature of laws and allows Pausanius to insinuate that what one city allows should be accept-able in all cities, though it does not seem to occur to him that what one city bans should also be banned in all cities.

Pausanius's second rhetorical trick is to partially agree with his critics. He urges that relations with *boys* be made illegal. Such actions are bad. This restrictive posture is really only a smoke screen for his desires. Pausanius wants his erotic desires to be commended by the city. By banning sex with the very young, he hopes to win praise for having sex with young men.

Pausanius believes he should be honored for his sexual affairs as a benefactor of the city. How will he pull this off? He declares that no ac-tion in itself is wrong, that morality depends on the results and the way a thing is done. He claims his sexual desires are really all about helping young men.

The impotent old lover rationalizes to get his way and to quiet any condemnation from Athens. The harm he does is bad enough, but the arguments he uses to justify himself are even more dangerous in the

---

[3]Plato *Symposium* 180e.
[4]Plato *Symposium* 182b.

hands of a capable person. Alcibiades can use Pausanius's moral reasoning to become a tyrant and a betrayer of the city. It was not Socrates but men like Pausanius who have ruined Alcibiades. Pausanius has spoken of his desire for piety, but his desires lead to the greatest impiety in young men like Alcibiades.[5]

Following Pausanius's speech, the comedian Aristophanes develops a bad case of the hiccups, and the medical doctor, Eryximachus, takes his place to give a speech. Plato creates comic relief: the comedian does physical humor, and the doctor cannot heal him but only talks about healing. Perversely, the new speaking order elevates the status of comedy and reduces that of science. The medical doctor becomes subordinate to the clown.

It is hard to imagine how comedy could be more important than science, but it might be when the topic is eros. Whatever science may discover, science cannot explain love because love is of the soul. Comedy was serious business in the ancient world, and it often gave deep insights into human psychology. In a democracy comedy is also a greater danger to philosophy than science because it shapes a person's worldview, the people and the city.

Eryximachus represents Greek medicine, which emphasized a balanced diet, clean living and "doing no harm." It was a successful craft the effectiveness of which was not matched until modern times. Eryximachus is a good doctor, but his devotion to his craft blinds him from any other consideration. He does not make the youthful errors of Phaedrus and has no interest in the political posturing of the old sybarite Pausanius. He reduces the mystery and glory of love to regular bowel movements.[6]

Eryximachus gives the dullest speech in the entire dialogue, contributing almost nothing new. He begins as if love is a great god, but he ends up making it the science of "repletion and depletion." He follows Pausanius in dividing love into two types, but he speaks of healthy and unhealthy love. There is not much left of the soul or of Mind, and he continually reduces humans to bodies. Love becomes such a scientific idea

---

[5]Plato *Symposium* 180d.
[6]Plato *Symposium* 186d.

that Eryximachus claims it exists in plants.[7]

Eryximachus predictably claims that the doctor is the best lover because he adds or subtracts from the body as needed. Eryximachus is not a fool like Phaedrus or a genteel monster like Pausanius, but his speech on eros has the singular defect of being utterly unerotic.

Eryximachus does compare love to a harmony, which is a key term in Greek science. At the end of his speech, almost as an afterthought, he also says:

> Such is the power of Love—so varied and great that in all cases it might be called absolute. Yet even so it is far greater when Love is directed, in temperance and justice, toward the good, whether in heaven or on earth: happiness and good fortune, the bonds of human society, concord with the gods above—all these things are among his gifts.[8]

Eryximachus wants love to be directed to the good! Nothing immediate comes of this great insight, since Eryximachus has given no argument for it, but it is a beautiful insight. The love of the scientist toward his craft is very great. This devotion is not motivated by self-interest. The love of science is not the love of wisdom, but it is much closer than the self-interested love of beautiful bodies. So even dull Eryximachus is better than the flashy speakers before him.

THE SECOND SET OF SPEECHES:
ARISTOPHANES, AGATHON AND SOCRATES

Aristophanes begins with a myth both absurdly funny and deeply meaningful, an odd mix of tragedy and comedy. Aristophanes is comfortable with being amusing in a serious speech. Unlike Eryximachus, he does not think it impossible to speak the truth in jest.[9]

According to Aristophanes the gods created three types of humans: males, females, and male-females. In the original creation humans were spherical with four hands, four legs and two faces. Humans rolled about, like medicine balls with limbs, and were very powerful. Eventually these

---

[7]Plato *Symposium* 188b.
[8]Plato *Symposium* 188d.
[9]Plato *Symposium* 189b.

roly-poly humans rebelled against the gods, and to defeat them Zeus cut each roly-poly in two, leaving two weak, incomplete humans from each whole roly-poly. One roly-poly woman made two half-women; one roly-poly man produced two half-men; one roly-poly male-female turned into a half-man and a half-woman. Through millennia of reincarnation these half-people desperately search for the lost half of their original self.

The myth is a strange blend of the absurd and the romantic. Who can avoid smiling at the picture of a spherical human rolling up the sides of Mount Olympus to battle Zeus? No one can believe that the details of the story are serious when Aristophanes describes the gods carefully sculpting breasts for the newly divided humans with a shoemaker's tool. And yet Plato has written some of the most romantic passages in literature for his Aristophanes. These lines are frequently quoted by the passionate, with Plato getting the credit, but they are antithetical to his views.

According to Aristophanes' myth the original males are now present as homosexuals in search of their missing half. Men seek this reunion in sex with other men. Since men are the most rational and powerful humans, homosexuals are the best persons. Homosexuality in men is natural and should not be condemned.[10] The original females are now lesbians and reunite with other women through sex. The original male-female human is the heterosexual.

Procreation is merely a duty owed to the city. Originally humans procreated like some sea creatures, conceiving and bearing children externally, but then the gods made procreation internal. Since it is necessary to have babies for the survival of humanity, sex with women becomes a chore that homosexual men must perform. Making babies for the brightest and best—that is, homosexuals—is a duty performed, not the result of love. Real love is found only in the quest for the soul mate and ideally would leave behind the physical altogether.

However amusing or beautiful it sounds, this is the great error of the myth. Eros is designed for baby making. What other purpose does a penis or a womb have? Aristophanes divorces sexual desire from reproduction, but he still needs it, and humans are designed for it.

---

[10]Plato *Symposium* 192b.

Aristophanes substitutes the search for a soul mate for the desire for children. Each man seeks his other half, usually in vain, but occasionally a miracle occurs and the right halves meet. Aristophanes says, "And so, when a person meets the half that is his very own, whatever his orientation, whether it's to young men or not, then something wonderful happens: the two are struck from their senses by love, by a sense of belonging to one another, and by desire, and they don't want to be separated from one another, not even for a moment."[11]

It is *not* just sex that these lovers want from each other. There is a hidden mystery to their desire: the union of souls. Pausanius and Phaedrus listed benefits for the lover, but Aristophanes creates mutual need. Pausanius and Phaedrus had a lover and a beloved, but Aristophanes has two lovers. In another moving passage from a speech full of them, he says:

> Suppose two lovers are lying together and Hephaestus stands over them with his mending tools, asking, "What is it you human beings really want from each other?" And suppose they are perplexed, and he asks them again: "Is this your heart's desire, then for the two of you to become parts of the same whole, as near as can be, and never to separate, day or night? Because if that's your desire, I'd like to weld you together and join you into something that is naturally whole, so that the two of you are made into one. Then the two of you would share one life, as long as you lived, because you would be one being, and by the same token, when you died, you would be one and not two in Hades, having died a single death. Look at your love, and see if this is what you desire: wouldn't this be all the good fortune you could want?" Surely you can see that no one who received such an offer would turn it down; no one would find anything else that he wanted. Instead, everyone would think he'd found out at last what he had always wanted: to come together and melt together with the one he loves, so that one person emerged from two.[12]

Aristophanes has captured the longing for completion that is in each human heart. Most humans look for completion in eros, which usually amounts to mere sex, but Aristophanes demands that eros heal the soul and not just the body.

---

[11]Plato *Symposium* 192b.
[12]Plato *Symposium* 192d-e.

Not everyone would agree to Hephaestus making them one. Phaedrus would not want to be joined forever to his aging lover. Pausanius wants a string of young lovers. Eryximachus is too busy tending people's physical health to worry much about romantic longings. These three intellectual lightweights are too badly trained to understand their own desires. Their inability to hold their liquor symbolizes an inability to contain deep passion. They need to become stronger men.

The romantic Aristophanes is an improvement over them since he longs for something beyond sex in love: another human soul, the only eternal thing he has experienced. Each human soul is infinitely more interesting than any physical object. More accessible than the gods, human souls are the closest thing to divinity humanity can grasp. Aristophanes uses another soul to fill the gap in the human heart.

Aristophanes has misunderstood and forgotten the body. The lovers want to be joined with each other, but they do not desire the destruction of self in that union. Healthy lovers do not wish to consume or destroy their beloved. Sex brings a physical union that leaves the individual bodies of the lovers intact. The real union of lovers comes when the two become three through the making of a baby. Since Aristophanes wants to praise homosexual love, his view is sterile, leading only to death and a shrinking number of humans. His lovers begin as two but become only one, with no third.

In fact, the deepest problem with his seemingly romantic vision is that it depends on the destruction of the beloved. This is true even in sterile heterosexual love. Imagine two deeply passionate lovers, such as Tristan and Isolde, who are given the choice of Hephaestus. A true lover would reject it. Tristan would say, "You have misunderstood our love. I wish to create new life with Isolde while holding and cherishing her. The last thing I want is anything that would harm her or cause her to become something other than what she is." If Tristan loves Isolde, then he loves *her*. The healthy lover makes the beloved more like what he loves. He does not destroy her in the hopes of a better thing that will meet his need. The romantic who wants a soul mate wishes the death of the person he claims to love.

The union Aristophanes describes sounds good, but it means that both

Tristan and Isolde disappear. How could they want this? Of course, Aristophanes justifies the destruction of the lovers by saying that Tristan and Isolde were originally one, but this myth cannot cover up the stench of death. The romantic love of Aristophanes is that of a spider that consumes her mate. Worse, it is like a spider that consumes her mate and herself in the hopes that the monster that is produced will be better.

Plato gives clues to the wickedness of this loss of personhood by the comic but inhuman and even monstrous description of men he puts in the mouth of Aristophanes. Aristophanes believes every human that now exists is not really human, but incomplete with bodies that are scarred and ugly. Ideally all of existing humanity would be destroyed, and the number of humans would be cut in half. But if he is wrong, then Aristophanes is asking humans to put the entire future of the race at risk by his story. Both lovers will be consumed into a new and monstrous third. If Aristophanes is right, soul mates do not even love each other, but the monster that their destruction will produce.

It gets worse. Aristophanes creates a potential tyranny of lovers. A lover could justify almost anything in order to be restored to his beloved. The separation of lovers is the deepest truth, and reunion with the soul mate answers the man's deepest longings. What would any vow or loyalty be against this? Individuals are not the only ones who would be hurt by the tyrant romantics. Society, norms, laws will all fall to the powerful call of eros. Any custom that prevents reunion will have to fall. If the lover must betray his city, then the highest morality demands he do so. Love is a powerful god indeed.

Of all the speeches, this one is most dangerous to the romantic. The myth of Aristophanes promises to sublimate sexuality into something higher and better while keeping the sex. It promises an answer to the deepest human longing. Longing for a soul mate may be "higher" than longing for a one-night stand, but if Plato is correct, then it is a path that leads to death.

This speech is also the least hopeful in the *Symposium* because it is the most unreal. No one ever becomes one with another person. Even if it were desirable, it has never been done. The speech is all poetry with no reality. Plato is presenting the danger of storytelling unconstrained by philosophy or religion. Aristophanes cites no examples from traditional mythology or history. He has made up a new myth with no examples in tradition or science. Aristophanes has boldly taken control of all of Greek culture in service to his desires. He creates reality out of his own head.

Plato goes to war with this kind of poetry and artist. The lover of wisdom submits himself to the good, the true and the beautiful. Aristophanes submits himself to nothing. However, Aristophanes' utopia does not exist. It can never come to be. It is not even a dialogue that another person can enter into. It is a speech to be believed or not believed.

The entire speech is a fraud. Aristophanes pretends that he and his followers can simply deny that they want sex and yearn for higher things. They think they are above the body, but they are not. Aristophanes' hiccups were a reminder to him that he still has a body.

Aristophanes' speech is the first one that might appeal to a potential lover of wisdom. Plato does not cheat by giving Aristophanes a foolish speech, but one that is in turn profound, amusing and seemingly wise. Readers may choose it, but this is the risk that Plato must run if he is to cure the soul of the romantic. He must show the romantic that he gets it by writing a dazzlingly romantic speech, and then he invites the romantic to move past it by following the Logos.

At the end of Aristophanes' speech, Phaedrus prevents Agathon and Socrates from beginning a discussion. He knows that if Socrates begins the dialectic, the speech making will end. Phaedrus loves speeches and not truth. All he has is an erotic attachment to speeches and drinking parties.

Agathon gives a speech full of flourish. Like his plays, the speech sounds good, but it is difficult to remember anything in it. He begins, "I wish first to speak of how I ought to speak, and only then to speak."[13] This is typical. Like Phaedrus, Agathon enjoys talking about talking. However, there are real differences between the two. Agathon is brilliant and has great potential. Even his name sounds much like the Greek word for "good," which is significant later in the dialogue. His speech is an improvement on that of Aristophanes, but it has dangers of its own.

---

[13]Plato *Symposium* 194e.

Agathon is not interested in defending his own lusts. Agathon is much more interested in praising Eros. He says, "So now, in the case of Love, it is right for us to praise him first for what he is and afterwards for his gifts."[14] Agathon has turned from praising love for the sake of what Eros does for humanity to praising love for what love is. The human-centered view of love has consistently led to the mere fulfillment of sexual desire. Instead of praising love, the previous speakers have ended up praising making love. He is speaking badly; he still recognizes that the eternal ideas matter and that love is valuable for its own sake.

Agathon describes the god Eros as beautiful, supple and young. Agathon modifies the deeply held idea from Greek religion that Eros is an ancient god, but he still relies on Homer and the ancients for his basic view of reality. Like Aristophanes, he is willing to rewrite mythology, but unlike Aristophanes, he does not do so radically. Agathon is more moderate in his assault on traditional religion. As a result, his speech is less novel but also safer. He will not become a tyrant like Aristophanes because he is willing to be moderated by the culture. This is praiseworthy, allowing for change without the dangers of revolution.

Agathon exalts in love because Eros possesses all the virtues. Agathon's final reason for praising love is that it does good things for humanity and the gods. He praises virtue and doing good deeds. Nothing very controversial here. By trying to say things that will be accepted by the multitude, Agathon cannot build on his original insight that love should be praised for its own sake and not for what it does for human beings.

It is significant that this speech ends in applause. Agathon has perfectly captured the mood of the city of Athens at the time of the writing of the *Symposium*. He has just won the drama prize and is the man of the hour. His empty words perfectly capture the mood of Athens in its declining years, but his work will not endure. Agathon starts to examine ideas but allows his love for the approval of the masses to stop him. The crowd loves fancy words, at least for the short term, and Agathon is their ideal. If Socrates can speak to him, then he can speak to Athens.

---

[14]Plato *Symposium* 195a.

THE DIALECTIC

There is a funny thing about the *Symposium*. The speeches praising love are not very erotic. In fact, each speech marks a decline in the *feeling* of eros. The partygoers are listening, occasionally moved, but passive. Making love requires two active participants. Speeches are self-serving, but dialectic requires at least two active participants.

Socrates says he has misunderstood the terms of the speech making. Instead of speaking the truth, each person has simply praised love in any way he could. Since the room is filled with eloquent people, they have done this very well. He, however, will speak differently: "You will hear the truth about Love, and the words and phrasing will take care of themselves."[15]

Before Socrates begins his speech, he turns to Agathon and says, "Allow me to ask Agathon a few little questions, so that, once I have his agreement, I may speak on that basis." Socrates recognizes that Agathon (whose name, recall, sounds like the Greek for "good") represents the current "good" of the city. Eros appears as the questions begin.[16]

Socrates asks, "Is love of something or of nothing?"[17] This is an odd question. How can love be of nothing? The student of Socrates anticipates him asking, "What is love?" But he does not, which suggests that there is something different about love. Humans might not be able to see love by looking directly at it but only by looking at the thing that is loved.

Agathon's reply is most emphatic: "Of something, surely!"[18] Socrates follows his strange question with an even odder command: "Then keep this object of love in mind, and remember what it is." How can Agathon remember what it is if they have not yet identified it? Socrates is asking Agathon to recollect in the Platonic sense. There is something that Agathon knows that he does not remember he knows. Agathon must remember the unknown that he really knows. There is a mystery to love that the other speeches have glossed over.

---

[15]Plato *Symposium* 199b.

[16]For the source of many of my ideas on this topic, see Al Geier's brilliant commentary *Plato's Erotic Thought: The Tree of the Unknown* (Rochester, N.Y.: University of Rochester Press, 2002).

[17]Plato *Symposium* 199d.

[18]Plato *Symposium* 200a.

Socrates then says, "A thing that desires desires something of which it is in need; otherwise, if it were not in need, it would not desire it. *I can't tell you, Agathon, how strongly it strikes me that this is necessary.*"[19] Those who say they love a possession only mean they wish to go on having it. They prove by their implied fear of loss that it is not truly theirs. A man who is alive and loves his life implies that he wishes to go on having life. He cannot desire a thing he already has. His desire is to go on being alive. Socrates concludes that a person "loves things of which he has a present need."[20]

Agathon's contention in his speech that "love is beautiful" is now destroyed. If love desires the beautiful, then eros must not possess the beautiful. Agathon can believe that love desires beauty or that love is beauty, but he cannot have both. Agathon abandons his speech saying, "I didn't know what I was talking about in that speech." Just so, but Socrates points out that at least the speech was beautiful. Agathon has created a speech that would attract love. Whatever the limits of rhetoric, the beauty of the flowing words attracted the passion of Socrates but could not satisfy him. Socrates argues in *Phaedrus* that the really beautiful speech will also be true.

Love cannot be good either. How does Socrates know? Ancient Greeks could use the same word for "good" and "beautiful," creating the impression that they are the same. Athenians also believed the good was divine, but how could a divine thing be ugly? If love lacks the good and beautiful, then it cannot be a god. The great god Eros has been reduced to poverty. It is a longing *for* something, but something humans have forgotten.

The object of love is almost forgotten, but humans very dimly recall it as a divine good. Humanity has forgotten an image of the good that it once knew. Limited humanity never knew the infinite good as itself, but men could see feeble reflections of it and feel its absence. Positive definitions of such mysteries are impossible for unaided reason, but it is easier to say what the good is *not*. The good is the known unknown.

Plato often "knows" by knowing what a thing is not. It is hard to define justice but easier to know what is not just. This is not skepticism because

---

[19]Plato *Symposium* 200b (italics added).
[20]Plato *Symposium* 201a.

Plato does know something. He knows by negation that the thing he does not remember is there. The hole reminds him of the donut. The man who forgets the name of his beloved knows that he has forgotten *someone*.

Agathon says a sad thing: "I am unable to challenge you. Let it be as you say."[21] Socrates agrees, "It's the truth, my beloved Agathon, that you are unable to challenge."[22] Socrates cannot continue his search for the thing he does not know without the challenge or the negation of the dialectical partner. It is not hard to disagree with Socrates, but in the dialogues his partners are constantly giving up. Because they are used to the false education that depends on lectures and gurus, they are overwhelmed by Socrates. They are too quick to agree. Socrates must create his own dialectical partner in his speech.

SOCRATES AND DIOTIMA

Socrates begins his speech wondering if love must be either ugly or beautiful. Couldn't there be something "in between"?[23] Love is a poverty of goodness and beauty. In his speech Socrates invents Diotima, a wise woman, to be his teacher while he acts as the ideal student. Diotima describes Eros as born of Penia (poverty) and Poros (way). Penia gets herself pregnant by Poros. Poverty finds a way! Their child is Eros, or Love. Eros is the poverty-stricken spirit that always finds a way.

Diotima teaches Socrates that eros must pursue the beautiful, which must also be wise. Love must be a lover of wisdom, a philosopher. As a lover of wisdom, love desires what is lacking. Eros is not totally ignorant since it knows what it does not want and that it wants something. Eventually Diotima describes the ultimate object of love as the good. "What is the real purpose of love? . . . It is giving birth to beauty whether in the body or in soul."[24]

Reproduction is the only immortality that animals can know, and humans also become immortal by giving birth. Some humans seek immortality in physical children, and others seek it by bringing forth great

---

[21]Plato *Symposium* 201c.
[22]Plato *Symposium* 201c.
[23]Plato *Symposium* 202b.
[24]Plato *Symposium* 206b.

deeds. Diotima asserts that humans can become truly immortal by birthing the good in their souls.

Diotima begins to describe new religious rites to Socrates as she acts as a transformed Pythia, the new prophetess and oracle of Delphi. Plato's metamorphosis of Greek religion is complete, but as a result Socrates is cut off from Athens. Diotima is acting immoderately in destroying the old customs and imposing new ones that are disconnected from the old ways. Diotima has given Socrates truth, but in a manner most Athenians could not understand.

Diotima describes the ascent of love to the good using the metaphor of a ladder stretching to Platonic heaven. The ladder is not firmly grounded on earth since the dialogue between Socrates and Diotima is not real but merely imagined. A philosophy that is disconnected from citizens and their customs cannot save a real city.

There are six steps in the ladder, one for each speaker in the dialogue so far. Each step of the ladder represents a stage in the beautiful birthing of the good in the soul of a human. Each step is a response to the errors of the previous speaker.

First, a young man will love another person's body. If the lover thinks about his beloved, he notices that one beautiful body is much like another. He admires the beauty in all bodies. Plato does not despise physical love or merely transform it, but he builds on it. The love of bodies leads to a higher concern: because I do love your body, I must love your soul.

If one loves the soul of another, then he wishes the soul to be properly educated. He comes to love and care for the laws and customs of the city that shape the souls of the people. This love will cause him to develop a passion for knowledge. He will want to shape the city's laws and customs with wisdom. He will give birth to many ideas in this cause. Finally, these ideas will draw him toward the Platonic forms. His love will grant him a vision of the beautiful itself. Once he sees this vision of the form of the beautiful, "only then will it become possible for him to give birth not to images of virtue . . . but to true virtue."[25]

---

[25]Plato *Symposium* 212a.

Here is Diotima's ladder in chart form:

Phaedrus: Love of one body
Pausanius: Love of all bodies
Eryximachus: Love of the soul
Aristophanes: Love of the laws of the city
Agathon: Love of knowledge
Vision of the beautiful

We now see the confirmation of what the text hinted at in each speech. Phaedrus loved being loved. He was in love with being the beloved, and he loved his own body. He loved one body, his own, but this love trapped him. In a culture without mirrors, it was actually difficult for Phaedrus to see Phaedrus. Self-love is fruitless love of one body.

Pausanius loved young men. This love was indiscriminate. However, his sensual nature kept him building on his desire. He could not see that sexuality needed to be *fruitful*. It is no accident that Diotima is a woman. It is no accident that she uses images of giving birth. Pausanius's homosexuality is barren.

Eryximachus loves his craft. He loves curing the body. He also would cure the soul if he could. However, because of his love for the medical craft, which is mostly concerned with the body, he cannot escape his impotent love and give birth to something greater.

Aristophanes wants to be a new mythmaker. He has created a tyrannical love that demands total obedience. This love is not the love of the actual city. He only loves his own monstrous myth, which traps him in the fourth level of development.

Agathon is the saddest case of all. He is named after the good, but his speech lacks knowledge. It begins well but does not produce the fruitful ideas that make knowledge grow. It is all rhetoric. Agathon pleases the public instead of seeking the truth.

It would seem that Socrates has made the perfect speech, but it is not so. Humans cannot live on the mountaintop with the gods. Homer describes Odysseus as unhappy living with the goddess Calypso. All his physical needs are met, but he is not with human beings. He misses his home. Socrates leaves the philosopher in a place where he cannot live; it is not his home.

Socrates comes close to the error committed by Aristophanes. Aristophanes totally destroyed bodily love and love of the city in the pursuit of the soul mate. Of course, Socrates does not go quite that far. His ladder moves *through* love of the body to the good. He does not say that love of the soul is a substitute for love of the body, as Aristophanes did, but he does not return philosophers to the place where they can love bodies.

Socrates is so drunk on his speech at the symposium that he forgets that humans must live in community with other humans. Alcibiades soon enters to remind him that the philosopher must live in the city. There is no exit. For Plato there is an eternal cycle of birth and death. In the end a person must return and play his or her role in the affairs of this world.

SOCRATES AND ALCIBIADES

Socrates ends on a high note. He says of Diotima's speech, "This . . . was what Diotima told me. I was persuaded. And once persuaded, I try to persuade others too that human nature can find no better workmate for acquiring this than Love. That's why I say that every man must honor Love, why I honor the rites of Love myself and practice them with special diligence, and why I commend them to others."[26] For only the second time in the dialogue, people applaud. This is a bad sign. Instead of dialoguing with Socrates, the audience claps for the good show. It trivializes Socrates' speech. Instead of giving them a vision and bringing them back down to earth, Socrates has merely made a fine speech. All is not lost at first. Aristophanes starts to question Socrates because he wants to defend his own speech. Suddenly there is a loud, even frightening noise. Conversation becomes impossible. Alcibiades bursts into the room "very drunk and very loud."[27]

In the *Meno* we saw Plato's expectation that a good philosophy would produce good people. The entrance of Alcibiades into the *Symposium* is the toughest challenge to that view. Alcibiades was a student of Socrates. He was handsome and brilliant. He was also the worst Athenian of his day. He had the greatest gifts of any of Socrates' students, yet he betrayed the city to its enemies.

---

[26]Plato *Symposium* 212b.
[27]Plato *Symposium* 212d.

Among his other crimes, Alcibiades defiled the gods of the city. He dishonored the herms, which were statues of Hermes placed at street corners. These frequently had large erections and were symbols of fertility. Alcibiades became infamous for mutilating these statues around the time of this dialogue.

Alcibiades' drunken entrance would have reminded any Athenian of his nighttime orgies and blasphemies. Alcibiades betrays Athens again and again, but he is so verbally skilled and so handsome that he is forgiven repeatedly. He is the slick and skillful manipulator of public opinion.

Alcibiades was raised by the great Athenian statesman Pericles. In the *Meno* Socrates pointed out that these great leaders were unable to raise their sons well. They could not teach them virtue,[28] but somehow the statesmen escape blame for the corruption of their sons while Socrates is killed for it. It is safer for the city to blame philosophers since statesmen rule the city. To acknowledge their failure would be to admit difficulties at the very center of politics. Philosophers by their very nature are usually found at the margin of positions of power.

Alcibiades gives the last speech of the dialogue, and it is a necessary corrective to Socrates. Alcibiades gives a bad speech that has the good effect of reminding Socrates of his job. When Socrates leaves the party he immediately returns to the marketplace of Athens and attempts to find good students to become his dialogue partners. He gained important insight in his mental dialogue with Diotima, but his fearful confrontation with Alcibiades reminded him of the urgency of his work in the city.

Alcibiades is very drunk, but in this drunkenness he speaks the truth about himself. His spiritual blindness is symbolized by his pushing his hair ribbons over his eyes. He sits between Agathon, who admires him, and Socrates. This talented and wicked man comes between the good of the city and Socrates. The real value of Socrates to the city of Athens will be forgotten in comparison to the degenerate behavior of this young man.

When Alcibiades discovers he is near Socrates, he becomes enraged. He may have meant for his rage to be amusing, but in his drunkenness it

---

[28]Plato *Meno* 94.

is actually frightening. Socrates seeks protection from Agathon, and Alcibiades crowns both Agathon and Socrates. The old community, formed by Phaedrus at the start of the dialogue, is destroyed.

Socrates says that he is in love with Alcibiades, and Alcibiades accepts this praise as his due. He accuses Socrates of being a jealous lover, confusing Socrates' love for his soul with erotic love of his body. Eryximachus proposes a new round of speeches, and Alcibiades agrees, but his behavior prevents any speech but his own.

Alcibiades comes as a tyrant and a god. He insists on "naming" anyone who speaks, describing their character. He hands out the crowns of victory, like the god Dionysus in *Frogs*. He demands wine and bullies Socrates. There can be no other speeches after Alcibiades' speech, for he castrates the gods of the city and leaves it barren. Socrates begs him to "speak the truth," but Alcibiades can only see himself. His physical eroticism overwhelms everyone at the party and attracts even more drunken revelers.

Alcibiades speaks in praise of Socrates, describing him as a Satyr. A Satyr was half goat and half human, with a great sexual appetite and frequently portrayed with an erection. Alcibiades tries to "castrate" Socrates in his speech just as he did to the herms. One of the two men will be silenced by the end of the dialogue.

Alcibiades claims that there is a magical erotic power in the words of Socrates. These words disturb the young man for they "upset me so deeply that my very own soul started protesting that my life—*my life!*—*was no better than the most miserable slaves.*" He continues, "Socrates is the only man in the world who has made me feel shame."[29] Philosophy has moved Alcibiades, turning him from his narcissism and giving him a glimpse of higher things,[30] but Alcibiades does not want to pursue wisdom. Alcibiades thinks that if he can possess Socrates, he will possess the forms. The city has trained him to desire only sex, but Socrates will not cooperate. Alcibiades complains that when he tries to bed Socrates, Socrates refuse again and again.

---

[29]Plato *Symposium* 216b (italics added).
[30]Plato *Symposium* 217a.

Despite this, Alcibiades cannot leave Socrates alone, for he has all the virtues most Athenians lack. Socrates courageously saves Alcibiades' life in battle and offers him friendship. Alcibiades says he has been bitten by philosophy like a snake, but he cannot love ideas.[31]

Like every tyrant, Alcibiades attributes his own motives to every human. He believes Socrates is trying to control him or make fun of him. The best of potential students has been destroyed by the Athenian educational system. With his own words Alcibiades condemns himself and the culture of the city that raised him.

Alcibiades came to the party loudly, but he disappears from the dialogue with no mention of the fact. He is just gone, neutralized by Socrates. Agathon, the good of the city, chooses to be with Socrates on the basis of Alcibiades' speech. Without knowing it, Alcibiades has shown Agathon and the rest of the company a better path of love. When Agathon moves next to Socrates, Alcibiades is allowed one complaint, and then he is gone. Alcibiades vanishes, but Socrates' work goes forward.

WHAT IS TO BE DONE WITH ALCIBIADES?

Socrates leaves the party alone: the postlude matches the prologue. A large group of drunken revelers appears and destroys any chance for further conversation.[32] Eryximachus and Phaedrus leave, and Pausanius disappears from view.

Only the last three speakers before Alcibiades remain to carry on the dialogue. These were the men strong enough to drink and talk. Socrates now attempts to unify Agathon the tragedian and Aristophanes the comic, but both eventually fall asleep. The room becomes as still as a tomb. The text says, "But after getting them off to sleep, Socrates got up and left and Aristodemus followed him, as always. He said that Socrates went directly to the Lyceum, washed up, spent the rest of the day just as he always did, and only then, as evening was falling, went home to rest."

Socrates has put the speakers to sleep or driven them away. He has given up on the men at the symposium. They are not merely clueless but

---

[31]Plato *Symposium* 218b.
[32]Plato *Symposium* 223b.

dangerous. The best thing he can do for the city is to allow them to frit-
ter away their time in parties or put them to sleep. It is bad for the city
when its intellectual leaders are in this condition. By their very failure to
lead Athens in the right direction, the city is beginning its slow decline.

This is Plato's justification of his master's teaching. These bad men,
especially the brilliant Alcibiades, are not truly the students of Socrates.
They may hang around him as an interesting figure, but they do not follow his lifestyle. Socrates is a celebrity to them, like the winner of a
drama prize. He would save them if he could, but they love their passions
more than wisdom.

If we have followed the argument, Plato has shown us a great feast of
words. He has shown us how he knows *(Meno)*, why it is necessary to
know *(Euthyphro)* and where this knowledge leads *(Phaedo)*. Erotic desire
powers the quest for the truth *(Symposium)*. Now the good student who
refuses to turn back comes to the greatest question of all: what is the just
life?

6

THE CITY IN WORDS

On Justice

REPUBLIC OR *ON JUSTICE* (MIDDLE PERIOD)

"I went down with Glaucon to the Piraeus." So begins a book that is exhausting and exhilarating in its complexity and message. In all pagan literature it is the single book that never fails to teach something new and wise each time it is read. *Republic* is also a sad book. It comes close to the truth, perhaps as close as humans could come before the incarnation. Being so near the truth but never quite reaching it left Plato well aware of his own inadequacy.

A few comments on the title are in order before we begin. *Republic* is a dreadful translation of the Greek title, which is the Greek word *politea*. This word describes the structure of a Greek city-state. As I pointed out in chapter one, the polis was much more to the Greeks than what is captured by the Latin word *republic*. The polis was to the Greek the entire culture, religion and way of life. It is too limiting to ask only political questions of the text in the modern sense of *political,* for the *Republic* is about every area of human life. The subtitle, *On Justice,* was added much later and is a clue pointing to what the dialogue will keep asking: what is the appropriate place for each citizen, each human being, in the city?

Some have tried to use *Republic* as a guide to building an ideal city, but this begs important questions. Is the polis examined in *Republic* a city in words or a city in speech? Is it possible that *Republic* is a thought experiment and not a constitution that Plato hoped would be implemented in an actual city? The text strongly suggests that Plato is building his community in words in order to see justice in the souls of humans. If the city built in *Republic* is an aid in this task, then using the dialogue as a detailed road map for practical affairs in modern times would be a misuse of it.

After all, wouldn't the taming of one Alcibiades be a worthy political project? If *Symposium* had no answer to the question, What is to be done with Alcibiades? the *Republic* will propose an answer. A young man named Glaucon, which means "bright eyes," is Socrates' main interlocutor and becomes the antithesis to Alcibiades.

BOOK 1

As a whole, book one of *Republic* reads like an early Socratic dialogue, but careful reading of the very first line tips the reader off to the fact that Plato is doing something bigger. Though this introduction cannot look at every line in detail, careful examination of the first line of the dialogue shows the depths found in the entire book. The English translation of the first line reads, "I went down yesterday to the Piraeus with Glaucon, the son of Ariston, to pay my devotions to the Goddess, and also because I wished to see how they would conduct the festival since this was its inauguration."[1] This descent to Piraeus, the port city of Athens, is a key to understanding the dialogue, as a bit of Athenian geography demonstrates.

Ancient Athens was built around seven hills. These hills included the high Acropolis with its stunning temple dedicated to the virgin goddess Athena, the Parthenon. The Parthenon was built on the highest fortified point of the city. Most Greek cities had an acropolis, but the one in Athens was so spectacular that it became *the* Acropolis. The Parthenon at the top was the religious center of the city-state and was visible for miles. With its brilliant colors and perfect proportions, country folk must have been overwhelmed as they walked up the steep steps to reach it. Most days the Parthenon is framed by the intense blue of the Greek sky. The Acropolis seems to be the spot where heaven meets earth and gods meet humans.

Directly beneath the Acropolis was the business and arts section of the

---

[1] Plato *Republic* 327a.

city. On this level were found the theaters and the marketplace. To one
side of the Acropolis were the large performance areas for music and theater, where the Western performing arts were born. Aristophanes performed his comedies and Agathon won the prize for tragedy here. On the
other side of the Acropolis were the marketplace of Athens and the smaller
temples, where Socrates could be found daily engaging in philosophy.
Down toward the sea were the shops and homes of the city, surrounded
by a wall that marked the end of this second level of the city.

The third area of Athens was the countryside around the city, containing the farms and country homes that fed Athens and provided relief
from the dust of the city. *Phaedrus* is set in this countryside. Visually the
area was dominated by the long wall that connected Athens to its port,
the Piraeus.

This port formed the fourth area of greater Athens. Many of the people
who dwelt here were metics, foreigners who did business in Athens. Like
all port cities it was full of new ideas and strange practices. The Piraeus
was vital to the survival of Athens, a naval power by necessity. The highly
populated city could not feed itself without constant trade. The city ended
in the sea, which mirrors the sky with its intense blue. Shallow and
changeable, subject to sudden storms, this chaotic realm of Poseidon was
in sharp distinction to the orderly realm of Zeus above. Athens sat as
"middle earth" between the deep blue sea and the vault of heaven.

Socrates' descent to Piraeus is remarkable. He is famous for never leaving
the city and his work in philosophy. We saw in the *Symposium* that even after
an all-night party, he would go right back to his work. But here Socrates
makes the long walk to Piraeus. This steep descent to the sea is symbolical of
the entire course of the dialogue. The greatest dialogue of Plato occurs not in
the city or on the Acropolis but in the home of a foreigner in the port city of
Piraeus. Socrates has learned the lesson of Alcibiades. He engages young men
of business at the heart of that part of greater Athens most dedicated to
change. Piraeus represents the future, while the Acropolis represents the past
of Athens. The new polis in words will be founded in Piraeus.

Nothing in the dialogue takes place where it might be expected to
take place. Philosophy had a home in the marketplace, and religion was
for the temple, especially the Acropolis. But Socrates goes down to the

port city, the home of commerce, to see a religious event and ends up doing philosophy. This social inversion is an important clue to the dialogue. The *Republic* innovates and challenges the social, cultural and legal conventions of Athens.

The sea with the chaos it represents is a metaphor for danger in the dialogue. In book five, Socrates claims that the discussion is endangered by "great waves." By book nine, the conversation partners will be forced to look at the most evil of persons, the tyrannical man whose soul is disordered like the sea. Book ten describes the great sea monster Glaucus, who is so marred that "his original form can no longer be discerned."[2] The similarity of the name Glaucus to the name of the promising young Glaucon shows that the threat of the sea remains throughout the dialogue. Glaucon is in constant danger from the great waves of intellectual chaos that could mar his soul. Socrates has gone to a dangerous place to discuss dangerous things.

The religious festival in Piraeus cannot long hold Socrates' attention. It is a "great sight," but he is not interested in mere spectacle. Socrates is a pious man and has come to Piraeus hoping to find a real god, a rational Mind of the sort he postulated in *Symposium*. As an Athenian he longs to worship a goddess of wisdom, a real Athena, but she is not well represented by the idol in the Acropolis. He will be executed by Athens for impiety, but it is Athens that is bringing strange and inadequate gods to the city.

Socrates went down to Piraeus, but at the start of the dialogue he is trying to go back up to Athens. He seems oddly resistant to talking to the young men of Piraeus, as if his experiences in *Symposium* discouraged him from attempting dialogue during a party. A gang of young admirers led by Polemarchus grabs him and forces him to go to the house of Polemarchus's father, Cephalus. Cephalus, whose name means "head," is a wealthy metic. He lives comfortably, pretending that infirmity keeps him from Athens and dialogue with Socrates, though he is able to move easily when he wants to worship the conventional gods of Piraeus. Cephalus is not a promising conversation partner, but as the head of the house he cannot be ignored.

---

[2]Plato *Republic* 611c-d.

Plato teaches several obvious lessons in this part of *Republic*. Philosophy can take place anywhere, even in the most unlikely of places. The home of the brilliant Athenian writer Agathon seemed ideal, but nothing came of the discussion in *Symposium*. Cephalus, the foreign moneymaker, hosts a much less promising party, yet it is here that the greatest progress is made.

The desire to see spectacle cannot match the erotic attraction of philosophy. Glaucon has come back down to Piraeus to see a horse race at night, lit with torches, but once the discussion begins nothing more is heard of the horse race. In fact, the entire city of Athens fades away. Plato carefully places the dialogue in a geographic setting, but then building the "city in words" causes the real city of Athens to disappear. The care given in placing the conversation in the geography of Athens draws attention to its gradual disappearance.

Finally, Socrates needs the spirited nature of the young men to make progress. He was heading back to the city disappointed, but a newly formed community of young men forces him to return. Without these young men Socrates would have missed the discussion of the *Republic*. No teacher, no matter how great, can make progress without promising students. In *Symposium* the brilliant gathering lets Socrates down. In *Republic* the young men come through, two in particular.

Superficially, book one is like an early Socratic dialogue, but Socrates never gets to ask his famous question, "What is ____?" Socrates is being forced to speak, and it makes the early part of the conversation strained and awkward. Cephalus and the young men are using Socrates and his conversation as just another amusement.

Cephalus's protestations to the contrary, he is not interested in open-ended discussion but is conventionally pious and dutiful, the true head of his family. Like many older men, he likes to talk about his life and the complaints of old age. He expresses his gratitude for wealth since it allows him to make his peace with his fellow citizens and the gods. He can look forward to death since he will have justly paid all his debts.

Socrates twists this general observation into a discussion about justice. "But speaking of this very thing, justice, are we to affirm thus without qualification that it is truth-telling and paying back what one has received from anyone, or may these very actions sometimes be just and sometimes unjust?"[3] After all, nobody would return a borrowed weapon to a friend who had gone mad! Cephalus agrees and accepts that his definition of justice is inadequate. He then "wills" the entire argument to his son Polemarchus and goes off to sacrifice to the gods.[4] He cannot wait to get away from Socrates and the uncomfortable questions of the dialectic.

But Cephalus has one virtue: he miraculously leaves and allows the discussion to continue. This is a rare bit of fortune for the group, as Cephalus does not force them to decide between respecting convention or critical discussion. Socrates shows respect for Cephalus's traditional position and even admires the old man for his concern for the gods and the afterlife. By taking Cephalus seriously, Socrates mollifies his concerns, and Cephalus can leave his son as heir to the argument. Cephalus gives Polemarchus "everything."[5] Socrates has "killed" Cephalus and helped Polemarchus receive his heritage without actually harming the father. Plato presents a conservative strategy for change without revolution.

Polemarchus cites Simonides, one of the greatest Greek poets, who defines justice as "to render each his due."[6] Just as in the *Symposium,* the power of philosophy is immediately matched against the power of the traditional poets. If any poet is censored in the city built in *Republic,* it is the poet who cuts off free thought, not the one who encourages it.

Polemarchus goes through the normal Socratic process leading to bewilderment. He tries to refine his definition of justice several times but fails miserably. His views are conventional like his father's. His first attempt is to argue that "to benefit one's friends and harm one's enemies is justice."[7] However, Socrates points out that a good man cannot harm even his enemies since harm would make them worse.[8] Polemarchus cannot defend his point of view, and he and Socrates end up "brothers in

---

[3]Plato *Republic* 331b-c.
[4]Plato *Republic* 331d.
[5]Plato *Republic* 331d.
[6]Plato *Republic* 331e.
[7]Plato *Republic* 334b.
[8]Plato *Republic* 335.

arms"[9] against anyone who would make such claims.[10] Polemarchus, whose name means "chief in war," has become an ally of the Logos.

The *Republic* is a dialogue of surprises, often seeming to come to an end only to restart. At 336b one of these startling moments occurs with an angry interruption by Thrasymachus of Chalcedon. Having betrayed Athens, Chalcedon sent its master rhetorician, Thrasymachus, to plead its case. This urbane man is so frustrated with Polemarchus's childish arguments that he tries to interrupt several times. Shockingly, the master rhetorician and diplomat loses control of himself, and like a "wild beast he hurled himself upon us as if he would tear us to pieces. And Polemarchus and I were frightened and fluttered apart."

A new and better community had been forming between Polemarchus and Socrates, but Thrasymachus drives them apart. The formation of an enduring philosophical community is difficult, and before it can happen the wild beast with the tongue of a clever man must be tamed.

Thrasymachus defends the allegedly realistic position that injustice is more profitable than justice. He defends the right of the strong to do as they please. "Justice is the advantage of the stronger."[11] Thrasymachus claims that the entire Socratic method is a dodge "since it is easier to ask questions than to answer them."[12] Socrates is afraid of his angry passion and resorts to every dialectical trick he knows to tame him. Thrasymachus defends the tyrant against the philosopher and in a sense acts as a lawyer for young men such as Alcibiades. Thrasymachus insults Socrates and behaves like a "lion."[13]

Socrates points out that through ignorance tyrants often harm themselves through their commands. He also argues that the arts are for the benefit of the weak, not the strong. The shepherd acts for the benefit of the sheep, including the weakest. Though Socrates advances fairly weak arguments, Thra-

---

[9]Plato *Republic* 335e.

[10]Plato has a tricky way of disagreeing with a great poet. Because the poet is great, Plato simply denies that he could have said anything evil. Therefore Socrates and Polemarchus decide to take up arms against anyone who claims that Simonides said what he plainly did say.

[11]Plato *Republic* 338c.

[12]Plato *Republic* 336c.

[13]Plato *Republic* 341c.

symachus does not challenge them. In an impassioned diatribe he reasserts that injustice is best because it leads to the good of the ruler. After this speech Thrasymachus gets ready to leave since he wants to make speeches and not discuss, but the other members of the community make him stay. Socrates forces Thrasymachus, sweating and blushing, to admit that only justice allows a ruler to act in the ruler's best interest. Thrasymachus admits that even thieves who act unjustly destroy themselves. Eventually Socrates' questions wear Thrasymachus down, and he becomes cooperative.[14]

Book one ends badly. Socrates claims they have had a feast of words, but through his own fault he has "behaved like a glutton."[15] He has silenced Thrasymachus at the cost of ending the pursuit of justice. Socrates recognizes this, saying, "So that for me the present outcome of the discussion is that I know nothing. For if I don't know what the just is, I shall hardly know whether it is a virtue or not, and whether its possessor is or is not happy."[16] In a role reversal from most of the dialogues, Socrates is the one who ends the first book of *Republic* in bewilderment.

BOOKS 2-4

Whatever community had been forced upon Socrates is dead by the start of book two. The first word of this section of text is "I." Socrates stands alone, but most important, he says a frightening and uncharacteristic thing. Socrates, the founder of philosophy, reports that he thinks he is "done with the Logos." He believes the discussion is concluded because his bewilderment will not let him continue. Though Plato does not appear in his own dialogue, he has his two brothers force his old master to defend his position.

These brothers, Glaucon and Adeimantus, restore Socrates to the Logos. The two young men refuse to give up as easily as Thrasymachus because they recognize the importance of really defeating injustice. Many practical political men agree with Thrasymachus that "might makes right." Glaucon and Adeimantus want to defeat Thrasymachus's viewpoint, not just Thrasymachus. Better still would be to somehow co-opt a

---

[14]Plato *Republic* 351c.
[15]Plato *Republic* 354b.
[16]Plato *Republic* 354c.

person like Thrasymachus and make him part of the moral community. The erotic power of such a wild man can accomplish much and should not be wasted. Somehow his power must be harnessed for the needs of the philosophic community. This they succeed in doing, but only because they do not stop with book one. Socrates, Glaucon and Adeimantus end up as partners standing together to pursue the Logos.

Glaucon and Adeimantus passionately press the central question of the rest of the dialogue: "Is it really better to be just than to be unjust?"[17] The two young men want to know if justice is only praised because it is beneficial. Thrasymachus was defeated partly by the hidden assumption that the just person will do better in the city. What if all the external benefits were stripped away? Can justice be praised for its own sake?

Glaucon and Adeimantus make their case against justice in several ways. Most famous is the "ring of Gyges" story. Gyges was a shepherd who discovered a magical ring. This ring allowed him invisibility, which he used to enrich himself and to commit all manner of crimes. Since he was invisible, he was able to be respectable while gaining all the benefits of crime. Crime does pay, but only when no one knows about it.

On the other hand, if the just person is stripped of all the rewards of justice, he or she will be the most miserable of human beings. Most who are just are known to be just, with all the benefits society gives to good people. What if a person is just but is thought to be unjust? Glaucon describes the fate of such a person:

> We must tell it, then: and even if my language is somewhat rude and brutal, you must not suppose, Socrates, that it is I who speak thus, but those who commend injustice above justice. What they will say is this: that such being his disposition the just man will have to endure the lash, the rack, chains, the branding iron in his eyes, and *finally after every extremity of suffering, he will be crucified,* and so will learn his lesson that not to be but to seem just is what we out to desire.[18]

Can Socrates show that such a person is happier than Gyges, with his ill-gotten gain and good reputation?

---

[17]Plato *Republic* 357a.
[18]Plato *Republic* 361e (italics added).

This passage is such a remarkable premonition of the fate of the just person that Christians have always been puzzled about what to do with it. After all, the thought experiment of Glaucon came to pass on Golgotha. The just person was thought unjust and was tortured and crucified. It happened not just *in* the Logos (Plato's discussion), but *to* the Logos (Jesus Christ). The Logos did not stay dead but triumphed, thus making the cross of Christ the ultimate symbol of the just man overcoming the injustice of culture.

Through Socrates, Plato struggles mightily to see the same point. Socrates admires the two brothers for their courage in facing the problem so boldly.[19] Glaucon, Adeimantus and Socrates decide that the soul of a human is too small to see clearly if one wishes to know whether justice is greater than injustice. They hope that in a carefully constructed city in words they will see justice and be able to apply this larger vision to individuals.[20]

My children and I like to play simulation games on the computer. We set up cities and watch the people in them go about their own lives. We have noticed that the makers of these games have not been very careful if their goal is to demonstrate justice. In some games cheating is rewarded, or the situation is so unrealistic that it is useless. One game has children that never grow up. The simulations are not constructed with the idea of seeing justice. Often the opposite occurs, and we see injustice rewarded. Socrates and the brothers are better simulation builders. They isolate the just person in a carefully constructed just city.

The city and the residents are tools, which is appropriate since they are not real. If they were real, then the lawgivers (Socrates and the brothers) would be using them, treating them unjustly. Justice could not arise from such injustice. However, in simulation Socrates and the brothers are able to be lawgivers that do not have to worry about the happiness of the individuals of the city.

As a result the city of the *Republic* cannot be Plato's final advice on politics. Plato tries to signal this by setting up what he thinks are obvi-

---

[19]Plato *Republic* 367e.
[20]Plato *Republic* 368d.

ously foolish societal rules for his simulation, such as women and children being held in common by the men of the city. Philosophers like Karl
Popper rail against Plato as an enemy of open society, based on the alleged totalitarian details of his utopian republic, but they have missed the
point of the dialogue.

The three men act as founders, constitution givers, of the city. Since it
is only a city in words, they construct a very simple city. Only the bare
needs of the city are met; there are no luxuries. Each citizen has a job
that provides for the needs of the citizen and the city. One man is a
farmer, and another makes shoes. Justice is already becoming visible as
each man finds his place and fills it. Equals are treated equally, and those
not equal are treated unequally.

Glaucon begins to take the simulation seriously. He imagines living
in it and finds that it is not good enough for him. It is a city of pigs without any of the relish that makes life worth living for a cultivated Greek.[21]
Socrates goes along with Glaucon and complicates the city so that it
more closely resembles a city-state Glaucon would find desirable. Like
any good teacher, Socrates does not tell his student what he should want.
Socrates understands that Glaucon is trying to find himself in the city.
Only if he can do so will he be forced to wrestle with his own position
in Athens. Can Glaucon, a member of the ruling class, sacrifice his immediate happiness for the good of the city? Glaucon cannot imagine
himself in the simple city, so Socrates builds a more complex model.
The more complicated city requires a more complicated governmental
structure. Socrates invents the guardians, whose role is a combination
of educator and police.

The description of these rulers and their formation takes up the better part of books two and three. The guardians live austere lives, giving
up most pleasures for the good of the many. One of their jobs in particular strikes many as distasteful: the guardians censor the arts to prevent
the youth from being corrupted. At least in this thought experiment,
citizens are denied access to morally corrupting art.

Plato's concerns about music and poetry are controversial but rele-

---

[21]Plato *Republic* 371e.

vant. People are passionate about the arts. The arts affect them, and through them influence the cities in which they live. As a result Plato believes there is a compelling state interest in censoring the arts. Plato himself is the consummate artist, so he does not hate poets. He is reacting to the harm he has seen Homer and other traditional Greek poets do to the souls of the citizens of the city of Athens. Does the artist have the right to corrupt the souls of the youth? What if certain art helped destroy Alcibiades?

Plato carefully considers government power since misuse of such power led to the death of Socrates. It is easy to urge censorship of the arts in his simulation since nobody is being harmed and there is no chance of making such a disastrous mistake. The censorship in the simulation does cause Plato's reader to question whether censorship would be good in a real society. The argument could be made that recent American failure to continue mild civic censorship of the arts, including movies and television, has led to moral decay. At the very least, Plato reminds the reader that *personally* censoring the art one consumes may be a moral necessity. Even someone who is an extreme libertarian about government's role in censoring the arts need not be a libertine in his personal life.

In discussing education of the guardians, Plato deploys his famous tripartite structure of the human soul. Humans have a rational part, a spirited part and an erotic part. The rational part controls thinking and, in a good human, governs. The spirited part corresponds with the higher passions, like courage. The erotic part deals with the passions of the body, such as the desire for food and sex. Just like modern scientists, Plato cannot know the structure of the soul, so he constructs his best model to cover the observations he has made about humans. He would happily accept another model if it better explained the way people behaved and helped the philosopher see justice.

It is this moral element of theorizing that is so unique to Platonism. Plato knows many different explanations can account for the facts. Why not pick the one that has the better moral outcome? Having been raised on Homer, Plato feared moral chaos and saw no worth to theorizing that was value free. Any psychological model that removes moral responsibility from humans is dangerous, and the job of the philosopher is to find a model without such bad ethical implications.

Families complicate social structures in real cities, so Plato gets rid of them in his simulated city. In a series of steps that Greeks would have found fantastic, women are treated with perfect equality, the state controls the procreation of children, and there is no marriage. Plato creates an absurdly complex eugenics plan for his city and a tyranny of the brightest and best who maintain their rule by lying to the people. The greatest of the guardians would govern as philosopher-kings.

Experience with the planned economies of the twentieth century and the massive human-rights violations that have come with them makes it hard to read this part of the dialogue fairly. One must remember that, by book seven, his plan will depend on the rule of philosopher-kings, which guarantees that he did not intend his city to be constructed. Despite the hopes of countless dictators, from Alexander to Napoleon, there is no evidence that Plato believed such a divine being as a philosopher-king could exist. In fact, claiming to be the philosopher-king and desiring to rule is conclusive evidence that one is not the philosopher-king in Plato's writings.

The goal of the simulation is to see justice in the city as a whole, so to see it in the life of a single person. Each person in the city is treated like a body part in a single human being. Highly rigid social structures would be most unpleasant to live in, but they would have the advantage of simplicity. In words, Plato can simply assert that his mechanisms work and that the people believe the lies of the city. Plato constructs a city that helps educated Athenians like Glaucon and Adeimantus to see justice. It needs to work for them, and it seems to do so. The thought experiment must be complicated enough to show them a plausible picture of justice but not so complex as to introduce too many variables for them to track. In fact, Socrates says something like this to the complaint of Adeimantus that he has made a hard life for the guardians:

> We will say that it wouldn't be surprising if these people were happiest just as they are, but that, in establishing our city, we aren't aiming to make any one group outstandingly happy but to make the whole city so, as far as possible. We thought that we'd find justice most easily in such a city and injustice, by contrast, in the one that is governed worst and that,

by observing both cities, we'd be able to judge the question we've been inquiring for so long. We take ourselves, then, to be fashioning the happy city, not picking out a few happy people and putting them in it, but making the whole city happy.[22]

Socrates, Glaucon and Adeimantus regard only the happiness of the whole city-state, which is thought of as a single person.

There is a *second* city being formed in the dialogue. Glaucon, Adeimantus, Polemarchus, Thrasymachus and Socrates are becoming a fellowship of learning. Of course, as the readers participate mentally in the discussion, they too become part of this second city. This community is the real city of the *Republic,* and its progress is the most important thing to monitor in the dialogue. The details are so fascinating that it is tempting for the group, and for the reader, to get lost within them. This is precisely what the group does at the end of book four and the start of book five, and it is very dangerous.

Socrates and the young men need a city ruled by reason for the experiment. There could have been multiple evil cities not governed by reason, but that would not have served the goal of seeing justice. Evil cities are interesting, however, and the group turns from construction of the ideal city to look at the "forms of evil."[23]

What does it mean to look at the forms of evil? One dare not imagine the evil itself. In fact, if the evil existed, then it would not be utterly evil, since it is good to exist. The good is basic to the universe, but evil can only be a twisting of the good. As a result most commentators think this phrase is not to be taken technically. There is so much in Plato about the form of the good that the phrase "forms of evil" is evocative. Ignoring it is inappropriate.

The forms of evil are found in the cities that are not best. These evil forms do not exist in themselves but as shadows of the form of the good city. Humans can look at and study shadows. Forms of evil are the degraded shapes of cities that are no longer governed by reason. They are dependent on the good city for existence, but they twist the good in several

---

[22]Plato *Republic* 420b-c.
[23]Plato *Republic* 445c.

different ways. Because they are formlike, they can be categorized. If they were not forms at all, then ordering them would be impossible.

There is the great danger. Looking at the wicked cities is turning from the good! Will such an examination corrupt Socrates, Glaucon, Adeimantus and the reader?

BOOKS 5-7: A GIANT DETOUR

The conversation takes an odd turn as Socrates is about to move forward to a study of the constitutions of the basic types of cities. The young men stop him, and the dialogue takes a long detour. Not until book eight will Socrates be free to return to the evil cities. Oddly, this detour contains the most famous passages of *Republic*. Without it there would be no philosopher-kings, no divided line and no cave analogy. The detour is necessary because the group becomes fascinated with the ideas related to women and children. Socrates fears they will drown in the "waves of difficulties" from such problems, but the young men are curious, and their curiosity will not let them move forward. As a result Socrates must digress and discuss the issues that concern them.

This is the last point in the dialogue where characters other than Glaucon and Adeimantus speak. Socrates and Glaucon begin to dominate as even Adeimantus slowly becomes silent. The others, including a newly cooperative Thrasymachus, are the ones who encourage the detour. It is all reminiscent of book one and marks a third start for the *Republic*. The important thing to notice is the unity of the group and the taming of Thrasymachus. He is now interested in the dialogue, no longer behaving like a wild beast.

Book five introduces the paradox that the lovers of wisdom must rule.[24] Philosophers must be kings. This seems so absurd that Socrates is afraid of being drowned out in a sea of ridicule and laughter. Even in his day, philosophers were thought of as impractical. Most philosophers don't even have good social skills. How can philosophers be rulers?

Plato despises the public intellectuals, the Sophists who use their rhetorical gifts to enrich themselves. Plato has nothing good to say about

---

[24]Plato *Republic* 473d.

people who simply use learning to justify their own prejudices. Philosophers are not obsessed with their own opinions or any opinions at all. Plato would have been disgusted by the people Paul met on Mars Hill, always waiting to hear something new.[25] Philosophers want to know the truth. Philosophers are "ones who can grasp what is always the same in all respects."[26] People confuse Sophists with philosophers—there are very few real philosophers—and so philosophy gets a bad name.

Someone who really loves wisdom will be rational in decision making. The difficulty is in how to persuade the philosopher to rule. The philosopher's pursuit of the good does not leave the time or the inclination to make political decisions. However, for the sake of the city in words, Plato forces the philosopher to govern. This city is unlikely but conceivable.[27]

At 502c Socrates begins a discussion of the good. He reflects that most citizens of Athens think pleasure is the good, but more sophisticated types assume it is knowledge. Both groups are wrong. Pleasure and knowledge can both be bad. Some pleasures should be forbidden, and some knowledge is destructive. Who wants to satisfy the pleasures of the masochist? Who wants torture to be taught? Knowledge is good, but not *the* good. Pleasure is good, but not *the* good. What is the good?

Socrates is hesitant to explore such an important topic, but he finally says:

> So that what gives truth to the things known and the power to know to the knower is the form of the good. And though it is the cause of knowledge and truth, it is also an object of knowledge. Both knowledge and truth are beautiful things, but the good is other and more beautiful than they. In the visible realm, light and sight are rightly considered sunlike, but it is wrong to think they are the sun, so here it is right to think of knowledge and truth as goodlike but wrong to think that either of them is the good—for the good is yet more prized.[28]

The good gives intellectual light. As in the *Symposium* the good is known to the extent that it is known by being the postulated cause of all effects.

---

[25]Plato *Republic* 475d.

[26]Plato *Republic* 484b.

[27]Plato *Republic* 502c.

[28]Plato *Republic* 508d-509a.

Knowing the good is like being in a lit room where the source of light is too intense for human eyes. One can never see the light source directly, but one can assume its existence from the light in the rest of the room.

Plato believes that since we can think and make judgments, we know that the good exists. It is super-rational, but it is there. The good is simply not visible in itself. Humans cannot contain it and would burn out if they tried. The good is known from its images and from thinking. It is the hole in the explanatory mechanism, the foundation of thought. *It is the known unknown.*

Plato relates knowledge to reality in the image of the "divided line."[29] Socrates divides a line into two unequal parts. The larger of the two parts represents the world of the invisible, and the smaller, the world of the visible.

Socrates further divides the invisible between the realm of the forms and the realm of mathematics. The truth can only be known fully in relation to forms, which are the only fit subjects of reason. The forms cannot be doubted once seen, and gaining this vision is the goal of all true philosophy.

Mathematics achieves *understanding* by moving from axioms to conclusions. Euclidean geometry *assumes* certain first principles and then derives conclusions from those principles. The conclusions are as firm as the principles are true. Since the basic principles are assumed and can be doubted, the conclusions are not certain, as they are in the world of forms.

Below mathematics is the world of the visible, which is further divided between science and fantasy. Both science and fantasy are matters of opinion. The further down the divided line one goes, the less certain such opinions become.

Opinions about the objects of the visible world are certain enough to be called *beliefs*. These beliefs can be the product of reflection or simply

---

[29]Plato *Republic* 509d.
   World of the Invisible and Intelligible
   • The good or the forms known by reason.
   • Mathematics known by understanding.
   World of Vision and Opinion
   • Science known by belief.
   • Phantasms known by fantasy.

assumptions. Something *like* knowledge is possible about some of the objects, like stars and the earth, since they are very stable. Science is made up of the "likely stories" or myths humans tell about such objects. These stories can be valuable aids for life in the shadow lands.

Finally, there is the realm of imagination, utterly unreflective imitations of what is visible. Here are the crude phantasms and tricks of the human imagination. These fantasies are thoughtless and function more as prejudice than as good guides.

Plato does not place great art in the realm of phantasms. As Francis Cornford suggests, fantasy is thoughtlessness that fails to separate the imagined from the visible. The hard work of the artist to think about the world is science and not fantasy.

J. R. R. Tolkien's writings never confuse the seen with the unseen or the imagined. His books are the product of great thought. They contain deep truths and are the type of mythmaking Plato loved. In the Platonic sense, they are more science than fantasy and better opinions than much of what passes for modern science. The best reason to think that Plato would not condemn all art to the lowest realm is that the *Republic* is a great work of art containing great images such as the divided line.

Each thinking person slowly moves from fantasy to the visible and then to the invisible. Imagination is a stage in this process and is not an evil thing unless it is never outgrown. Fantasizing is for children, and not for grown men and women.

At the start of book seven Plato drops the image of the divided line for the story of the cave. The image of the cave is so powerful that it has haunted countless other works of art, including poems and movies. The cave is simply told, but each detail is meaningful. It is a powerful myth, a gripping explanation of the condition of humanity.

Like all good stories, it can be a trap if the unwary reader is tempted to try to understand all of Plato through it. This is dangerous since the cave is not all of Plato but only one image in one dialogue. Socrates is faced with young men who love the visible world, but he wants them to love the invisible world more.

This is a hard job, and Socrates uses the cave image as a mental sledgehammer to break open their thinking. The world that seems so impor-

tant is much less important than the unseen divine reality. Citizens of the
city often mock the philosopher for loving the invisible, while the philosopher despises the visible city as unenlightened. The cave story cautions against both attitudes by showing the people of the city that they
are prisoners of their ignorance and revealing to the philosopher that he
must live in the visible city. The duty of the enlightened philosopher is to
serve the city.

Plato offers no description of how the first man gets out of the cave,
saying only, "When one was freed from his fetters . . ."[30] How did this
miracle happen? Chains don't fall off simply because the prisoner notices
them. Even if he can recollect the invisible lands, he cannot go there because of his chains. His memory would be uncertain, and the power of
the wardens too absolute. Who releases the first man? How is it done?
This is the great unanswered question of *Republic*.

Socrates uses the images of the divided line and the cave to develop an
educational program for the simulated city. Education is offered freely,
but it is not compulsory since "nothing taught by force stays in the soul."[31]
The students are to be sound in body since sound bodies will make possible the hard work of learning. Young people are to learn all the normal
Greek fields of study. At age twenty the best are taught how all fields
form a unified whole. Socrates warns that dialectic is not for the immature, since the immature use it to become lawless. Having been confused
by argument, they rush out and confuse others. Instead, only the most
mature should be taught dialectic to use in service of the city.

This is the educational system of the city in words. Real people took
this speculation seriously and built the Western educational system
around its principles. The training of a stereotypical Victorian English
gentleman followed this course of study almost exactly. Modern American education still has the remnants of this liberal arts system without
any comprehension of the philosophy behind it. Building on the ideas
of *Republic* worked and became the best way to educate ever discovered. How can this be, since I have cautioned so often that Plato is

---

[30]Plato *Republic* 515c.
[31]Plato *Republic* 536e.

building a city of words that is not prescriptive?

Plato has no commitment to the details of his educational proposal, but he does present principles that are valuable. When Socrates is asked if a course of study should take five or six years, he says, "It doesn't matter. Make it five."[32] On the other hand, at times in *Republic* Plato is basing his city in words on certain metaphysical beliefs he takes seriously. These ideas are not found only in *Republic* but in all the other dialogues. It seems fair to attribute them to Plato. When the education program is based tightly on these ideas and when *Republic* itself is using them to educate the reader, then they are ideas that Plato wants practiced in the visible world.

BOOKS 8-9

Book eight begins as if the detour of books five through seven never happened. Socrates and Glaucon examine imperfect cities and their imperfect citizens. The ideal state cannot endure since nothing humans create, even in speech, is perfect. The city in words contains its own destruction.

The city that Socrates and Glaucon built, the best city, is ruled by the best people, the aristocrats. Corruption comes from the children of these aristocrats, who love only the rewards of high position. Glaucon in book two of *Republic* worried that humans love the good only for honor's sake; now Socrates tells how such humans come to be. Education, duty and service are hard work, and the degenerate children try to maintain their high position without hard work. They love the praise their fathers received for service and so create the illusion that they are working hard. These are the timocrats, the lovers of honor, who are not good but appear to be good.

Corruption once it has begun cannot be stopped. Timocracy becomes oligarchy, the rule of the rich. The lovers of honor, the debased nobles, beget children who love only wealth since it can buy them praise and happiness without any moral effort. The prosperous, such as Cephalus, no longer see why they should submit to the rule of ignoble nobles.

Oligarchy crumbles into democracy. The mob knows there is no reason to respect the debased children of the oligarchs. They wallow in

---

[32]Plato *Republic* 539e.

their wealth until they are no longer able to defend the city, then the masses seize power for themselves. The effete cannot stop them, as law is replaced by popular opinion, and the voice of the people is confused with the voice of the gods.

Democracy inevitably leads to tyranny. The citizens get "drunk on the unmixed wine of freedom."[33] Hard choices are avoided, and the city sways from one decision to its opposite. Eventually one clever man well trained in rhetoric becomes a wolf in the fold. This werewolf preys on the citizens like the beast-man Thrasymachus in book one. Eventually the city kills any philosopher who questions the wisdom of the tyrant, who can then gather all power to himself and fulfill his every desire.

The soul of the tyrant is badly harmed by his own tyranny. He lives in fear and wretchedness.[34] He can trust none of his slaves and deserves no one's respect, including his own. Though everyone flatters him and says he is just, the tyrant knows the truth. He lives for his erotic lusts, but they are insatiable, for the more he consumes, the more he desires. He has all power, but he pays for it with the terrible scarring his wickedness has done to his own soul. Despite appearances, he is miserable.

The tyrant's soul is disordered. If the three parts of his soul are pictured as a man, a lion, and a multiheaded beast, then he is governed by the erotic part of his soul, the multiheaded monster. Reason, the human part of the soul, is silenced; his spirit, the lion, is cowed. The happy person is the one who learns to tame the lion and the monster and use their power to pursue the good. The most miserable person, the tyrant, is the one who is so governed by the monster that his own humanity is destroyed beyond recognition and hope of redemption.[35]

What of Alcibiades? Sadly, Alcibiades is becoming a tyrannical man and should not be envied but pitied. It is bad to be unjust because injustice destroys the soul of the unjust person. No one has to know, but the tyrant will always know. Now Socrates can use the images of the city in words to answer Glaucon in book two. The best man, the happiest man will be the one who strives for a virtuous soul in a sound body. He will

---

[33]Plato *Republic* 562d.
[34]Plato *Republic* 578.
[35]Plato *Republic* 589b.

direct his education toward that goal and tame his spirited and erotic nature by using music and poetry to achieve harmony in his soul. Finally, "he will look to the constitution within himself and guard against disturbing anything in it, either by too much money or too little. . . . And he'll look to the same thing where honors are concerned."[36] He will take part in politics if he can, but he will long for the city that does not "exist anywhere on earth."

Socrates says:

> But perhaps, there is a model of it in heaven, for anyone who wants to look at it and to make himself its citizen on the strength of what he sees. It makes no difference whether it is or ever will be somewhere, for he would take part in the practical affairs of that city and no other.[37]

A kingdom, Plato notes, is better than any form of government if one can only find a philosopher-king. But where can one find a philosopher-king? Christians know the only answer: his kingdom come, his will be done, on earth as it is in heaven.

BOOK 10

Commentators have described book ten as unnecessary and anticlimactic. Julia Annas says it is far below the rest of the *Republic* in terms of literary quality and philosophical content. Does Plato, the master artist, just not know when to stop?

Book ten is important because it deals with Delphi, the great enemy of philosophy. First, Socrates argues that Homer and the poets of traditional religion should be excluded from Athens for the time being. Having finished his great thought experiment, Socrates can express his views not just for the city in words, but for Athens. Socrates honors Homer by taking him seriously, yet he believes that Homeric religion is evil.

Plato does not just ban Homer but replaces him with a new mythology. Glaucon and Adeimantus wanted to know that the good was worthwhile now, without reference to future rewards or punishments from the gods. Having done this, Socrates completes the cosmic picture by includ-

---

[36]Plato *Republic* 591e.
[37]Plato *Republic* 592b.

ing the world of the divine. The good is good for its own sake now, but it is also good in the world to come. The tyrant is not just punished in his own soul here, but also in the life to come.

The myth is the account of the after-death experiences of a man named Er. This myth of Er prefigures the cosmology of *Timaeus* by placing poetry, science and religion in the service of philosophy and presenting a unified picture of reality.

The main purpose of the myth is to show that justice is *natural*. It harmonizes with the very pattern of the world. There are rewards for justice, but they are not arbitrary or the result of the whims of the gods. The gods are just because they are good.

Homer had his great hero Odysseus visit the realm of the dead. *Republic* is a philosophical retelling of the *Odyssey*. The brave philosophers leave the city and journey to their true home, the heavenly city over the dangerous seas. Homer said that a person cannot be happy away from his hearth in his own hometown, while Plato argued that the good person is a pilgrim in this present life. Plato appropriates Homer's poetic vocabulary in the service of philosophy by picturing the world of the dead in his own way. Many of the same characters are there, but notably missing is Achilles. The great hero of the *Iliad* with his fearful rage is not just tamed, he is gone.

Each soul is presented as choosing their own future life as they stand before the gods. The gods let them choose their fates. Erotic people desire bad things and so pick reincarnation in futile and meaningless lives. Philosophers are rewarded because they choose wisely as a result of the care they have taken for their soul in life. Book ten is not unnecessary but a beautiful, artistic capstone to the dialectic process. Philosophy does not end in the visible but leads to right choices and bliss in the world to come.

That has been my experience in twenty years of reading *Republic*. In a battered blue notebook in my office is my proudest professional award. It is a pair of wings cut out of paper by a little girl, the daughter of a great teacher, given to me at the completion of a two-year voyage of discovery through the *Republic*. She created a pair of wings for each of us who endured to the end. I suppose in our dim way, we *had* learned to fly.

I nearly destroyed myself during those two years with bad choices, but the dialectic showed the wages of sin to my own soul. When I was too dull for the Bible, *Republic* brought me back to Jesus Christ. My noble teacher is teaching my children now, and his little girl is a colleague, yet I am still reading and being changed by the power of *Republic*.

Republic is great, but it finds no resting place. How *does* one escape the cave? Plato turned from the image of the city in *Republic* to the even larger image of the cosmos in *Timaeus,* hoping to find a way where there was no way.

7

THE LIKELY STORY

The Timaeus

SUMMARY

Timaeus is the first part of what was to be a three-part project written at the end of Plato's life, but he would never finish the second two works. *Critias,* a detailed account of Atlantis and ancient Athens, was not even half finished. Of *Hermocrates,* we have nothing, not even good guesses of what it would have contained. The *Laws,* which may have replaced the aborted project, was the last dialogue of Plato.

From the trial of Socrates to the nature of the soul in *Phaedo* to heaven and hell in *Republic,* Plato's scope and power increased, but the themes remained the same. First, there is a world beyond that is eternal, unchanging and utterly good. Second, this world can be known through recollection. Third, this truth would transform if the seeker had the courage to pursue it through the dialectic. *Timaeus* is the final expression of the third theme.

For nearly one thousand years after the fall of Rome, most of Plato was lost, and *Timaeus* was essentially all that Western Europe had of his writings. As a result *Timaeus* had a tremendous impact on the cosmology and thinking of the European Middle Ages. Every scientific scheme owed something to the ideas in *Timaeus,* which helped shape the scientific revolution. It inspired Kepler, and Neo-Platonists like Ficino followed its example by making mathematics central to science.

Perversely, science would outgrow Platonism as mainstream science forgot metaphysics in pursuit of physics. The mandarins of science adopted a simplistic philosophy that had no room for divine causes and assumed that science was the only source of knowledge. Platonism limited scientific investigation to the visible world while at the same time suggesting that the visible world was not all there is. That made Plato the foe of scientists who wanted to reduce everything to scientific explanations.

Science limited to natural causes cannot explain mathematics, the language of science, and it cannot defend the assumptions that helped create it. These secularists, by limiting themselves to a narrow philosophy of science, cut themselves off from the humanities and much of what makes life worth living. If assaults from the secularists were not enough, some conservative Christians have also attacked Plato as an enemy of science.[1]

In his own time, Plato had to criticize scientists who refused to consider Mind as an important cause. He pokes fun at pompous men of science like Eryximachus in *Symposium,* and he urges practical men to remember their souls and the forms. Of what profit is it to a city if it gains material wealth and misses the good itself?

Without the dialogue *Timaeus,* it might be fair to think Plato anti-science, but his spoofing of Eryximachus has a counterpoint in Timaeus of Locri. Put in modern terms, Plato would like Phillip Johnson and dislike Richard Dawkins.

"One, two, three . . . where's number four, Timaeus? The four of you were my guests yesterday and today I am to be yours."[2] Plato starts with a question and numbers. He loved numbers, and this is more than an amusing game to try to discover the "missing fourth" in the dialogue. Is it the reader? Is it Glaucon, Socrates' main companion in *Republic?* Is the missing person the philosopher-king, who is not mentioned in the recapitulation of the *Republic* that follows? Or is it a more philosophical concept such as harmony?

Equally intriguing is the identity of Timaeus, who will be the main speaker in the dialogue. He is called a prominent citizen of the Sicilian

---

[1]Karl Giberson, *Worlds Apart: The Unholy War Between Religion and Science* (Kansas City, Mo.: Beacon Hill Press, 1993).

[2]Plato *Timaeus* 17a.

city of Locri, a great philosopher, leader and astronomer. But who is he? Nobody knows. Plato made the name famous, so later authors often adopted it to give their works authority, but there is no conclusive information regarding the existence of a Timaeus of Locri prior to this dialogue.

Why might Plato invent a new character for his main speaker? *Republic* depended on the courage and farsightedness of Glaucon to continue, but he had been marred by the bad education of Athens. He might be saved, but he will not teach. Timaeus is an unknown and so can be written as a plausible wise man to *teach* Socrates, while Glaucon had to be *guided* by him.

This explains the strangest part of the dialogue, the great myth of ancient Athens and its triumphant war with the imaginary island city of Atlantis. Plato is telling a story, creating what may have been the world's first intentional myth.

The plot of the story is drawn from the recent history of Athens. Athens led the Greeks in a great victory over the Persian Empire. This was the proudest moment in all Athenian history, and Plato utilizes it in creating his story.

In the dialogue Socrates regrets that the city in words of *Republic* books two through five[3] was not real. Critias replies that ancient Athens had been exactly like it. This mythical Athens faced a foe far more formidable than Persia: the empire of Atlantis. This great island state, west of the Pillars of Heracles, was rich, proud and militarily awesome. Eventually it was destroyed by the gods for its pride, drowned in the ocean that bears its name.

Socrates asks that the city of *Republic* be made real, but instead he is given an even more elaborate myth. The myth is not history, but it is not exactly false. The Atlantis story did not happen, but it is like events that did happen. Athens did defeat a proud and gigantic Persia, and the Atlantis story borrows credibility from that history.

Plato might call the Atlantis myth "bastard history," or the sort of thing that would have happened given a simple, counterfactual set of circumstances. If circumstances were as they are in the story, the story would have

---

[3]Another fascinating textual question is to ask why the philosopher-king is missing from the summary of *Republic*.

turned out the way it does. No city-state like that of *Republic* ever existed, but if it were to exist, it would defeat an evil empire like Atlantis.

The historical patterns found in the actual events of history can be discovered and used to create alternative history. These general truths are rules of thumb that work in most cases at most times. Plato's Atlantis myth contains such a rule: cultures ruled by virtue do not fall in the end to cultures governed by mere power and pride. This is the lesson Plato learned from recent Athenian history. Even if a culture is militarily conquered by a lesser nation—Jerusalem by Babylon or Athens by Rome—it often triumphs in terms of ideas, as Jerusalem and Athens did.

Plato calls such stories likely myths. Such likely stories cannot unfold in any direction but must follow the cosmic order and illuminate deep truths. The author of a likely story has less control over his characters than the author of a lie. Christ's parable of the prodigal son and the forgiving father is a likely myth of this sort. It never happened historically, but it is the sort of thing that would happen. The parable has to move as it does not just to relate some predetermined lesson to the audience but to remain plausible. Christ's parable has so many parallels in history that it seems *more* factual than many singular historical events.

Of course, authors may tell unlikely stories. Such stories are total fiction. They move in any direction the author chooses, regardless of the patterns of history. They cannot teach anything and often teach harmful ideas. This is the sort of story Plato does not think should be told to the simple.

Some stories are true at the deepest metaphysical level and are also fact. The historical victory of Athens over an overweening Persia is such a story. The death of Socrates is another such tale. Both have profound lessons to teach. The history recorded in the Bible and the works of Plutarch is composed of this sort of true story.

Plato describes four types of tales: the true, the singular, the likely and the unlikely. Facts shaped by a skilled artist that conform to the rational pattern of the universe are true stories. Facts that happen outside the normal pattern are merely singular and serve to remind the philosopher that the cosmos contains agents not fully predictable. Likely stories (such as classic fairy tales, the parables of Christ and the Atlantis story) did not happen, but are so like the things that do happen and so well illustrate why things happen that such stories are very much like the truth. Finally, there are the stories that are unlikely, those that did not happen, are fantastic and contain no moral.

Timaeus says that the creation accounts that follow the story of Atlantis are likely stories. He presents two such myths. The first creation account presents the actions of Intelligence in the universe using the image of a divine craftsman shaping the world by the pattern of the world of the forms. A second creation account describes material causes, the laws of motion and existence. The Platonic god cannot create laws, as the forms are not in the divine Mind but stand outside of the cosmos to be used as a pattern for creation.

Plato advocates a dualist cosmology and ontology, a dualist view of causation, and a high role for mathematics and music in explanation and education. His methods move from Socratic questions to hypothesis to mythmaking. As a later dialogue the likely myths of *Timaeus* must be understood in relationship to the whole Platonic canon, just as *Republic* book ten relates to the rest of *Republic*. *Republic* book ten mythologizes the worldview presented in books one through nine of *Republic* while Timaeus mythologizes *all* of Plato.

Plato shapes the cosmos from a basic duality between the world of becoming and the forms. The physical world has only a secondary reality; it is always becoming or changing and dependent for existence on the forms. The world of the forms and the world of becoming are separated by an unbridgeable gap. Parmenides puzzled over motion and existence. Could both exist? Plato solved the problem by creating a middle way between pure being and nonexistence.

Since the cosmos exists in this middle place of being "about to be," science can be done, but never with certainty. Science searches for patterns in the cosmos. These patterns, which would be closest to forms, would be very stable. Any given event in the cosmos is the product of change, but this change is lawlike and mathematical, and therefore predictable. A Platonic scientist proposes a model (usually mathematical) to explain the world and then examines how well that model fits the everchanging and vast collection of particular data.

Plato accepts two types of explanations for causation: reasonable mind and natural law. In his first creation story, Plato accounts for the order and beauty of the cosmos. The god creates the cosmos as a great, perfect living animal ordered by Mind. Why then is there any imperfection in that universe?

In the second creation story, he must account for the defects. The cosmos is not always reasonable and controlled by the divine mind. Fire burns, even when it should not. Water runs, even where it should not. Natural laws that make the cosmos possible also create the possibility of disorder. A basic natural law that Plato inherited from the pre-Socratic scientists was "like is attracted to like," but this attraction will happen even when it should not. A reasonable mind will sometimes want water to move toward fire, but the very nature of water will force it toward other water. Natural law is not reasonable, it just exists.

Since Plato's god is not omnipotent, Plato is able to account for the imperfections of the cosmos. His god wants all the cosmos to be reasonable but lacks the power to make it so, as natural law guarantees a constant motion toward disorder. Natural evils are caused by natural law.

Plato has more difficulty accounting for moral or human evil. In his myth the creator god hands over the creation of humans and animals to the lesser gods. These gods create the human soul and thrust it down to earth, where it becomes confused by the irrational motions of the material world. This confusion can be fixed by proper education, but proper education is rare, so most humans become wicked.

Why do the lesser gods, who are supposed to be as good as they can be, leave humanity adrift? Having created humankind, don't they owe it more parental care? Why don't they provide training for this sphere of existence? Without the Christian notion of the Fall and human sin, the failure of the Platonic gods to provide better care for humankind is impossible to justify. Whatever the merits of his cosmology, Plato's theology is inadequate to support it.

MATHEMATICS AND MUSIC IN SCIENCE

Like the Pythagoreans, Plato has a mystical interest in math. He creates Timaeus from the center of Pythagorean philosophy to advance these ideas. Why does Plato think mathematics is the ideal bridge between the forms and the visible world? Math is ideal, but it also works in the real world. This is the great insight that makes the duality between forms and material substance plausible to the modern. If the universe must imitate the real in order to have any type of existence, mathematical objects are the prime substance from which the most enduring things in the cosmos would be constructed.

Plato believes that the universe is best understood by math and best communicated in music. He demonstrates this by making his ideas mathematically precise and tying this math to theories about harmony. If a "theory of everything" were possible, then it would be heard in music and not spoken. Music is the expression of mathematical reason, guided by emotions, driven by erotic passion and performed by an incarnate soul. One cannot play good music without the exercise of mathematical reason, higher emotions and erotic passion. Each plays its proper role and then becomes audible by being played by the physical self. Science at its best would play the music of the spheres. This view helped create the modern world in the writings of Christian Neo-Platonists like Kepler. Though presently out of favor, its revival presents the hope of a more humane and honorable end to modern warfare between the humanities and the sciences.

PLATO, RELIGION AND SCIENCE

Timaeus says, "If we can furnish accounts no less likely than any other, we must be content, remembering that I who speak and you my judges are only human, and consequently it is fitting that we should, in these matters, accept the likely story and look for nothing further."[4] Here is a solution to endless debates on the roles of religion and science.

Though Plato was not dealing with the modern problems of religion and science, he did develop many of the basic categories and arguments still in use today. In *Laws* (book ten), he gives what is the most concise and persuasive case against atheism from the natural sciences. He also had a robust philosophy of science that allowed for both mind and natural law as causes.

Sadly, Christians have not benefited from this friendly philosophy of

---

[4]Plato *Timaeus* 29c.

science. Ironically, many Christians in science have more in common with David Hume than with such religious figures and Neo-Platonists as A. E. Taylor or George Berkeley. Meanwhile, secular science is locked into an established Darwinian view that does not allow for Mind as a cause.

Too often Christians in science have adopted methodological naturalism while rejecting philosophical naturalism. No Christian scientist can believe that nature is all there is, was or will be, but such scientists act as if naturalism were true in their research. They will not allow a miracle or consider evidence for divine intervention any more than their secular peers. But methodological naturalism closes the door to God's detectable action in nature. Plato would caution moderns that truth is hard to find and would suggest that stories are all one can tell about the cosmos. It is simply a subject about which developing any orthodoxy is impossible.

Timaeus shows that scientists can never have all the facts and must be skeptical about any scientific hypothesis. No such story or theory, no matter how secure, is beyond the reach of revision. One adopts these theories after all, not because one is compelled to do so or because of logical necessity, but for societal or social reasons. Incompatible theories that fully explain the data are possible. If one allows for a broader view of science with supernatural explanations, then the possibility of such logically incompatible theories is even greater.

Of course, Plato would accept that some theories are very secure or, in his language, likely. Many, like theories about gravitation, are very secure. One should not discard very secure theories on a whim but only for good reasons. Unlike mathematical relationships, however, scientific theories are human artifacts. Mathematical relationships are necessary relationships. No mathematician will discover that two plus two is not four. On the other hand, while it may be hard to imagine what would cause scientists to revise certain theories, the history of science (Newton to Einstein) shows that even the most secure theory can be replaced.

Plato argues that science is storytelling and that these stories should account for all of human experience. In the case of human origins, for example, to pretend that only data from the external and visible world is relevant is too limiting. Plato suggests that humans know more about

themselves than they do about anything else. To discard the internal human experience when doing science is not wise. Most humans experience being an "I," which is not reducible to matter. Radical Darwinian
theories that attempt to reduce everything to matter and energy should
provoke dissent based on this experience, which is the deepest that humanity has.

Does there have to be an alternate and equally compelling story before
rejecting another one? Since alternatives are always possible, it is rational
to look for another story simply because the old story seems false or for
the sheer joy of developing new theories. Denying the human joy of seeing things from a new perspective would be anti-intellectualism in the
name of scientific orthodoxy. So long as the person deals fairly with the
evidence and the rules of rational discourse, Plato would say he or she
should be free to pursue other vantage points.

In the case of human origins, it is clear that large numbers of people
have powerful and rational reasons to seek a new scientific theory. The
conservative Christian has a powerful and satisfying set of religious experiences and explanations of those experiences and is perfectly rational to
seek to preserve those. Doing so at the cost of reason and honest dealing
with the data would not be in line with Plato's cosmological ideas, but
exploring openly and honestly for some compatible theory is a reasonable
action. Why shouldn't a person value his metaphysical orthodoxy over a
scientific one?

Of course, not every story is as likely as others. A Platonic philosophy
of science says that developing incompatible theories is possible, not that
all stories are possible. The "myth" of Genesis is a powerful one and has
helped humans for centuries. Desiring to preserve it is not irrational unless the researcher refuses to consider alternatives. Can scientific theories or stories be developed to explain the appearance of the world and
save a traditional reading of Genesis? Whether or not it can be done,
Plato would find the search rational.

Even if traditional Christians are wrong, if they are working carefully,
their failure would be illuminating to everyone. Considering the possibility of divine agency, as Plato suggests, helps even secular people look
at the world in new ways through critiques of secular theories and refor-

mulations of data. Imagine the opportunity for biologists to examine a completely creationist biological classification scheme developed from the principles found in *Timaeus*. Like the intellectual stimulation that comes from the contact between two radically different cultures, both secularists and theists would benefit from the cross-fertilization. If secularists continue to exclude Platonist or Christian worldviews from consideration, then such open dialogue will be impossible or will take place only in heated debates.

If all scientists would admit to telling likely stories, then they could continue to use their metaphysical assumptions to spin new theories to explain the ever-increasing amount of data collected, but do so with openness, humility and care. Lives can be at risk if scientific assumptions are not open to scrutiny in this way. Feminist philosophers have shown that medical research limited to a male perspective has harmed women's health. *Timaeus* suggests that colleges and universities should free individual scientists, philosophers and theologians to work on their own individual theories about the way the cosmos works. Platonism is not antiscience but wishes to incorporate science into a view of truth that includes knowledge gained from all the disciplines, including theology.

Platonism also avoids relativistic postmodernism since Plato believes in truth and that some kinds of truth are knowable. Scientific stories can be *likely* or *unlikely,* so while never certain of scientific truth, Plato can still find good reason to prefer one answer to another. Theories that are internally coherent are preferable to those that are not. Given the goodness of his god, the creator will create beautifully, giving a reason to prefer an elegant scientific theory to a clumsy one. Platonism is not triumphalist in its scientific expectations, but it does allow for progress.

CHRISTIANS AND PLATO

Plato started most of the great discussions. No one has escaped him; certainly the first generations of Christians did not. None of the fathers of the church followed him slavishly, but they used his vocabulary and ideas often. The Greek Old Testament used by the early church was a translation based on Plato's language and concepts, thereby bringing Platonic philosophy to even the most remote Jewish synagogue. Augustine's most famous image, the man hopelessly chained in sin, is an appropriation of the image of the cave in *Republic* book seven.

Plato gives Christianity tools to combat the difficulties of this age. He provides a philosophy of science that allows for intelligent design and urges humans to account for ideas, the soul and matter. He does not allow humanity to ignore any experience! Plato also gives a way for humans to know and *know* they know and communicate this knowledge to others. Platonism can escape the foolish certainty of fundamentalism and the intellectual chaos of postmodernity.

Plato was rejected when the Enlightenment ripped Europe and the West loose from its intellectual roots. Now that the Enlightenment has reached a point of futility, perhaps a reexamination of Plato will give the church new direction. His questions are most important because they are still fresh and demand the attention of any Glaucon willing to examine them.

This appropriation must be done with care, and the church fathers provide a good model of such scholarship. They would blister Plato for his errors while happily using his best work and ideas. Any subordination of Christianity to Platonism must be rejected since Christianity must ultimately be most important; but Christianity enriched by Platonism, like that of A. E. Taylor, C. S. Lewis, Charles Williams and J. R. R. Tolkien, has promise.

8

BREAKING WITH
THE MASTER

Aristotle and the "Other" Path

AFTER PLATO

Socrates taught Plato, and Plato taught Aristotle. While the Academy refused to appoint him as leader upon Plato's death (making the safe but dull pick, like many educational institutions since), Aristotle was the great intellect of his age. He thought about everything, creating and organizing whole disciplines and discovering the necessary tools to explore them. His ideas on theater, politics, ethics and many other areas are still the starting point for serious thinkers. At the same time, Aristotle was a man of the world, a sharp dresser with good connections and a cultivated, educated accent. He was tutor to Alexander the Great, who would conquer the known world by the time he was thirty-two.

Aristotle was proud of his polished prose, but those works have been lost, and what remains today are his lecture notes from advanced classes. They are dense, complicated and require a technical vocabulary that he does not bother to introduce. Once a reader begins to understand the structure and nature of these notes, then Aristotle's careful arguments are beautiful and illuminating. Aristotle is complete: a scientific man of affairs with a poetic soul who discovered logic.

ARISTOTLE'S METHOD AND LOGIC

Formal logic is so basic to education and to modern life that it is difficult to remember that even as great an intellect as Plato knew nothing of it. Of course, people reasoned well before Aristotle, as Plato did, but they did so more or less instinctively. Rhetoric could sometimes mask bad arguments. Aristotle discovered basic principles that allowed anyone to check and see if an argument was sound.

Aristotle grasped that a good argument had three basic characteristics: truth, persuasiveness and validity. A conclusion in an argument should only receive assent when it is true. The beauty of logic is that it creates rules that, if followed, allow the discovery of new truths from others.

Conclusions also need that fickle element called persuasiveness. If the conclusion seems outlandish or absurd, then it will be difficult to accept. A single argument will rarely move even a reasonable person from his or her position, especially if it sounds tricky or contradicts too much of what he or she believes.

A good example is the ontological argument for the existence of God. As formulated by Anselm, the argument says, roughly, that if God could exist, then he must exist. Why? Since God is the greatest possible being, and it is greater to exist than to not exist, then if God is the greatest possible being, he must exist. The argument sounds like a verbal trick. Though recent formulations, like those of Alvin Plantinga, seem sound enough, few atheists are persuaded by it. In fact, the argument strikes even most *theists* as unpersuasive.

Aristotle loved studying rhetoric and believed that in the past persuasive techniques had not been dealt with in a systematic way. If Plato's great strength was in presenting an *attitude* toward investigation, his great weakness was in the *systematic* investigation of any question. A complex dialogue like the *Republic* might move from questions of theology to cosmology and then to epistemology in a single page. Aristotle believed such treatment too haphazard to be trusted with finding the truth and too scattered to be persuasive when the truth was found.

Aristotle believed that good investigation would first divide all knowledge into disciplines. A discipline would be a constricted area of learning with its own questions and methods for arriving at the truth.

First, the area of investigation is carefully defined. Second, previous writings are mined for ideas. Third, the investigator establishes first principles for the area.

Aristotle developed general explanations for his specific findings. Of course, such a method meant the need to develop specific findings! Given this, he was the greatest ancient advocate of experiment and exploration of the natural world. Following the discovery of first principles, the investigator could rigorously deduce further conclusions using logic.

Logic is concerned with the validity of arguments. An argument consists of premises and a conclusion that putatively follows from the premises. In a valid argument the premises cannot be true and the conclusion false.

Here is a valid argument:

1. Premise: If Damon Gough is Badly Drawn Boy, then the *About a Boy* soundtrack was by Damon Gough.
2. Premise: Damon Gough is Badly Drawn Boy.
3. Conclusion: Therefore the *About a Boy* soundtrack was by Damon Gough.

Given the form of the argument, if one and two are true, then three must be true as well. As a matter of fact, one and two *are* true, and so three must be. Suppose, however, that we change the argument in the following way:

4. Premise: If William Shatner is Badly Drawn Boy, then the *About a Boy* soundtrack was by William Shatner.
5. Premise: William Shatner is Badly Drawn Boy.
6. Conclusion: Therefore, the *About a Boy* soundtrack was by William Shatner.

The form of the argument has not changed, but the name Damon Gough has been replaced with the name William Shatner. This argument is still valid, but it contains falsehoods. Even though premise (5) is now false and the conclusion is false, if both premises (4) and (5) *were* true, then the conclusion would necessarily be true.

A valid argument may have some false and some true premises, or a true conclusion and false premises. Consider the following:

1. Premise: Men with black hair and only men with black hair are mortal.
2. Premise: Tigger Reynolds is a man with black hair.
3. Conclusion: Therefore Tigger Reynolds is mortal.

Premise (1) is false, since more than black-haired men are mortal. Since Tigger Reynolds is our charming cat and not a man, premise (2) is false. It is true that Tigger Reynolds will die, so both premises are false while the conclusion is true. What of the validity of the argument? It is a valid argument. If (1) and (2) were true, then (3) could not be false.

Finding several forms of valid arguments was a tremendous accomplishment on Aristotle's part. Once he had done so, given some known-to-be-true premises, numerous further known-to-be-true conclusions could be drawn. These conclusions become premises in their own right and produce further conclusions! Starting with true premises, logic produces a huge amount of knowledge.

The truth for the logic machine would come from *first principles,* or ideas that humans either could or would not doubt. This quest for first principles might sound naive to some in the postmodern twenty-first century, but Aristotle was not foolish enough to insist on certainty. He knew that certainty about first principles could be discouragingly difficult to get, but he believed that certainty was setting the bar too high. He demanded that first principles be subject to no *reasonable* doubt. Aristotle had little patience for propositions that *could* be true but that no *reasonable* person believed. Aristotle was confident that first principles could be found, and that if a discipline were based on those principles and ideas were carefully deduced from them, it would prove persuasive to a reasonable and well-educated person.

Aristotle used intuition as a starting point. By limiting useful intuitions to those held by sane and well-educated persons over a long period of time, there was less risk of starting with widely believed falsehoods. After all, in a good cosmos, especially one formed by a good craftsman, there is sound reason for trusting human intuition. Generalizing from observation, experience and experiment strengthens confidence in intuitions. This process is known as *induction.*

Aristotle formalized *logical deduction,* but he also recognized that many premises used in logic are gained through induction, and there is a limitation to the certainty of induction. Human observations are always incomplete, and conclusions drawn are therefore, at best, *probably* true and lead to *probable* generalizations. Using those generalizations as propositions in a logical argument produces results only as sure as the original generalization.

If the goal of the philosopher is certainty, then induction means failure. Since the conclusions of induction (e.g., "All humans are mortal") form the premises of arguments from deduction, the persuasiveness of those deductive arguments is weakened. A deductive argument may be perfectly valid, but if any of its premises were formed by induction, then the persuasiveness of the conclusion will hinge on how convinced the reader is that the induction used is probable.

The gap between reality and evidence is the problem of induction, but Aristotle was optimistic about induction and the science based on it. Certainty is a good thing, but the quest for it need not hold back the researcher from the next best thing: highly probable conclusions open to reexamination based on further evidence.

But why believe reality allows the philosopher to form highly probable conclusions? Plato was comfortable with radical uncertainty in the study of the natural world, but Aristotle was not. Aristotle rejected an independent world of forms in favor of forms that exist within the material world. In this way Aristotle anticipated gaining sufficient certainty from observations.

ONTOLOGY RESCUES EPISTEMOLOGY
BY WAY OF PSYCHOLOGY

Any natural object has some essential and some inessential properties. The essential property is the form: what separates it out from other things and makes it like other things of its *genus,* or natural kind. A researcher apprehends the genus through study of numerous examples.

Beyond the material substance, what makes a human human? By studying many humans, the form of humanity is discovered: humans are *essentially* rational animals. Aristotle could be confident of this conclusion because his forms were in the natural world. Aristotle was confident in the ability of human beings to come to the truth about the essences of things. This leads naturally to questions about human psychology. Aristotle presents his fullest description of his psychology in a work titled (naturally) *On the Soul,* or *De Anima.*

DE ANIMA

Aristotle believed all things are composed of matter and form. By itself, matter has only the potential to become something. Without form, it is just "stuff," and all stuff is alike. Form makes stuff into the thing it is. Aristotle argues that form or essence is that precisely in virtue of which a thing is a called a "this."

The form of a living creature is the soul, but the soul is not just the form. Without the soul there would not *be* a form, but soul also enables human functions. A bell is a bell not merely because it is made of metal or has the form of a bell, but because it can ring. Likewise, humans are not humans merely because they are made of human stuff or have human form, but because they can *function* as humans. A bell is a bell only when it can ring. A human is a human only when he or she can reason.

Breaking with Plato, Aristotle rejects the idea that the soul can exist apart from the body. Body matters. The soul must have a body that contains the proper organs, or the ability to produce the proper organs, to allow the soul to function. All living things have a soul, so psychology, the study of the soul, embraces the entire biosphere. Everything that lives has at least one function that is performed by the soul.

Aristotle borrowed much of this vocabulary and many of his ideas in psychology and other disciplines from other philosophers, especially Plato. Plato and many of the pre-Socratics believed in a material body that possessed an immaterial soul, and Aristotle accepted this basic psychology. With Homer and Hesiod, Aristotle accepted that the soul was the cause of life. Aristotle inherited the view that the soul was the source of motion and the seat of reason.

Aristotle was the first philosopher who systematically surveyed the views of his predecessors. If Plato founded the Academy, then Aristotle is the first academic, seeing himself as the culmination of a tradition. His summaries of prior philosophers preserve many ideas of pre-Socratic philosophers that otherwise would be unknown. He is not often fair to the predecessors he quotes, but at least he acknowledges their existence.[1]

Aristotle was the first to argue that the soul has a disposition, or potential, to produce vital functions in bodies. Each soul begins with potential to do an action or have a trait that will be an actuality when the incarnate soul does the action or has the trait. Aristotle draws a further distinction between knowledge that is not used (first actuality) and the exercise of that knowledge (second actuality).

There are three kinds of Aristotelian soul, defined by the functions they can potentially perform. For Aristotle souls do not really have parts but different functional potentialities. The three basic functions souls can possess are *nutrition, perception* and *reason.*

Every soul can perform the nutritive functions. Nutrition includes eating and elimination, reproduction, growth and decline. All living things have a nutritive soul to acquire and dispose of the matter needed to flourish. Having reached that fullness, living things wither and die. Plants possess only a nutritive soul since they do not require any higher functions to flourish as plants.

Despite their simple appearance, Aristotle discovered through his experiments that plants have organs. Plants must have reproductive parts, or organs, in order to reproduce, or nutritive organs in order to take in energy. Aristotle demonstrates that all functions of any soul (save one) have a specific organ that is the *tool* of the soul in helping bodies flourish.

Every animal has a nutritive soul *and* a perceptive soul, whose functions include motion and appetites. Perception includes the five senses, divided between the distant senses (smell, sight and hearing) and the senses that depend on contact (taste and touch). The organs of perception include all the standards organs of the senses: the nose is the organ of smell, the eyes of sight, the ears of hearing, the tongue of taste. For touch Aristotle imagines an organ that lies just below the skin and stretches throughout the body.

Perception begins with any object that can be perceived by the appro-

---

[1]Comparing what Aristotle says Plato wrote to what Plato actually wrote does not leave a happy impression about his charity in dealing with pre-Socratics, where there is no way to check his conclusions.

priate organ of the animal. According to Aristotle, if one wishes to see, then one needs an object that has color, such as a bluebird, since the proper sensible object of sight is color. Each sensible object is perceived by a single organ; for example, the eye for sight of color. The eye would perceive a bluebird to be blue. But the proper sensible object of hearing is sound, so a new organ, the ear, perceives the singing of a bluebird. The soul actualizes potential in material organs (eye or ear) to function (seeing or hearing).

Most objects possess some common sensible qualities, including number, shape and motion, that are common to more than one sense. Both an eye and an ear can detect that there is *one* bluebird (number), because either seeing the color of the bird or hearing its lonely song would trigger the perception that there is one bird. Aristotle grouped the proper sensible objects and the common sensible qualities as those that could be *directly* perceived.

In virtue of the direct perceptions, there were also certain incidental perceptions that could be generated in animals. If I see a certain color and hear a particular sound, then I may know (incidentally) that this is Shirley's bluebird. This perception of Shirley's bird is incidental to my direct perceptions, connecting the perceptions with reason in higher animals.

Only humans have a soul that can perform the functions of nutrition, perception and reason. The reason or intellect in a human, the nous, has no specific organ. Aristotle centers reason in the human heart, but the heart was not reason's sole organ. (Aristotle believed the brain was there to cool off the body.) Reason is capable of so many perceptions of so many different kinds that it cannot have just one organ.

Unlike other functions, reason can start thinking without any external stimulation. The intellectual soul contains both the potential to think and an active intellect that energizes thought. Just as light causes color to be seen, so the active intellect causes the rational soul to think. One can start thinking based only on other thoughts one has been having. Since reason has no organ, it might exist apart from the body, which allows some hope for an afterlife, but Aristotle himself betrays little interest in the subject.

In virtue of the senses the intellect is able to move from the direct and indirect perceptions to broader concepts. It is able to apprehend universals from the particulars that the senses present to it. The sight of many bluebirds singing can lead to a general description of the species and an ability to classify the song it sings. The intellect is also able to apprehend geometric objects, such as squares, suggested by perceptions within the physical world but having no actual existence in it.

Based on wishes or desires, the rational soul can decide to move the body according to reason. Only a reasonable person could decide to act against his short-term interests and in favor of the long-term interests of his city. When a person pays more money for a fuel-efficient car, which works less well for himself but is good for the community, his rational soul is at work, motivated in part by his desires.

Aristotle is unclear about whether the *desiring* soul is a fourth function of the soul in addition to nutrition, perception and reason or whether it is a function of perception. However categorized, desire allows most animals to move. Sponges are animals but do not move. The tiger perceives the bluebird, desires lunch and so moves. Motion is necessary for most animals to flourish, since an immobile tiger is an unhappy, hungry and soon-to-be-dead tiger.

Some desires are the result of pleasure or pain and are very simple. If you prick a tiger, will it not scratch you? If you pet it, will it not purr? These are mere reactions and do not require the use of the intellect. As a result, these desires and the motions that follow from them may be a mere byproduct of perception.

Imagination is a byproduct of perception and desire, and not reasonable. Aristotle believes humans think in images. These images come from actual perceptions by the sense organs that are then imagined. I perceive the color of the bluebird with my eyes, and the organs of perception recall this and repeat it for me in images. Dreams and memory are byproducts of this production of images.

Some desires, such as a wish, are the product of reason. If I wish to play soccer, then this might be despite the immediate sense of pain that comes from a rare workout. Humans can make plans to accomplish their goals. They can also wish to think about things that they never could perceive, such as a perfect square. This wish seems less related to perception; there are no round squares to be perceived in the natural world, and so it must be a desire of pure reason.

METAPHYSICS: **FIRST PRINCIPLES**

"All men by nature desire to know."[2] In one of the most powerful opening sentences ever written, Aristotle presumes that human beings as human beings are mentally restless. Human curiosity knows no limits, and humans can be defined as a species that wants to know *more*. Humankind knows of no other animal that has the desire to learn. Though some animals "learn" things through training, there is no evidence that any beast other than a human being *desires* to know.

There are no real exceptions. Some humans accept simple pleasures, such as television and beer, as the only good in their lives, but even these are mentally restless. They might desire to know how to steal cable or find the perfect sofa or the best beer, but one can always find mental activity. The religious fundamentalist might seem thoughtless, but in actuality it is never so. The fundamentalist community is often alive with intellectual controversies. These often seem absurd to outsiders ("Is the New King James Version of Satan?" "How much fellowship should one have with folk outside the community?"), but they are still the signs of badly directed intellectual ferment. Humans can misdirect and weaken their mental restlessness, but they cannot escape it.

If Aristotle is correct, both the hedonist and the fundamentalist in weakening their desire to know are attacking their own natures. That they cannot destroy their intellects totally is a mercy; that they try is folly. Education is the central task of humans, who are learners by nature.

Epistemology, the study of knowing and knowledge, is the study of the central human activity. Aristotle's *Metaphysics* begins with the nature of human thinking, followed by a description of science, then turns to the nature of things and only then to God. If Plato grounds human cognition in abstract forms, then Aristotle bases abstracts, or higher things, in human cognition. In that sense, Aristotle is the most humanistic of all the ancient philosophers.

---

[2]Aristotle *Metaphysics* 1a.

NATURE OF HUMAN THOUGHT

Most living things function at the level of perception. Many living things can first perceive and then remember pleasure or pain. Perception leads to memory, and memory accumulates as experience. This natural experience is not much different than the training a pet receives except that the unguided events of nature are the trainer.

The human possesses a rational soul, the intellect, which builds on experience to create knowledge. The intellect receives experience and starts to question it. Out of that questioning, the human begins to search for universals that will unite experiences.

A puppy may experience the dryer, a place that has one particular smell, as painful and thereafter avoid climbing into it. If the master gets a new dryer with a different smell, the puppy may be in trouble since dogs cannot universalize from experience. A puppy has no notion of the universal category of dryers, and so any change in the dryer is dangerous for him.

Even the youngest human child can do something that the puppy will never do. Babies begin to universalize from their experience of one particular dryer to the class of dryers or even to the genus of machines. As a result, children move from experience with one machine to stoves and other hot objects. Their intellectual souls develop universal principles.

Art and science are born of broader and broader generalizations about the world as the intellectual soul imposes order on the world. Soon the human categorizes experiences in ways that go far beyond the direct experiences themselves. The sciences and the arts gradually allow progress that limited experience cannot match.

In sciences such as medicine, doctors universalize from experience to treat patients, but they also follow general rules learned from the experience of others. In the visual arts the artist imitates one thing in another. The painting is not the object being painted, but the painter finds rules and tricks that enable recognition. Only what is essential to the viewer (the redness of the apple, the roundness of the basketball) must be reproduced, and the rest can be left out. The artist's grasp of universals, learned from experience, makes representational painting possible.

"All philosophy is born in wonder."[3] Humans are curious, full of wonder, and this wonder motivates not just art and science but a desire to explain art and science. Philosophy explains experience from the top down through universal principles, and even reflects on the nature of philosophy. Aristotle's true science is philosophy that attempts an explanation of everything, even what makes things things.

STRUCTURE OF SCIENCE

Aristotle begins his examination of science not with explanations but with a description of what good scientific explanations look like. Here is no mere "likely story," as in *Timaeus,* but a rigorous examination of what scientific explanation should be. This process of finding a set of explanatory principles begins with an attempt to define the notion of cause.

Aristotle believes that attempts at scientific explanations of what causes a thing have failed in part because the earlier philosophers did not take into account all the possible meanings of the word *cause.* For many, looking for a cause almost always has to do with finding the reason for events. "What caused," says the angry father, "my pink lawn flamingo to get crushed by the minivan?" He is looking for a reason for an event. Aristotle is (mostly) speaking about things and not events in the *Metaphysics.* He wants to know the causes of things: fathers, pink flamingos and minivans.

Aristotle found four causes for the existence of things: the material, the efficient, the formal and the final. The material cause is the stuff of an object giving it substance. The material cause of the pink flamingo is the plastic that makes it up. The pre-Socratic philosophers' quest for the *archē* was a search for a material cause. They were looking for the matter that made up the object and gave it coherence over time. This is an excellent starting point, but it is not enough.

The efficient cause is what brings a thing into being or is the source of the change that produced a thing. The father is the efficient cause of the child. A Chinese factory worker is the efficient cause of the original pink flamingo, but the minivan is the efficient cause of the squashed pink flamingo.

---

[3]Aristotle *Metaphysics* 192b.

This Aristotelian cause is most similar to the way *cause* is used today. Though it does not deal with events, as *cause* does in most contemporary usage, the efficient cause accounts for any given thing coming into being as it is.

The formal cause is more complicated because the formal cause is closely related to the final or teleological cause. In fact, some scholars believe the formal and final causes may be reducible to one another. For Aristotle the formal cause was the form or essence of a thing that allowed it to perform its proper function or reach its intended end. The proper end of an object, the reason for its being, is the final cause. The final cause is that for the sake of which an object came to be. An eye came into being for seeing, and a plastic pink flamingo for lawn ornamentation. The formal cause of a pink flamingo is having a shape vaguely resembling a tropical bird, which allows the pink flamingo to serve its purpose (or final cause). The final cause of a pink flamingo is functioning as a low-cost and oddly attractive lawn ornament. To achieve this, it must be formed in a flamingo-like shape, be made of brittle plastic and be the color pink. The formal cause of a pink flamingo is its pink-flamingo shape and components (wire leg, plastic bird body). So, here is a look at the pink flamingo in terms of Aristotelian causation:

1. Material cause: plastic
2. Efficient cause: the flamingo-making factory worker
3. Formal cause: flamingo shape, single leg to stick in the ground, pink color
4. Final cause: being a low-cost lawn ornament

Almost all Aristotle's best examples deal with artifacts, things made by humans, because with artifacts it is reasonably simple to find the four causes. But what of natural objects? Controversially, Aristotle applies all of these same four causes, including the final cause, to objects found in nature. The human eye is *for* seeing, the ear *for* hearing and the nose *for* smelling. There is design and purpose to creation. This is controversial today because it implies purpose and order to natural objects at a level that secularist Darwinism finds unacceptable.

In one sense Darwinism does not dispense with final causes. A Darwinist can say that a nose is good at smelling, as it turns out, and that given the present state of the human organism, this is the survival function (the Darwinian final cause) of a nose. Nature taken as a whole favors (blindly, through natural laws) the most fit; therefore, the end or purpose of any organ is the survival value gained by the organism through that organ. Evolution itself is the efficient cause of this organ existing. It "designed" the nose to smell since smelling has survival value.

However, no Darwinist can go further and say that the interlocking organs of any organism were *intended* to be as they are by design. The nose isn't actually *for* smelling in some intentional sense; it happens to smell. The function was not intended but fortuitous. If the history of the world were replayed, then there is no reason to think humans would have noses that smell or eyes that see, or even that humans as humans would exist. There is no intentional teleology for a Darwinist, and so historically, Darwinists have been hostile to Aristotelian science. The historical marriage between Aristotelian and Christian natural theology in the writings of Saint Thomas Aquinas did not help matters.

Even the most secular biologists have not shaken teleological talk, however. When creationists are not around, they wax lyrical regarding the highly organized nature of living things. After all, it is not just one organ that seems highly specialized but also the relationships between organs. Any late-night PBS television special on the life of the orchid is apt to fall into shockingly Aristotelian language about the cause of any given structure that seems to go beyond mere evolutionary function to an inherent final design. This is natural. Given the highly organized and interlocking structures of most organisms and the irreducible complexity of some of the organs of living things, naturalists have begun to flirt with more robust forms of teleology. Is the cosmos hard-wired to produce the things that are produced? Does "life" organize itself? Perhaps cosmic history can go only one way, or in a very limited number of ways, making living things as they are probable and not improbable.

Since Aristotle uses teleology without being a creationist, his material universe is eternal. The modern secularist can make peace with him, but any reintroduction of strong teleology into biology will still favor theism. A hard-wired universe naturally causes curious humans to wonder who did the wiring. It seems strangely fortuitous that humanity should exist, and it is unsatisfying to end the questioning with the retort that humans can only worry about this because they exist. It is no accident that Aristotle's views found the greatest use only after they were adapted in a theistic direction by Saint Thomas Aquinas.

Aristotle did not just structure science around four causes; he developed many presuppositions of this science. These principles gave a formal structure to his classification and examination of the natural world. The laws became rules or theorems of his logic to help him develop his universal principles and do science. The two most important laws are the law of non-contradiction and the law of the excluded middle. The law of non-contradiction states that a proposition or state of affairs and its negation cannot be true or obtain at the same time. The statements "The flamingo is pink" and "It is not the case that the flamingo is pink" cannot both be true at the same time.

The fact that one or the other proposition must be true leads to the law of the excluded middle. This law asserts that either a thing or its negation is true. There are no other options. The flamingo is either pink or it is not the case that the flamingo is pink. With logic as a tool, certain noncontroversial principles of reasoning discovered and a theory of full causation explored, Aristotle is ready to explain what things are. He is ready to do science.

NATURE OF THINGS, INCLUDING
THE FIRST SUBSTANCE

All things perceived are substance. The *Metaphysics* is most obscure on the nature of substance. The Greek is difficult, and even some scholars have thrown up their hands at the difficulties. Even if Aristotle has worked out his ontology (theory of being), nobody thinks it is easy to understand, and there is real disagreement among scholars about what Aristotle proposes. Here is one way of looking at Aristotelian substance to guide further study of the *Metaphysics*.

Most things contain properties or functions that are accidental to them. The baseball on my shelf is designed for a game, but it is now a memento because it has been signed by Frank Pastore, one of my favorite radio hosts and a former major league pitcher. The Frank Pastore signature could be removed, though I hope nobody tries, and the baseball would remain what it essentially is—a baseball. It could still perform its function as a baseball if it lost its accidental function as a keepsake. What is it that makes a baseball a baseball?

If all things are substance, then what is substance? Is it a genus, an essence, a universal or something more complex—an underlying structure or substratum? Aristotle dismisses genus as not basic enough. Simply saying that substance is an essence seems to explain nothing, replacing one mysterious term for another. Aristotle was convinced by the "third man" argument and other difficulties that Platonic universals are incoherent. Aristotle also wanted to ground knowledge in the world so that his science can contain more certainty than was possible for Plato's theories.

This leaves the existence of a substratum, an underlying structure of a thing, as the favored Aristotelian explanation. This substratum, or basement, contains the characteristics necessary and sufficient for a thing to be that thing. An object may have some features accidentally, but there are some features it cannot do without and remain what it is. These features are found in the substratum.

The substratum could itself be a form, matter or a combination of the two. Not surprisingly Aristotle rejects matter as being an inadequate vessel for the essence of a thing. Matter for Aristotle is a shapeless stuff that lacks any independent characteristics. It is wonderful in that it can be the basic building blocks for anything, but it lacks the independent characteristics that could contain the essential features of a thing. Its plasticity makes it adequate as material but inadequate as a basis for essential properties. For Aristotle the "matter" of the pink flamingo is the same as the "matter" of the baseball. It is the *form* of the matter that allows necessary functions of flamingo or baseball.

For Aristotle things are *hylomorphic:* they are formed of both matter *(hylo-)* and form *(-morphic)*. This is important since matter is fully real and an important part of the substance in ways it could never be for Plato. But even for Aristotle it is the form that gives a thing its name and separates it out from all the other things. Nobody would call a pink flamingo lawn ornament "plastic." Nobody would call a baseball "leather and twine."

The Aristotelian form is the basic substance in a thing. Only it can contain the essential properties that will allow a substance to actualize its functions. Of course, in a secondary sense the form and matter combination is the substrate, since Aristotelian form never exists apart from matter. The form is the substrate that makes a thing a thing. It is the essence of any object and so the object of knowledge.

But this answer is a contradiction of earlier claims! In book seven Aristotle says that no universal is a substance, yet at the same time he says that substance is prior in definition and knowledge. Has he simply returned in a roundabout way to a universal, approaching it from beneath instead of from above? This seems unlikely.

Aristotelian essence exists in the *individual* alone. It exists by nature in *this* matter and makes *this* thing what it is. Because nature is orderly, the intellect can generate a universal from individual forms (found only in matter) and so "create" a universal existing only as an object of human knowledge. Platonic universals exist in themselves, but Aristotelian universals exist only in thought. A thing is the form that can produce essential functions necessary to maintain it as itself without changing into another thing. These forms can be organized into categories, such as living versus nonliving, and universal principles can be derived from them. The universal principles are the objects of science.

In living things it is the soul, or the form, that gives substance. Matter can only exist in potentiality whether in living or nonliving things. In discussing sensible things, Aristotle argues that there are those that can be destroyed and those that cannot be destroyed. Objects in the world are the first kind, and objects in the heavens are the second kind. Heavenly bodies change, but they are eternal and cannot be destroyed.

Aristotle erred, but he did so because of a rational induction based on a large set of observations. Humans had been observing the heavens and keeping careful records for hundreds of years. Aristotle could induce the fact of change in the heavens since they move, but he also sensibly induced the eternality of the heavens since they seemed stable over all of human history. In 1572 a supernova shocked scientific Europe not because it was a change in the heavens (as even some college texts teach), but because this change seemed to be a birth or destruction of an object in the heavens. Aristotle was wrong.

Aristotle postulated sensible structures that were mortal and immortal. Each, however, contained some potential and was not fully actualized since it contained matter. Each is sensible and so is capable of change, and each moves. What is the source of that movement? In *On the Heavens* Aristotle postulates a self-moving element, but he rejects this idea in *Metaphysics*. Nor is he content to accept motion as a given. He believes that he needs a cause of motion. Why? He rejects the possibility of an actual infinite, which would occur if he postulated an infinite regress of causes for motion.

If Aristotle is to avoid an infinite regress (i.e., X moved Y, but what moved X?) and self-motion, then he must have an unmoved first mover. The first mover must also be fully actualized or there would be potential for change and so movement. This first movement does not come in time, since Aristotle does not believe in any creation, but occurs in terms of causal priority. Everything in the heavens that is moving has always moved, but that eternal motion stems from the Unmoved Mover. To use an image, the Unmoved Mover is the external, unmoved engine to the movement of the heavenly machine.

In finishing off his picture of what exists, of all the possible substances, Aristotle is left then only to postulate the existence of pure actuality, or First Substance. This is an essence with only form and no matter. Aristotle proposes that there exists a being that is pure actuality. This being, the Aristotelian god, would be eternal in every way. This god moves the heavens but is himself unmoved. He only thinks, and these thoughts are only about thinking. He is oblivious, utterly unconcerned, about humanity.

The god of Aristotle is even less like the God of the Bible than Plato's god. The Unmoved Mover is not a creator or redeemer or even compassionate. This philosopher's god is not a creator since the cosmos has always existed as it is. Aristotle's god is a *motivator*. He has no thought to spare for humanity, and there is no chance that the thought to become incarnate would even occur to the Unmoved Mover. To worship or love the Unmoved Mover would be like loving the big bang. There can be no afterlife, no concept of future rewards or punishments. Aristotle presents the first fully worked-out ethical system totally disconnected from religious ideas.

9

THE MIDDLE WAY

Aristotle's Ethics

⚜

HOW SHOULD WE THEN LIVE?

What do people want? This is a broader question than the one Freud asked, but it is a more appropriate one. Aristotle believes he has an answer to this question. Keeping in mind his four causes, Aristotle begins his treatise on ethics, the study of how humans should live, with a careful examination of the options for the final end, the final good, of human action. From the poets to the philosophers, everyone is concerned with living the good life; however, merely saying that one wants to live the good life is not enough. What is the good life for a human?

Aristotle examines the plausible answers with care, but he warns the reader that *Ethics* is not physics. The results of his examination, because it deals with human things, will be imprecise. Humans and their civilizations are too complicated to expect to find a simple set of rules that applies in every case. The most that can be expected from any science dealing with human behavior is a set of general principles.

Because the study of human behavior is so difficult, it is tempting to abandon it. But the fact that one cannot reach perfection, or even be sure what perfection is, does not mean that one cannot improve. As humans study the nature of the good life, Aristotle suggests they begin to get a feel, an ethical intuition, for what the good life is. The thoughtful person will seek practical wisdom about human affairs, which consists of experience and knowledge about how events usually turn out. When this practical wisdom is combined with training in the virtues begun at a young age, the well-trained citizen can be expected to make better judgments in any given situation than the person attacking problems at random.

This is especially true if the ethical student has the end of human life in mind. The general end of human existence, what people are here to do in order to flourish in this life, *can* be known scientifically. While the student cannot always be sure what behaviors will contribute to achieving this goal, he or she can make better decisions than someone who has the entirely wrong end in mind. If a person thinks the highest good in life is to see a Packers game on the Frozen Tundra, then he or she may make all sorts of bad decisions in order to achieve that goal, sacrificing important things for an unworthy end. However great it would be to see a Packers game in Green Bay, that is an insufficient object to motivate an entire life. Bad or even inadequate goals will likely lead to bad actions. After all, the fan living for the Packers may be courageous in a particular situation (standing in line in subzero temperatures) because he thinks it will get him closer to his goal. However, he is also likely to sacrifice more important things for his bad goal. The fanatical Packer backer who ignores his wife and children to watch games has made such an error. The goal is unworthy of an entire life.

Aristotle believes that in most cases it is hard to know for sure what is right or wrong, but that does not mean he does not think some answers are much better than others. Aristotle believes that a limited number of emotions and actions are *always* known to be wrong. Just because most ethical rules in most situations are unknowable or even nonexistent does not mean that all are unknowable or that none exist. In fact, Aristotle concedes there are some actions that are base in and of themselves.[1] For example, there is never a good time to commit adultery. Some actions are simply known by any reasonable person to be base. Base actions do harm to the person's intellect and can be known to be wrong by definition. If an action is defined as essentially shameful, such as spite or envy, then there can never be a sensible time to do it. The essential nature and

---

[1] Aristotle *Nichomachean Ethics* 1107a10-25.

function of envy or an action such as murder can never be a good for humankind. There are not many of these actions and emotions, but it matters that a good citizen totally avoid them.

Aristotle has a pragmatic streak when it comes to human action. He is not interested in an ethic that will apply in a lawlike manner in every possible circumstance. He would have little patience with schools that give young children difficult ethical problems that they will almost certainly never face. Instead, Aristotle is looking for an ethic to help the average citizen maximize happiness. He concedes that if a citizen has very bad luck and lives in extraordinary times, he or she will face ethical challenges that will try all but sages. Even the wise may face extraordinary circumstances where experience and philosophy fail them. However, for most humans, worrying about this is like being deathly concerned about getting hit by lightning while speeding drunk down the highway without a seatbelt. Most citizens need to habituate themselves to doing what they should in the vast majority of cases where reasonable men and women agree about what is the right thing to do.

This eliminates the cheap relativism one so often encounters in some modern people. Such relativists take hard cases and use them to justify base actions. Others use the fact that ethical experts disagree in some situations or are not sure they are correct to abandon moral reasoning altogether. Aristotle would rightly have no tolerance for such folly. One can concede that ethics can be hard without giving up on the idea that some lives are better lived than others. The examined life, or living in a way calculated to bring human flourishing, is more rational. What then is the end of human existence?

TRUE ENDS

The quest for the true end for human existence begins in the common experiences of the individual citizens. If the seeker concedes that he or she should move from the general to the expert, what do those experienced in ethics say? One has to know what such an end will look like when one has found it. Otherwise, attractive options that are wrong will be too appealing, and bogus gurus may seduce citizens with answers that are harmful but seem attractive at the time.

First, the seeker must concede that not all ends are equal. Some ends are subordinate to other ends. This is a simple concept but one that is often overlooked in deciding how to live life. This can be a negative or a positive concept. Negatively, a good that a person can enjoy immoderately might cut off another good in the long term. For me, eating cheesecake and watching *Phantom* with my wife, Hope, is good, but if I do it too frequently, it will prevent me from having the physical fitness necessary to do my job and fully enjoy my relationship with my wife. It is too late to learn moderation when facing the buffet line at the local all-you-can-eat cafeteria. Virtues cannot be learned quickly, and the time not spent learning today may be time lost to vice when the price of immoderation has to be paid.

Positively, some goods can increase the enjoyment of other goods. One can only savor wine at a feast if one has taken the time to learn how to do so. The just person may understand the appropriateness of a particular courageous action and take satisfaction in it in a way that an unjust person cannot. Learning one virtue may be the only way to experience certain goods.

Second, one good might be needed while another good is not needed. Courage under fire is necessary on the field of battle, where other virtues may have to become subordinate to it for a time. All of this should convince a reasonable person that one cannot simply take goods or virtues as one comes across them. Such an unplanned life would lead to missed pleasures, virtues and goodness.

For Aristotle the best example of a hierarchy of values comes in the realm of virtue. The virtue of courage, for example, requires the virtues of practical wisdom and moderation. How? The one desiring to be courageous needs to know when his attempt at courage is rashness or cowardice. Only the virtue of practical wisdom will enable him to understand how he should act, and only the moderate person will know to what extent he should act. The life of moderation and practical wisdom is more fundamental to the good life than courage.

Aristotle has a few more clues to the nature of the final good. If a final end is the one to seek, what will a final end look like? First, other ends will be chosen for its sake. Second, it will be chosen for its own sake and, once chosen, will be self-sufficient. Nothing could be the final end for humankind if it itself is chosen for some other good. If that were the case, that other good would be the final good. So the best candidate for the good life will need no other justification.

Plato suggested that humankind should live in accordance with or in imitation of the form of the good. The good life is to be as much like the good as possible. Aristotle must reject this answer because he believes that he has demonstrated that forms do not exist apart from things. Second, even if one is a Platonist, Aristotle has shown that there is nothing very relevant about slogans like "living in imitation of the good." What does this mean? If one adopts it as a guide to life, then the same hard ethical examination that Aristotle is about to begin will be necessary.

A Platonist would respond that in the world of becoming, knowing how to live in accordance with the good will require a rough-and-ready sort of skill. A Platonist could agree the *Ethics* is necessary if Platonism is to be applied. Think, however, of the encouragement gained from the belief that ethics can be grounded in something eternal and unmoving, such as the good itself.

This Platonic reply is naturally only satisfactory if the theory of forms is coherent. A cheerful idea is a good idea only if it is also comprehensible. Aristotle does not believe that the theory of forms is metaphysically useful. His metaphysics does not need forms but grounds ethics and concepts of goodness in terms of the functions or final ends of organisms. Species exist and are not created; so, short of extinctions (in which case there is no further worry about behavior), their function and final causes are eternal. As a result, they are a sufficient ground for ethics. The difference between a Platonist and an Aristotelian need not be in the area of *how* they do ethics—both want to produce good citizens—but in *what* actually exists.

Most citizens think the good life is given to bodily pleasures, simple hedonism. Aristotle quickly dismisses this as fit only for beasts. "But wait," my students sometimes say, "isn't Aristotle too easily dismissive of the life of passions? Isn't that the problem with philosophers, that they do not understand the joys of the simple hedonistic life?" Philosophers "don't get it" because they live cloistered lives or they have to make a virtue out of thinking because that is about all they have the opportunity to do. There is no virtue in being chaste if that is one's only option!

Since Aristotle has called their own tastes bestial, it seems at least rhetorically fair that these students get to return the favor by calling philosophers social losers. As we have seen, Aristophanes and other prominent Greeks were happy to advance such assaults themselves. But if ever there was a philosopher who understood the potential benefits of animal pleasures, it was Aristotle. He lived well and spent time in what became the foremost court of Europe and the Middle East. He could have chosen, if he had wished, to have a closer association with the most powerful man of his age who had once been his student. Aristotle rejected the sybaritic life of the court for the life of philosophy not because he had no concept of the pleasures of wine, sex and power, but because he had good knowledge. He rejected what he knew.

The problem with the life of common hedonism is that there is not much pleasure there. It is also pleasure that, given a life of moderation, will always be available to a philosopher if one wants it, while the pleasures of the philosopher are not available to the confirmed hedonist. It is easy to drink and procreate—an animal can do it, after all—but it is much harder to experience the joys of understanding a very difficult but important idea for the first time. Those who have experienced intellectual pleasures rarely want to give them up for this very reason. So my students are wrong when they think that all philosophers adopt the life of thought because they have no choice. Both Plato and Aristotle did not fit this stereotype. The students are also wrong in their very calculation of pleasure. As we shall see, in the end Aristotle wants human beings to flourish, to live for pleasure, but he wants to be careful that we do not sell out too quickly. He wants us to be sure to get the best pleasures. Bestial pleasures are frequently mildly amusing at the start but come with a hangover later. The problem with bestial humans is not that they want to feel good but that they end up missing the best feelings while feeling bad due to the backwash of foolish decisions.

Aristotle was horrified with such a life for humans. Pleasures that are fit for beasts are not wrong for men since humans are animals; Aristotle was no monastic. Too much of these pleasures, however, can cut off access to the uniquely human pleasures. My dog cannot enjoy the subtle images in the films *Citizen Kane* or *Garden State,* but I can. If I as a man do not, then who will?

Aristotle's notions of appropriateness and function make this the conclusive argument for him. It may not persuade moderns, who sometimes act as if knowing what a thing is for is a good excuse for finding a new and novel use of the thing. But this is a cultural prejudice that should be subject to rigorous examination. It may not in fact be productive to a good life.

If the life of a hedonist is not the good life, then perhaps the life of the aristocrat is. The life of honor has commended itself to many people in many cultures. These people balance duty with pleasure in a way calculated to lend glory to their name, now and in the future.

The Greeks were not the only people to find such a life attractive. As recently as the early twentieth century, English aristocrats followed a code of honor. Standing on the deck of *Titanic,* an English gentleman of 1912 might have said, "I must not board a lifeboat in order to make way for the women and children. It is the only decent thing for a gentleman to do." Such men voluntarily joined the army or served in Parliament for minimal pay out of a sense of honor and duty. The same man might also refuse to cheat at cards not because of any grand moral theory but because cheating was beneath his dignity as an aristocrat. He had an honorable place in the society and meant to go on having it.

In theory such were the great men of the city-states of Aristotle's youth. While most aristocrats could not live up to their principles, popular writers such as Aristophanes still upheld the life of honor as an ideal. By middle age Aristotle witnessed the independent gentlemen of Athens giving way to sycophants of tyrants like Alexander the Great. Aristotle and his family were of the old class, and it would have been natural for him to commend it as the best life, but he did not.

The gentleman is a man of honor in the city. However, the benefits of honor are only received if the man of honor is known to be a man of honor. Self-declared gentlemen aren't. The man on the deck of the *Titanic* could not achieve the same honor for himself or his family by smoking his last cigarette alone in his cabin. He does not only need to do well but to be seen as doing well. This made the happiness of a man totally dependent on external circumstances. Aristotle had seen the politics of his age change so quickly that men who had once been honored were now dishonored. He could not commend as happy a life one so dependent on the good opinion of others.

Another popular candidate for the good life is the life of wealth, but wealth is for the sake of something else. Money, gold, excess cattle or land is of value only because it gives a person the ability to gain other goods. Wealth is not valued for its own sake, a characteristic Aristotle believed necessary for the greatest good.

Aristotle saw that one could never have enough wealth. People who are chasing wealth don't have time to enjoy it. Scrooge may be rich, but Cratchit has more fun. Wealth is good, but not *the* good. The wealthy may be able to purchase the leisure in which to pursue human excellence, but all the money in the world cannot buy them the moral fiber to choose it. Money seems at best an aide to living the good life, not the end of the good life itself.

Virtue seems the most likely candidate for the proper end of a good life. In discussing good living, the need for virtue has come up repeatedly. However, virtues are useful for living a good life, not the reason for living it. Like wealth, virtues are tools to build a good life, not the good life itself. All humans can agree that they want justice, but there seems to be little agreement for what end a person is just.

Aristotle finally declares that the end of all human existence, the good life, is to be happy as a human being. The simple hedonist is onto something when he says, "I just want to be happy." To this Aristotle replies, "Yes, but do you know what true happiness is?" True happiness is not a mere feeling, because feelings can be manipulated or even induced by a drug. True happiness for a human being is flourishing in humanity. The happy woman knows who she is and lives according to her nature. As with most things in Aristotle, the definition is functional, knowing what it is to act as a human. This is why ethical systems are always understood in terms of political activity.

Human happiness will be defined by the natural ends of the human genus and species. The student of human nature is most apt to become happy, though gaining such knowledge will never be exact or guaranteed. Seeking true happiness, or flourishing, is the unique job of every human being. In practical terms this work or function can be divided between practical wisdom *(phronesis)* and true wisdom *(sophia)*.

Human life will come to its full flowering when it culminates in true wisdom. True wisdom is the hardest to obtain, the most pleasurable and the wisdom for the sake of which all other education is directed. While a person must live in a city with other people in order to achieve sophia, practical wisdom is necessary for life inside the city, which provides distractions and the potential opposition of others to philosophy. Practical wisdom helps the wise to negotiate these difficulties and reach their goal.

WHAT IS MORAL VIRTUE?

The nature of moral virtue is the most prominent theme of books two through five and seven through nine. Just as today, moralists in Aristotle's day often praised the virtuous life but rarely told how to live it. Plato had complained about this problem, but Aristotle took on the task with his end in mind. Aristotle believed that moderation, living according to the mean, was the key to virtuous living that would lead to human flourishing.

All face a life of pain and pleasure, and all sane persons desire to avoid pain and maximize pleasure. Some pain may be necessary in order to gain great pleasure since higher desires and intense pleasures (especially of the intellect) can only be gained with sacrifice. As a result, practical wisdom must be used to determine when the cost is worth the gain.

Desire itself is a tricky part of the moral equation. Since the goal of human life is happiness, desire must be taken into account, but for many people such consideration turns into addiction to desire itself. In order to avoid this some humans try to suppress all desire. Both types of people end up miserable. Practical wisdom measures the pleasure and pain involved in the pursuit of desire and seeks to steer a middle course between the one who gets too little (the defective) and the one who gets too much (the excessive). The virtuous person, like Goldilocks in the fairytale "Goldilocks and the Three Bears," chooses neither extreme but rather the middle way, which is "just right."

This *golden mean* is one of the most useful ideas in ethics. According to Aristotle, it can be applied to any action that is not inherently base, such as eating or sexual activity. Courage is always a good thing, but knowing when an action is courage is hard. Merely seeing someone acting boldly in the face of danger is not enough. Is a soldier acting courageously or rashly? Excessive vigor in battle may not be good; it can put an army in danger. On the other hand, a soldier might become too prudent when it is time to act, which can be seen as cowardice with a college diploma. A wise soldier seeks a middle way between rashness and cowardice.

This kind of lesson does not apply only to virtues, but also to every other action that is not naturally base. It is good to wash hands. It is sanitary, helping reduce the spread of disease. The restaurant worker who never washes his hands is defective, but the obsessive-compulsive person who washes his hands after even the slightest physical contact is excessive. Moderation finds the mean between the two.

Aristotle's mean is not meant to be a precise guide to morally virtuous behavior, but a useful tool in decision making. The Aristotelian ethics of the golden mean searches for a useful outcome that will at the very least avoid being a very wrong outcome. Like a Greek physician, Aristotle wishes first to "do no harm." The mean will be most useful to a well-trained person who has received a proper education and experience in the politics of the city. Aristotle believes such a human will make mostly sound ethical decisions.

The quality of decisions made using the mean will improve with time and experience. Over time, virtue will become a disposition *(hexis),* and as it becomes more firm, a state of character or habit. A virtuous habit once acquired is easy to maintain since moral inertia now favors virtue.

Aristotle's arguments for moral education at an early age have impacted Western educators in the liberal arts tradition ever since. When the local school takes on bullying behavior in the schoolyard or decides that tolerance must be practiced in the elementary classroom, it is emulating the Aristotelian model. Virtue is to be acquired by learning and experience leading to good habits.

Plato had a simple explanation for virtue: one does what one knows to be good. Aristotle agreed with Plato that fundamentally virtue is tied to knowledge, but he allowed for weakness of the will. After all, some people may know and desire the good but may be unable to do it through lack of willpower. Just as good habits make doing the right thing almost automatic, so bad habits can make doing the wrong thing almost automatic. A given vice may be such an addictive behavior that the person who wants to quit cannot. What is necessary, if it is still possible, is a strict regime of moral training in which such persons teach themselves moderation, but a bad education or society may make this impossible.

The center of any of moral act is choice, which begins in desire. One of the first moral lessons a person must learn is that desire can be defective. Nobody defends masochism or stupidity, but some people desire pain or folly. Some people desire pleasures they are not capable of achieving or enjoying. They do not know their limits but dream of something they cannot have. To dream the impossible dream may make an appealing song in a play like *Man of La Mancha,* but in real life it leads to madness and danger.

Wanting what one cannot have is a recipe for unhappiness and frustration. There exists no indulgent screenwriter to write improbable endings to sate every human desire, but Hollywood has taught many that their dreams are sacred. As a result, by midlife (or even midcollege) many Americans feel cheated and even a bit angry. Their improbable desires have left them full of discontent and misery.

A good character channels desires to ends that are possible and beneficial. Aristotle, like almost every Greek of his time, accepted the message of the oracle at Delphi that a person should know himself and his limits. This self-knowledge leads to moderation of the desires to the beneficial and the possible. Because most citizens are badly educated, they have competing desires, some of which cannot be fulfilled and some of which are harmful. Part of a good education is to bring harmony to the desires of each citizen.

Becoming morally educated is not the same for everyone or even for one person at every moment of his or her life. First, some people are more morally perceptive than others. Just as some people grasp the meaning of art or literature more quickly than others, so some are quicker to grasp difficult moral issues.

Second, other people's perceptions do matter. While some actions are wrong even if everyone applauds, such as torture in wartime, other choices gain some of their moral force from public approval. A great-aunt is not successful as a gift giver if the recipient of her hand-knit Christmas sweater does not like it. Many actions require taking others' wants into account to be completed well.

Finally, circumstances affect what can or cannot be understood or discussed. The stress at the end of a semester makes reasonable discussion more difficult. Wartime limits the amount of time a nation has available to make moral judgments. A business partner may lack the education necessary to discuss an issue properly. The person of practical wisdom will have to do his best in such circumstances, and any future judgment about his behavior will have to take his circumstances into account. The good city will produce decent citizens, and these decent citizens may become capable of the greatest human happiness: intellectual excellence.

INTELLECTUAL EXCELLENCE, HUMAN HAPPINESS AND A QUESTION OF COHERENCE

Intellectual excellence is a rare thing and of ultimate value. All human beings can obtain moral excellence, but few can obtain intellectual excellence even in a well-run city. Intellectual excellence is the highest good for those living in a place and time with the necessary opportunities and education in moral virtue and who also have the character to make use of their blessings. Much more than moral virtue, intellectual excellence is a gift that not all human beings are able to share. Those that can fully grasp the intellectual virtues are amazing humans.

These special human beings are not Aristotelian supermen but human in the fullest sense. A superman has something most people lack, such as the ability to see through walls, but the intellectually virtuous person perfects what all people possess in some degree. Aristotle's intellectually gifted citizens have the ability to become the paradigm of what it means to be human.

Intellect is the chief function of humans that is unique among the animals. (The Aristotelian god may think, but he is not an animal.) As the unique end of human ethical existence, it is also perfect happiness: to think is to be a human and so to be happy as a human. Of course, not all thoughts are created equal, and some types of thinking make humans happier than others.

There are five intellectual virtues for Aristotle that form a hierarchy:

Higher Realm
1. Sophia—wisdom
2. Nous—intuitive knowledge
3. Episteme—deductive sciences

Lower Realm
4. Phronesis—practical reason
5. Techne—crafts or craft skills

The two lowest virtues, techne and phronesis, have as their subjects the changing objects of the world. Both apply universal principles to particular cases in their area of expertise. *Techne* includes such diverse arts as sheep-herding and medicine, which seek goods (i.e., food, health) usable by the other intellectual virtues. *Phronesis* deals with the final goods of variable objects. Phronesis is the practical reason, the application of moral virtues to civic affairs, that allows a good person to live at peace in the city.

The other three intellectual virtues—episteme, nous and sophia—discover universals among objects that do not change. *Episteme* is Aristotelian science, which as we have discussed deals with the nature of things. It is a derived and deductive science that uses Aristotelian logic. *Nous* is the intuitional insight that allows for the discovery of first principles. *Sophia* subsumes both of these activities into the contemplation of truth itself. Sophia is no longer *seeking* the truth but meditating on it as pure thought. By book ten of his *Ethics,* Aristotle urges the life of pure contemplation to the extent that it is possible as the best one for humanity, an access to divine bliss. Phronesis is good only as a means to greatest happiness. It is to a life of sophia that Aristotle directs the energies of the ethical person, but this presents a difficulty for understanding the *Ethics.*

In books two through nine of the *Ethics,* phronesis and sophia govern separate realms of human life and are treated fairly equally. Phronesis is given a secondary role in the hierarchy of knowing, but the good life is *balancing* the realms of sophia and phronesis. Sophia is the greatest good;

phronesis is not just good for the sake of sophia, but good as part of a balanced life. Is sophia the only good, as book ten suggests, or is human good as much sophia as possible in a life of phronesis?

Ethics book one contains both ideas, and Aristotle cannot seem to decide between the two. If he is to be consistent, however, Aristotle must abandon the idea that humans should strive for a life of contemplation. Aristotle knows all people must live in cities because it is not good for them to be alone. Even the greatest person needs friends, since it is better for a person's soul to be active and do good to others than to only passively have good done to him. The person of pure sophia in book ten is not a person at all but a god. Like his master, Plato, Aristotle has allowed his love of the highest things to cause him to forget not just the necessity but the glory of the lower things.

FRIENDSHIP AND POLITICS

Aristotle devotes two chapters of the *Ethics* to friendship, which might seem odd to moderns. Friendship has too often disappeared under pressure to make every relationship erotic, or it is viewed as unimportant to the good life. Aristotle was wiser and saw that there were certain human needs that only that unique thing called friendship can meet.

Aristotle believed that there are three sorts of friendship, and each kind meets particular needs in people. First, there is friendship based on pleasure. Some people are just pleasant to be around and gain friends for that reason. Attractive personalities are pleasant, and quick wit is enjoyable to be around.[2] Such friendships are easily made but are also easily broken.

The second type of friendship is based on utility. Both people want an external good that would not be available without the friendship. This sort of friendship is about *getting* from the other person. A good student becomes friends with a professor to gain knowledge, or a club forms so that the group can achieve something that the individuals could not. The first kind of friendship, for pleasure, hopes for an internal feeling; the second, for utility, seeks an external good accessible to both friends.

Are such friendships good? Some ethical systems, like Kant's, con-

---

[2] Aristotle *Nichomachean Ethics* 1156a15.

demn using other humans as means to ends. Such friendships can easily be exploitative and harm both people, but Aristotle would point out that this need not be so. Especially between equals who understand the limits of the friendship, such personal relationships are more like economic contracts that allow two people to achieve personal goals they could not obtain otherwise. Both parties can benefit in an economic transaction, both getting something they need; similarly, these "lower" forms of friendship can also meet needs of both parties.

Any friendship between persons who are unequal in power, virtue or happiness is risky. It is easy for the greater to exploit the lesser or for the lesser to merely use the greater. Yet such relationships cannot be avoided. It is risky to have children, to hire workers, to teach students, but it must be done.

Aristotle cautions that friendship in such unequal relationships must remain proportional. The greater should be loved more than the lesser. The one who benefits the most from the relationship (the child, the student) should be grateful. On the other hand, the person in a position of power and responsibility should be virtuous and act with justice. The limits of the relationship must be plainly spelled out for both parties. In no case, of course, would Aristotle allow for any friendship or relationship that harms the ability of any individual to achieve human virtue or happiness.

For Aristotle the third kind of friendship is the highest kind and the most apt to produce virtue. This friendship wants only the good of the other. Aristotle believes true friendship of this sort must be mutual; nobody can be a friend to one who hates him. Both friends make each other better. I love my true friends for their own sake.[3] As a result of my concern for my friends, I will spend time with them and experience their pleasures and pains.

Of course, in one sense this friendship is also a form of self-love. If Maria and Olga are friends, then Maria benefits by being good to Olga. She gains virtue by every act of goodness she does to Olga. Indeed, by befriending Olga this way, she loves herself by practicing the virtues. Aristotle rightly lauds such friendship as a practical necessity if people

---

[3] Aristotle *Nichomachean Ethics* 1166a1-9.

are going to live good and happy lives.

In *The Four Loves* C. S. Lewis points out that Christianity introduced a new friendship, a fourth kind: love and friendship of an unlovable person who cannot love back. This love can transform and enable the recipient to become the true friend of the one showing this Christian love. If Maria befriended Olga when she was an enemy, then she is no fool, as Aristotle might think, because she might win a friend.

Even if Olga does not change, Maria has acted in hope. She has tried to bring the beloved to friendship. Even if rejected, this hopeful action is good for Maria, since the attempt to do good is good for her whether it works or not. Of course, the model for such friendship is in the incarnation of Jesus Christ. God came down, emptied himself of his awesome powers and became human to befriend humankind. He loved each person even when they hated him and his law. In doing so God opened the way to becoming like God. At this point he enters into a friendship with humanity that brings nothing but benefits to humankind and brings nothing but the glory of his graciousness to himself. Humankind can only adore such a friend.

Despite Aristotle's failures and weaknesses, he still has much to teach the modern world. At his best Aristotle presented a complete picture of the cosmos and humankind's place in it. He tried to unify knowledge and did not leave any discipline alone. The breadth of his curiosity and research had never been seen before and only rarely since. The most important thing he gave to the West was a model for those with an insatiable desire to know. If in the end he was not the equal of Plato as a maker of myths, he was more than an equal as the master of those who would *know.*

THE INFLUENCE OF ARISTOTLE

Aristotle had few real disciples among the Greeks. His work was centered in the city-state and the free Greek citizen, but Alexander destroyed the city-states and enslaved the citizens. Even in Aristotle's own time, it was hard to interest Greeks in experimentation, and any chance at a scientific revolution was lost with the rise of Alexander. Greek gentlemen were simply not going to dirty their hands and dissect animals, and court sages were not going to ask hard questions of the state.

Some modern skeptics have argued that Christianity is the enemy of the development of science. They look to Aristotle and the Greek period as a lost golden age destroyed by the rise of Christianity. But hope for science died long before the birth of the Christ. Aristotle had provided an inadequate theological and social basis for his theories. He set them in the social context of the Greek city-state system, which would soon be dead forever. The pagan Greeks ignored the possibilities in Aristotle.

Christians always found inspiration in Aristotle. When the Roman Empire was divided, the western half plunged into chaos, and almost all of Aristotle's work was lost. The Christian philosopher Boethius salvaged some of Aristotle's writings on logic, and that fragment in Latin translation shaped Christian education in the West for centuries. The eastern half of the Roman Empire, Byzantium, also embraced Christianity but managed to fight off barbarian incursions. Byzantium retained many of Aristotle's Greek manuscripts and continued Christian education in Aristotle throughout its thousand-year life span. Some Western thinkers would visit the great capital of that empire, Constantinople, and return infected with Aristotelian ideas. When the Fourth Crusade sacked Constantinople, fatally weakening this great bulwark of Christianity against Islam, Greek texts and scholarship became even more available to the West.

Islam also was deeply influenced by Aristotle, but it is interesting to note that this did not lead to a scientific revolution. In several areas, but especially in Syria and Spain, Islamic thinkers inherited the work of the Christians and Jews they conquered, and on occasion built on them. Thinkers such as Avicenna and Averroes combined Aristotle with a religious Neo-Platonism and Islam, but unlike Christianity and Judaism, Islam was never able to maintain an educational tradition of free thought. In fact, by the time of his death the work of Averroes, the greatest of the Islamic commentators on Aristotle, could only safely be studied in the West.

Whether through Muslim Spain or from the declining imperial city of Constantinople, eventually Aristotle made his way to the University of Paris. There he eventually fell into the hands of an equal, Saint Thomas Aquinas, who used Aristotle and Neo-Platonism as a secular sounding board for a masterful synthesis of all knowledge of the time from a Christian perspective. Thomism helped make Aristotle the dominant pagan thinker. Dante considered Aristotle simply "the Master."[4]

This association made Aristotle part of the rejection of the medieval worldview that occurred in the Renaissance and Reformation periods. The study of Aristotle only began to recover in Protestant circles in the nineteenth century. Catholic and Protestant philosophers have shown a new interest in Thomas Aquinas and hence in Aristotle. Philosophers such as Alasdair MacIntyre in *After Virtue* revived interest in Aristotle's ethics as a good basis for regulating life in a pluralistic society. Of course, MacIntyre is not merely an Aristotelian, but many of his ideas and vocabulary imitate the *Ethics*. It is as an ethicist that Aristotle may provide the most help to a modern Christian living in a pluralistic society.

As far as he goes, Aristotle provides an ethic that allows for Christian flourishing but that can be argued for in terms acceptable to non-Christians. It would *not* be enough for Christian living, but if implemented, Aristotelian ethics would allow for such living and might even suggest it. After all, most Christians only aspire to community virtue set up as the standard by the noble pagan Aristotle. If Christians eventually surpass this standard in their own lives, then that will be all the greater witness to a secular culture.

A good grounding in Aristotelian ethics would also provide education and norms for non-Christians that would make them better neighbors and allow both communities to live in peace with each other. The decline in Christian teaching has left a cultural hole that Christianity should fill but might not be able to for some time. Having been recently rejected by much of the cultural elite, it might be too soon for it to return. In the meantime, one must live, and the culture must go on in a dangerous world where a vacuum of ideas cannot long be tolerated. Since Aristotle reaches his ethical conclusions in ways that are not calculated to set off cultural alarms and that could be taught in government schools, his system may represent a hopeful middle ground to end the culture wars, which benefit no one save the totalitarian foes of philosophy. There may be important work yet for Plato's best student.

---

[4]Dante *Divine Comedy* 4.131.

10

PREPARING THE WAY
FOR CHRIST

Hellenistic Philosophy

WHAT COMES NEXT?

Socrates begat Plato, Plato begat Aristotle, Aristotle begat Alexander, and the world of the classical Greeks came to an end. Alexander destroyed the old order, first in Greece and later throughout the entire rotting Persian Empire, but he replaced it with nothing stable. The Mediterranean world entered a strange shadow time during the period from 323 B.C. to 30 B.C., almost waiting for the coming of the Romans to reunite it and give direction to its history.

The rigorous logic of Aristotle and the passionate dialectic of Plato were not enough to preserve reason from the erotic and tyrannical nature of Alexander. It was just as Plato had feared in the *Symposium:* Alcibiades had not been tamed. Instead, this latter Alcibiades, Alexander, swept away Plato's world and declared himself a secular god. Alexander helped a strange brew of superstition and philosophical jargon triumph over philosophy.

THE RELIGION OF DELPHI AND PHILOSOPHY

The cosmos of Greek religion was vast, only slightly organized, and diverse. Its greatest classical shrine was at Delphi. Though there were many great shrines in the ancient world, there was none to compare to Delphi, which drew kings from all over the Mediterranean world to seek wisdom.

Delphi itself, as a physical shrine, declined with the power of the Greeks. It never really recovered from the destruction of the traditional Greek city-state culture by Alexander. Each of the warring Hellenistic empires that followed the godlike Alexander attempted to develop their own religious centers. Eventually, like Greece itself, the spirit and power of Delphi was transferred to Rome. The Romans would occasionally try to suppress superstition, but rationalism without religion was powerless to defeat the oracles that sprang up all over the empire. These oracles, especially those of the sibyl, had great power over the minds of every class of society. Every part of culture became Delphic, and in Rome the synthesis between philosophy and Homeric religion was perfected.

EARLY PLATONISM AND NEO-PLATONISM: THE CHIEF RIVALS TO CHRISTIANITY

In one sense Plato had no followers. His greatest student, Aristotle, abandoned Platonism. Even the Academy began to move in a direction inspired by Plato's canon but not necessarily consistent with it. By the time of the Academy's second leader after Plato, Xenocrates, larger discussions of spiritual beings (not just God) and purification were creeping into the mathematical and dialectical education Plato had begun. Plato's mythic conclusions were being drawn upon without the rigor of his dialectic method always preceding them. The ground was beginning to shift from philosophy into more of an accommodation with the language and ideas of Delphi. More frequently Platonism emphasized a public doctrine that sounded conventionally religious while teaching a more esoteric doctrine in private. This process would accelerate over time.

To its credit the Academy never fell into the worst sort of popular religion. As we shall see, to the very end of its history the Academy and Neo-Platonism in general maintained an active and creative agenda. Even in those last days Neo-Platonism was still capable of producing an important commentator and thinker like Proclus, whose commentary on *Timaeus* was an important reference work for my dissertation. However, the popular face of the Academy often allowed less-responsible thinkers to develop more mysterious and less rationally defensible versions of Platonism. These are often lumped together under the label of Gnosticism.

Gnosticism began its long career as a popular version of complicated ideas during the Hellenistic period. As a compromise between philosophy and popular religion, it was a middlebrow alternative for those not sophisticated enough to follow the arcane discussions of the Academy and other schools of thought, but who had just enough education to be discontented with the Homeric and Roman pantheon. It has never really died. I have books from Gnostic societies published in Victoria's England and in the early twenty-first century. One of the bestsellers is Dan Brown's *Da Vinci Code,* which appears to take Christian Gnosticism seriously.

Ancient Gnosticism developed four major themes that most groups shared and that continue to have appeal. First, Gnosticism denigrated the body while exalting the soul. This tendency had been present in Plato in dialogues such as the *Phaedo,* but the totality of Plato's teachings did not go this far. Unlike Plato, Gnostics hoped to dispense with the physical as much as possible. Because they despised creation, it was common for Gnostics to divide the gods of creation, who were mostly bad, from the gods of intellect. Many Gnostics viewed the entire cosmos as a stain that was offensive to pure intellect. As a result, they were frequently opposed to sex, and they were also misogynists and faddists about eating.

Rituals to cleanse the body and prepare it for heaven were common in most Gnostic cults and form the second common element of most sects. Many would engage in mysterious rites of purification, which became mixed up with magic and theurgy. Theurgy, which invoked the aid of good spirits against the material world, became particularly popular. Astrology, the most mainstream of the occult sciences, also assumed a dominant position as Gnostics looked for knowledge of the future so they could manipulate their own path toward the divine. This was a long way from the rationalistic religion of Plato, but it satisfied a popular craving.

Gnostics almost always claimed to have secret knowledge that could only be learned through rituals, magic or a great teacher-guru. These teachers often claimed to have a secret book of the knowledge of the universe. When examined, these books almost always contained a theory of emanations. As we shall see, the theory of emanations held that the good and purely spiritual god could be reached through a series of levels. Moving through these levels usually involved invoking a new spirit guide or performing some ritual act such as bathing in the blood of an animal or engaging in sexual acts.

Gnosticism had the advantage of being doctrinally flexible on almost every point. It was not tied to any particular holy book or people group (as was Judaism) and so could adapt the language and norms of the culture in which it found itself. The great Christian thinker Origen was influenced by Gnostic versions of Platonism. Christian views on sexuality and the material world always ran the risk of becoming heretical under assault from Gnostic notions built into the thinking of many members of the local church. Heresies about the nature of Jesus Christ often had Gnostic reasoning behind them.

Despite recent discoveries, such as the *Gospel of Judas,* we have little direct knowledge of Gnosticism. This is mainly because of the Gnostics themselves. The Gnostics wanted their texts and ideas to be hidden and rare. Gnostics had hidden gurus whose alleged apostolic credentials were only made available to insiders. While the early church invited anyone to examine their books and hear the teachings of their bishops, the Gnostics appealed only to the insiders. As a result, when they lost the intellectual battle, little record was left of their teachings.

By the middle of the third century, Platonism had reached an intellectual dead end and lost control of the intellectual agenda. Epicurean and Stoic schools of thought were attracting many of the best minds. Stoicism began to gain some popular appeal. In reaction to both these philosophical programs, but in particularly to Stoicism, the Academy evolved into what is now referred to as the Middle Academy. Arcesilaus (d. 241 B.C.) and Carneades (d. 129 B.C.) were the leaders of the Middle Academy, but it is important to remember that the leaders of the Academy in any period claimed and probably believed that they were recovering the real Platonic doctrines.

The emphasis in the Middle Academy was on the bewilderment and tentative nature of conclusions in the dialectical process. Of course, these ideas are prominent in the Platonic texts, especially in the early dialogues. The Academicians of this period emphasized those and placed almost no emphasis on the Platonic doctrines present in the later dialogues. The theories of knowledge of the time built human knowledge on impressions that compel action. The human being receives true impressions from the cosmos, apprehends those impressions, makes judgments and eventually acts. This process leads to knowledge. As the Middle Platonists pointed out, human impressions are fallible. As a result, humanity should greet the idea of knowledge with great skepticism. This moderate skepticism does seem in line with one reading of Plato's theories about the nature of reality.

Stoics in particular felt that this attack was not persuasive. The Stoics believed that one could develop tests that would allow humans to separate true impressions from error. One could develop a criterion of truth to separate judgments based on false impressions from those based on true impressions. The skeptical Platonists did not think there was such a criterion, but their very skepticism left them with no basis to criticize anyone. They also faced the problem of all skeptics: that one cannot live as if skepticism is true. As a result, skepticism does no work in the real world. If false, it is useless; if true, it cannot be lived and so is useless. Skepticism can therefore be safely ignored.

Carneades felt that this charge needed to be answered. He pointed out that in the end all human reason must, however convoluted the epistemological trail, depend on the input of the senses. Such sensation could never be any more than probable. Following Plato in *Timaeus*, Carneades argued that humans make nothing more than probable judgments; they can only reach persuasive statements, not truth. The Stoics could easily reply that this was simply a redefinition of terms on the part of the skeptics, who turned out not to be so skeptical after all. Probable judgments, after all, provide a standard for judgment, and no human except a great sage could ever expect anything else.

Platonism eventually moved away from skepticism, but skepticism did not die. Aenesidemus (d. c. 40 B.C.) revived the radical Pyrrhonian skepticism of the time of Plato. This form of skepticism refused even the possibility of probable knowledge of the nature of things. Humans are only presented with appearances, and appearances themselves can appear in ten modes. There are, after all, many diverse creatures, and there are also diverse sense organs. Mistakes in sensation may occur at such a deep level with a mismatch between an organ and the object that it cannot be told apart from a true impression.

As a result, a wise human does not trust any appearance or speak in terms of probability. Instead, he or she lives according to the appearances, with a total suspension of beliefs. Like other forms of skepticism, it is hard to see the appeal of the Pyrrhonian model. Even if it is true, living according to appearances will be functionally the same as living according to probability. Of course, it is better to believe the truth. If it is true that all things so disguise their true nature that even probable belief is impossible, then humanity will have to embrace the fact. However, it does not seem true in practice, and practice is all humanity has. Even the least-educated human being seems able to live in a world that does not seem designed to trick him. In any case, while Gnosticism flourished, skepticism remained the province of intellectuals proud of their tough-minded denial of all truth.

Around the time of the revival of Pyrrhonian skepticism, a New Academy returned to more orthodox teaching of Plato's doctrines around the year 110 B.C. under Philo of Larissa. Much of the excitement had gone from the program, and too often Platonism now seemed reactionary rather than a living intellectual program. There was still life in the pagan school of thought, however. Platonism had one last great flowering before being utterly subsumed by Christianity as a result of the magisterial writings of great early Christian Neo-Platonists such as Boethius and Saint Augustine.

Plotinus (d. A.D. 270) and his disciples Porphyry (d. A.D. 305) and Iamblichus (d. A.D. 330) brought a fresh rigor to the study of Plato. They developed a theory that was motivated by Plato's works, but they were unafraid to deviate from them. The Jewish sage Philo had a major unacknowledged role in shaping their thought. They freely borrowed from Christianity, especially the Gnostic sects of Christianity, and imitated such doctrines as the Trinity. If Christianity had the Father, Son and Holy Spirit, Plotinus postulated a divine principle that exists in three persons or manifestations: the One, the Noetic (Reason) and the Soul.

Late Neo-Platonism is complex and interesting. It is impossible to do more than touch on a few high points. Sadly, Neo-Platonism overemphasized the parts of Plato that denigrated the physical world and almost totally destroyed the balance between the life of contemplation and the life of action found in Aristotle. In many ways this form of Neo-Platonic thought was similar to Gnosticism in proposing a series of emanations from a spiritual principle down to the material world. For Plotinus, everything comes from the One and falls from the One to multiplicity. Even the Noetic and the Soul are less than the One and dependent on the One in a relationship that anticipates the Christian heresy of Arius (d. A.D. 336). The Arian heresy would make the Father the only true God, and Jesus Christ a lesser being begotten from him.

Later forms of Gnosticism became in many ways popularizations of Neo-Platonism, just as Plotinus can be seen in part as a rigorous expression of Gnosticism. In Plotinus's thought, reality consisted fundamentally of thought, not matter, which exists only in a derivative sense. The act of contemplation is the most noble and the only real action, and therefore it is the only path to truth. For Plotinus, thought actually shapes the world and is not just a passive reflection of some independent reality. The divine thought produced the world through contemplation, not through any active creation, and everything rushes back to that source of unity. Porphyry and Iamblichus modified and developed Plotinus's thought but were still dependent on him. Finally, Proclus (A.D. 485) brought an end to the long tradition of pagan Neo-Platonism. His writings span the knowledge of his day, making some contributions to mathematics and science, and he shows strong textual insight and skills. But the center of the intellectual world had left pagan Neo-Platonism, and in the main, nothing in Proclus could have changed that. Neo-Platonism had retreated from the careful synthesis of reason and theology found in Plato and moved into mysticism, which made much progress impossible. Late Neo-Platonism tended to reflect piously on the works of the masters rather than do much with them.

EPICUREANS

Intellectuals are often misunderstood, but perhaps no group from antiquity is more misunderstood than the Epicureans, who lived for pleasure.

I have heard Christians interpret this to mean a life of hedonism, but that says more about what the speaker enjoys than about what an ancient philosopher would desire. The Epicureans lived for the contemplative or higher pleasures in order to minimize fear, which they believed was the ultimate problem of humanity. Only by minimizing fear could they maximize pleasure. There is much to admire in their noble lifestyle, which was dedicated to philosophy and self-restraint. There were never many Epicureans in the Greco-Roman world, for a life of hard intellectual labor and rigorous morality based only on human opinion will appeal to few. Of course, among intellectuals, Epicurean thought has always remained a viable possibility. Materialists dedicated to the life of the mind and the good life without fear still exist in culture today.

Epicurus was a young man when Aristotle was coming to the end of his life. His main work was accomplished during the period of political confusion following the death of Alexander. This may partly explain his strong hatred of fear and his desire for contemplative peace. Epicurus built on the work of the atomist Democritus but modified it to answer the criticisms of Aristotle. Though little of his work survives, enough is left to sketch out his views. He founded a school in Athens called The Garden, and his movement never lacked for philosophical disciples from that point forward. It is the accumulated work of Epicurus and his disciples, the Epicureans, that we shall examine.

Both the Epicureans and their main intellectual competitors, the Stoics, responded strongly to the immateriality of Platonism. Both revived the atomism of Democritus and Leucippus (fifth century B.C.). Believing that the world was made up of indestructible atoms enabled the Epicureans to escape what had become the excessively contemplative outlook of the Neo-Platonists. The Epicureans were interested in the natural world and understanding humanity's place in it.

Wishing to establish the existence of the indestructible building blocks, the atoms, the Epicureans went in search of empirical evidence for atoms. This desire for proof from the natural world, using the senses and reason, was itself an important feature of the Epicurean school. They were not content to theorize but also wanted to explain the appearance of the world they saw. Their atoms would explain natural phenomena and ground thought in their unchanging existence. Study of the natural world could lead to knowledge because it is eternal and of the same substance with the mind, since both are made of atoms. Epicureans escaped skepticism about knowledge through atoms and materialism. This is another way that the Epicureans are a forerunner to the views of many contemporary scientists.

Like Parmenides, the Epicureans believed that the things that are must always be (things were not created or destroyed), and these were their atoms. Unlike Parmenides, Epicurus was not simply willing to dismiss the existence of motion, but this meant that he had to restrict existence to the atoms alone. The rest of the universe was just a changing combination of the unchanging and eternal substances.

Early atomists had not given an adequate explanation of atoms, their motion or how different objects could be made from one sort of thing. Epicureans provided the necessary development of the theory to keep it viable. Details of ancient cosmological theories might seem useless, but in this case (and in the case of the Stoics) they are particularly important as forerunners to the coming of the Christian church. As we shall see, this cosmology provided a materialist option for the early church if one was wanted. Instead, the church rejected materialism and sided with the Greek philosophical dualists. Having at least a quick overview of the options available to Paul and the apostles allows contemporary Christians to understand the world in which their faith was born.

Atoms came in an indefinite number of sizes to allow for an infinite number of combinations. They were all too small to see and were infinite in a limitless cosmos (one of many) that contained infinite space in which these atoms could move. As in traditional atomist thought, they continued in motion until acted upon, but Epicureans attempted to explain this motion by arguing that material atoms tended to travel toward the earth. From our perspective this is "down." They also had an inexplicable swerve, which allowed for motions that are not so simple or predictable. It also explained why atoms collide, something previous atomists had suggested but not explained.

The Epicureans were the first to place ideas and thought in mere matter. They believed humans to be thinking atoms. If madly materialist moderns believe that thought is a brain state, then Epicureans located the seat of human reason in the heart. Their theories of perception also could rely on matter. One atom collides with another, passing on motion and change from one object to another. How does this happen? Atoms that are contiguous develop a skin that will then admit atoms. These atoms impact the atoms of the sense organs, which pass motion on to the soul.

The human soul is just another set of atoms. This sounds implausible enough that the Epicureans developed an elaborate and, not surprisingly, a tripartite theory of the soul. First, the body contains air atoms that allow for neural transmission of the initial collisions from the human skin to the proper organ. Air is easy to move and is an ideal means for such transmissions. It can be carried along by wind or the motion of the air atoms. All the atoms of the mind are tiny, even in the world of atoms, but as a result they can be spread out over the entire body coextensively. They are centered in the heart region but function throughout. Second, heat atoms act as the central power of the soul for action, and they burn in the human heart. Third, certain unnamed but very "fine" atoms act as staples to join the soul atoms to the body. Perceptions cannot be mistaken at the lowest levels. However, the complicated motions within the body that any impression must pass through introduce the possibility of error. While humans can, therefore, make errors based on empirical or sense data, they need not fear that these errors will overwhelm knowledge.

Religion and divinity do not escape reduction to atoms. If one wishes to live for pleasure, and if this is defined as the absence of fear, then the gods must go. Gods are uniquely uncontrollable and wild. They cannot be tamed or studied like simple atoms can be. Epicureans were intent to avoid the charge of atheism, which was unpopular with the masses. They postulated gods but made them material and placed them in the furthest reaches of space. There they could not cause fear in the Epicureans either by acting in a manner that could cause fear or by official nonexistence, which would have angered the neighbors of the Epicureans.

Ethics can now be placed on a safe and rational foundation. Epicurus believed his ethics could avoid skepticism by being strongly empirical, and determinism (lack of freedom) by the atomic swerve. The highest good, the natural end of humanity, is seen in infants and animals. The

Epicureans thought that ideally persons should live without becoming upset or fearful. They were happy. This happiness or absence of fear can only be the absence of pain from the body and the mind. Pleasure may be relative, but pain exists and it is bad. Getting rid of it is the highest good for the Epicurean. Epicurus believed that all events produced either pleasure or pain and that neither could be reduced to the other.

As a result, Epicureans wanted to minimize activity since activity leads to the possibility of pain. They also wanted to minimize pleasure, especially erotic ones, since pleasure, too, can lead to pain, if only the pain of their withdrawal. This constrained life of the Epicureans borrowed from Aristotle the idea that the contemplative life was the best, but the Epicureans did so for utilitarian reasons. There is no right or wrong in fact for an Epicurean, only what is likely to lead to pleasure or pain. Epicureans were often accused of being immoral, which is technically accurate since they denied that morality existed. All that existed was the useful principle that pain should be avoided and thereby pleasure gained.

Of course, Epicurean thought suffers from the difficulties of all materialist philosophies but has the same attractions. It is attractive because it is not skeptical, but it is also not dogmatic. It avoids the dangers religion runs with mysticism. On the other hand, Epicureans must explain many varied phenomena, including all of religion, with one simple explanation. Simplicity can be a virtue, but it can also get in the way of understanding by failing to allow for important distinctions. Epicurean philosophy also reduces ideas, beauty and mind to atoms. This is difficult to accept. How does an atom think? Did an atom produce Narnia? If so, then where is that atom?

At the heart of it all is the problem of substance. What makes up things? Ideas seem to exist, and matter seems to exist. The relationship between ideas and matter is difficult if not impossible to understand. Most theists, including Christians, have tried to secure the existence of both and have been willing to live with the problem of the relationship between the two. However, just as some idealists abandon matter for ideas, so materialists solve the idea-matter problem by getting rid of ideas. This much is certain: the church has never existed during a time when it did not face intelligent advocates of materialism and its deficiencies.

STOICS

Though the Stoics are often held as opposites of the Epicureans, they agreed on much. First, they agreed on rejecting Neo-Platonism. Second, both camps were materialists and atomists. However, like many quarrels in families, the feud between Stoics and Epicureans was intellectually fierce. The Stoics disagreed with the Epicureans about the highest good for humankind, advocating a life according to human nature with the highest reward achieving peace of mind. The Stoics looked back to Heraclitus as their legendary founder, and though they rejected both Plato and Aristotle, their philosophies were deeply indebted to them, as are all thinkers.

Zeno (d. 262 B.C.) founded a school that met in the porches of Athens, where people could cool themselves and do business away from the heat of the Mediterranean climate. These porches, called *stoa,* gave their name to the school. Zeno was followed by Cleanthes (d. 232 B.C.) and then Chrysippus (d. 206 B.C.). This series of strong leaders put Stoicism on strong footing and enabled it to adapt to the first waves of criticism. Stoicism became widespread and had much more public and political appeal than Epicureanism, capturing the attention of emperors and the better read of the middle class. The emphasis it placed on duty and virtue made it a particularly apt philosophy for the Romans and their military leaders.

As a large-scale movement that existed right up through the triumph of Christianity, Stoicism went through an early, middle and late period, just as Neo-Platonism did. Stoics divided their project among logic, physics and ethics. They divided logic into rhetoric, which was the study of arguments, and dialectic, which involved the philosophy of language, epistemology and the nature of certainty. The Stoics were very concerned with skeptical objections to knowledge. They wanted to know how they knew as well as answer certain logical puzzles that had been presented. In physics they tried to account for the world in physical terms. Finally, they viewed ethics, as most people did at the time, as the central feature of philosophical investigation. Stoicism narrowed toward the end, becoming merely an ethic for some of its followers. Here we shall try to describe the basics held by most Stoics in most places at most times.

The most lasting contribution Stoicism would make is in the area of logic. Here they expanded on the simple tool left to them by Aristotle, allowing for arguments of much greater complexity. Aristotle had worked in simple propositions that followed basic patterns. Two simple propositional premises led to a conclusion based on an assured relationship. (For example: If A, then B. A. Therefore B.) Critics had attempted to confuse the logician with a series of puzzles, showing that the language of logic needed further reflection. This is what the Stoics provided.

Stoics were faced with logical puzzles such as the heap argument. How can one tell how many beans one has to have in order to make a heap? Is it four? Is it five? The Stoics quickly saw that the trap could only be sprung if the terms of the argument were not clearly defined. The wise person, the Stoic sage, would suspend judgment until the terms were clarified. This was an important reinforcement of the important Aristotelian traits of rigor and clarity in the use of language in argument. It also caused the Stoics to become committed to a key assertion: no impression could be false. Given time looking at heaps of beans, eventually the wise Stoic would know that, for example, three beans is not a heap but four is. As we shall see, however implausible this might seem, such an assertion helped escape a seemingly lethal skeptical argument.

The analysis of such arguments led the Stoics to recognize that some but not all statements were created equal. Some sayings could be true or false propositions that could be used as Aristotelian premises, while other sayings were incomplete. They are mere terms. Incomplete sayings could not be used in logic.

Other sayings have suppressed tenses or hidden referents that can cause confusion if not brought to light. For example, suppose a boy named Luke meets a hooded man named Darth. Luke is asked if he knows Darth, and he replies that he does not. However, the hooded man is actually Luke's father, Anakin, whom Luke *has* known since childhood. Does he know the hooded man or not? The critic can chuckle: Luke knows and does not know the hooded man at the same time.

The Stoics pointed out that this puzzle depended on confusing the question. There is only one man, but the boy experiences him in two different modes. Luke should hesitate in answering the question "Do you know this man?" and ask for clarification. Which is the question being asked?

- Does Luke recognize Darth, the man with the hood?
- Does Luke know the identity of the man who is under the hood?
- Does Luke know the man under the hood?

Luke can say no to the first question without fear of contradiction, and no to the second as well. On the third question a wise Luke should demure. He does not know if he knows the man under Darth's hood. The tricky original question could be understood several ways and was used to catch Luke in a seeming paradox. A wiser Luke who was slower to speak would never be caught in this way. One result of such puzzles was that the Stoics placed a high value not only on precision in speech but also on slowness to speak, which became stereotypical of philosophers of the period.

Finally, there is some evidence that Stoics' investigation of logic expanded the number of sayings that could be allowed in an argument. They did this by allowing for conjunction and disjunction between two "full sayings" to form new premises. Two full sayings could be combined in rulelike ways to form new full sayings. These sayings could also be used in arguments, since they were constructed out of good sayings, and this allowed for greater variability in argument.

Stoics were atomists, believing that nothing that was immaterial exists. It appears that the Stoics were like Aristotle in believing in a material "basement" substance that was permeated by the active principle that makes it distinct: wind, spirit or pneuma. Pneuma finds its most basic existence in structure. Pneuma allows things to be what they are by organizing them and holding them together. Connected to it, and over all, is a burning, rational fire, the god Logos, which acts as soul to the cosmos and to all animals (but not plants), and is the active principle that organizes the whole. Organic things are composed of inorganic substance with every thing, organic and inorganic, connected to every other thing in a great cosmic circle of fire.

The cosmos of the Stoics was cyclical, with a first material principle of fire. In much of this the Stoics did indeed echo the ideas of Heraclitus from centuries before their own time. One difficulty of atomist or materialist theories is determinism, but Stoics were comfortable with this outcome and the belief that every action is predetermined. Everything that is was and will be again. There is no changing history or future, as it is all part of a vast, rational and material chain of causes. The sage can only mentally assent and relax in the face of this predestination. Each cycle of the cosmos ends in the living fire, which penetrates the world. This only real god, the divine Logos, who holds together all things through the pneuma, brings the cycle of life to its conclusion and then starts it again. This fire, of course, is itself material. Stoicism is therefore a pantheistic theory with a material and rational god who permeates everything and brings about everything.

Stoic theories of perception seem most motivated by the desire to avoid skepticism. Stoics apparently believed that one could gain a firm grip on an idea at the level of impressions. Stoics loved to use the analogy of a hand to explain their theory of knowledge. The atomic soul has a perception of the world that it receives from impressions of other atoms striking it. The soul is presented with an impression of variable strength. The strength of the impression can be compared to the strength of a grip that a hand has on an object. The stronger the impression, the stronger the grip of the mental hand on the object. In other words, as the force of the impression of the atoms grows stronger on the soul, the thinker is justified in assenting to it progressively more strongly. No thinker should be in a hurry to give assent, and the amount of assent given should be measured to the strength of the impression. This does not lead to any relativism however, because the impression could be so strong that it could not be denied. This is compared to a tight grip by one hand with the other hand grasping the first hand.

Confidence in this regard was justified by the simplicity and rationality of the Stoic cosmos. Humans assert X based on an impression from the cosmos, and skeptics ask how the person asserting the proposition could know it to be true. But the Stoics believed that X, if true, would so strongly correspond to an actual X in the cosmos that the rightly ordered human would know X was true of X beyond any ability to doubt. This Stoic sage would simply never make errors. For obvious reasons, the Stoics were hesitant to identify any but historical sages.

This measured assent to reality was the key to Stoic behavior. In its declining years, Stoicism would be an ethical system attractive to the Roman ruling class, as it seemed to buttress an acceptance of an established order that was often under fire. The good life was the reasonable life, and there was no excuse for vice. Humanity's natural impulses could only be appropriately realized through reason. Reason must accept that externals such as health and wealth are incidentals not under the control of humans. The cosmic cycle is what it is and must be accepted. Social norms should be accepted in public to avoid trouble, but insiders understood that much of it was nonsense. All things being equal, why shouldn't a wise person eat his parents after they had died? Why waste the meat? Weren't many clothing customs and sexual practices irrational? In this way, Stoicism continued the double life of the ancient philosopher in the community.

The Stoics were not always consistent in talking about moral progress. Sometimes they seemed to assert that perfection could be reached once the key insight of assent to reality and living according to reason had been reached. Since, however, errorless Stoic sages were thin on the ground, Stoics would often speak as if they were willing to allow most to live a life of practical wisdom. In this regard the system was not so different from that of Aristotle.

A main target for the Stoics was the skeptical Academy and an avoidance of skepticism. Since their assault on skepticism was one of the most carefully made in the ancient world, we will examine it at some length. As we have seen, the Stoics divided humanity into two groups: the wise and the ignorant. The wise possessed scientific knowledge, and the ignorant did not. Thinking or cognitions that cannot be shaken by reason is scientific knowledge. Some cognitions might of course lead to conclusions, falsely called knowledge, that could be shaken by reason. The impressions and cognitions were trustworthy, but the rapid conclusions were not. These conclusions, if accepted, would lead to opinions and ignorance. The Stoic Stobaeus refers to these as "weak suppositions."

A weak supposition was an attempt to generalize to scientific knowledge based on insufficient cognitions. The less-than-wise Stoic might view a glittering stone. He receives the impression of a glittering stone. He assents to certain propositions about the stone and fully grasps them. He has cognition. He then attempts to go further and pronounces the stone a diamond. This bad Stoic thinker believes he has achieved scientific knowledge only to discover that his "diamond" is merely cubic zirconia. What went wrong? The cognition was trustworthy, but the supposition based on the cognition had a weak grip. The impressions and thinking were not at fault; the ignorant Stoic just gathered too few. He is ignorant of an important something, unlike the sage who is "ignorant of nothing."[1] Opinion and ignorance could only be avoided by becoming a person who "supposes nothing weakly, but rather securely and firmly."[2]

The other route to ignorance was the route of the "precipitant thinker." This person assents in advance of cognition, which leads to error. Imagine a person speculating alone in his academy. He might make many wrong guesses. To avoid this, a Stoic was urged to embrace nonprecipitancy. Scientific knowledge could only come after careful cognition; there was no shortcut to knowledge.

The belief in knowledge placed the Stoics in conflict with the skeptical Academy, which had rejected the possibility of all knowledge. The Stoics faced two main attacks from the Academy on their views regarding cognition. These attacks are found mainly in the writings of Sextus Empiricus. As with all skeptical claims, there is a temptation just to ignore them, but this is not safe. Skepticism left unanswered can undermine an entire worldview. First, the skeptics point out that cognition takes place in both the wise and the ignorant. Where is the variation in these cognitions except for location? How can cognition produce knowledge in one person and ignorance in another?

The second attack on knowledge is even trickier:

1. All true impressions could be false.
2. Cognitive impressions are based on things that are true and false.
3. Things that are both true and false do not exist.

Therefore:

---

[1] Stobeus frag. 257, G3.
[2] Stobeus frag. 255, D1-3.

4. Cognitive impressions do not exist.

5. Cognitive impressions are the basis for cognition.

Therefore:

6. Cognition does not exist.

Therefore:

7. Every thought is noncognitive.

8. According to the Stoics, every noncognitive thought is an opinion.

9. According to the Stoics, a wise person refrains from assenting to opinions.

Therefore:

10. A wise person will refrain from all assent.

Therefore:

11. To refuse to give assent is to suspend judgment.

Therefore:

12. The Stoic wise person will suspend judgment in everything.

Using this argument, the skeptical Academicians have shown the Stoics that their own system urges them to adopt a skeptical position. Their own sage is a skeptic.

Do either of the skeptical attacks succeed? The first objection plainly does not. The Stoics simply accepted that both the wise and foolish have cognition. It is the misuse of cognition, through hastiness or errors in judgment, that causes mistakes. Only the foolish will make foolish errors, so the same raw material may produce opposite effects in different people.

The second argument is trickier but no more successful. It may be long, but the entire chain depends on the plausibility of number one: all true impressions could be false. This is the very assumption that underlies many of the logical paradoxes that the Stoics addressed. In order to address these arguments, the Stoics were willing to accept that true impressions could *never* be false. They could only lead to false and overly hasty judgments. The argument is only as successful as the previous attacks on the reliability of impressions. There is not much use in an argument to convince Stoics that relies on notions that the Stoics reject.

In many ways the Roman emperor Marcus Aurelius is the perfect ending to paganism. There is much that is appealing about this all-powerful leader who tried to live according to reason and to moderate his own desires. In his day the empire was fading, and at least for his lifetime Marcus Aurelius held off the outer manifestations of that decline. His written work, *Meditations,* is a nearly unique insight into the mind of someone ruling a mighty empire and trying to do so as a Stoic. He was aware of the growing Christian religion. He did not understand it, but he wanted to stamp it out. He despised any group that would embrace martyrdom. He did not understand that pagan philosophy was at a dead end. Why? He had not considered the message of a Jewish rabbi delivered two hundred years before his time. However, his own worldview had no mass appeal, and so the masses had to be sated not with reason but with bread and circuses. This message had taken the creative juices out of Delphi and out of any philosophy that tried to defy it.

Surely it was no accident that this taciturn military man, who provided entertainment to keep power, raised as his heir the weak Commodus, who ineffectively presided over the end of the Roman peace. Stoicism was the philosophy of duty and acceptance, but it could not produce the revolutionary change, social unity or freedom that the empire needed. In an expanding empire it was a ticket to ride, but in a contracting one it was a death wish.

PAUL AT MARS HILL

Athens at the time of Paul was a city that in many ways lived in the past. It had ceased to have much economic importance. The school of Alexandria surpassed it in many ways. Still, however, the great Parthenon towered over the center of the city on the great rock of the Acropolis, covered with the wonderful friezes that now are the prizes of world-class museums. If it still dazzles the eye with its beauty in its nearly ruined state, imagine how it must have appeared to Paul when it was still in one piece. Though the city had been looted many times, pagan benefactors who honored the classical period had also filled Athens with temples, theaters and artwork to honor the intellectual gifts Greece had given to Rome. The marketplace was still there, and even if it was less busy than before, one could still remember that here Socrates had begun philosophy. The Athenian porches (stoa) that had given their name to the Stoic school could still be enjoyed to beat the heat. The Academy still carried on its mission, even if it had little to do with the actual teachings of Plato, a short walk away, and on the walk one could remember the teachings of Aristotle. In between the great Acropolis and the marketplace stood a small hill that the ancient Athenians called the Areopagus. It had served from antiquity as an Athenian court, where the archons, or members of the court, met. Even under the democracy they retained some power, especially over murder and sacrilege cases. By the time of Paul, the Areopagus was a favorite meeting place for intellectuals where the judgments were more over ideas than individuals. So Saint Paul would have walked through the marketplace where philosophy was born to the hill where religious judgments had traditionally been made in the shadow of the greatest temple of the religion of Homer and of Delphi. Athens was still symbolically one of the great centers of ancient paganism, and as a symbol it had no equal for it contained great icons of both pagan religion and pagan philosophy. The Areopagus, or Mars Hill to the Romans, stood right in the center of the life of Athens.

Like Socrates, who was also accused of worshiping strange gods, Paul is brought to the Areopagus. Some scholars question whether the site of Paul's sermon was literally the hill of the ancient Areopagus or a meeting of the council of the Areopagus,[3] though modern Greeks mark the hill as the site with a plaque containing Paul's message. In any case, Luke uses the literary symbolism well. The physically unimpressive Paul was to stand before the Athenians as a symbol of the new and greater philosophy.

Paul's message is deceptively simple. Rhetorically, he uses the same technique that worked so well in his debates with the Jews. Paul will divide his audience, winning the majority by implicitly attacking unpopular but still numerous minority opinions. In the case of the Jews, Paul divided the Pharisees from the Sadducees by appealing to his common

---

[3]See Craig S. Keener, *The IVP Bible Background Commentary: New Testament* (Downers Grove, Ill.: InterVarsity Press, 1993), p. 373.

doctrinal beliefs with the Pharisees. Here he will split the Neo-Platonists and the Stoics from the Epicureans by appealing to his common ground with the Neo-Platonists and the Stoics. He was spectacularly successful.

Paganism and pagan philosophy never recovered from Paul's message. When Paul begins his sermon by saying that he perceives that the citizens of Athens are very religious, he is driving a wedge between the popular religion of Delphi and the religion of the persons on Mars Hill (Acts 17:22). Paul decries the idols in the city of Athens. Since Luke intentionally points out that Stoics and Epicureans are present, and Paul quotes the Stoic poet Aratus, the reader can be sure Paul knows that the Stoics are not idol worshipers. In fact, Luke is at pains to show Paul's erudition, as he also has the apostle quote Epimenides, a sage of the sixth century B.C. So at the very start of the speech the compromise with Delphi is exposed and used by Paul to make a point. No Epicurean or Stoic believes in idols, but over their shoulders looms the great temple of Athena, and all around them is a city given over to the worship of objects made of matter.

Philosophy has allowed the city to continue full of idols. The common people are permitted to continue in their gross ignorance, to the benefit of the establishment. Through fear and through hope for gain, philosophy has allowed itself to become co-opted by evil. Christianity as presented by Saint Paul does not need this compromise. The great thinkers and the common churchgoers will have the same beliefs. There will not be a god of the philosophers that is distinct and hidden, out of fear, from the person who kneels at the Christian altar.

Paul goes on to say that he has found an altar with an inscription to an "unknown god." In all probability Paul has seen one of many altars to unknown gods and has made the perfectly logical move that an altar to an unknown god is also an altar to the unknown God. The unknown gods in Greek thought are those that were propitiated in order to avoid accidentally missing a local or obscure divinity and so bring down divine wrath.[4] It is not so much a god that anyone is looking for but one about which the locals might be ignorant. This is a point that Paul makes when he says that what they once worshipped in ignorance, he will now pro-

---

[4]Pausanias *Description of Greece* 1.4.

claim to them openly. This proclamation is also an attack on the Gnostics, who hide their gospel from public view.

Paul then points out that the true God cannot live in any temple made by humans and that no human could ever serve him. This was an obvious philosophical truth. If there is a God, then no temple can hold him. He also creates all things and provides a basis of unity for all who are his children. Paul is establishing points of agreement between his gospel and some of the philosophies of the Greco-Roman world. There is nothing in the sermon thus far that would have offended or even educated a good Neo-Platonist or Stoic. Paul's statement that God is the Creator might have been controversial if it were understood as Paul meant it, but both Plato and the Stoic philosophers demonstrated that they would use the language of creation even if they did not believe in a literal first moment in time or creation out of nothing.

Paul's assertion that humans are called to seek God with the hope of finding him has Socratic echoes. Paul recognizes that there is a quest for the divine and does not believe that this quest can be ended by any human effort. Instead, this knowledge will come as a product of divine revelation, an idea that Plato seemingly allows for in construction of the liver in *Timaeus*.[5] Four centuries of interaction with philosophy had now proven beyond a doubt to the Greco-Romans on Mars Hill that humanity is not only political, not only desires to know, but is also religious. Humans wish to know God. Paul has not found God, but God has found him.

At this point, Paul has utterly separated himself from the Epicurean philosophers. They cannot accept his religiosity. He will increase this gap by quoting from the Stoic sage Aratus, who says that humans are the "offspring" of God (Acts 17:28). Any Neo-Platonist present can also accept what is being said since, as we have seen, Neo-Platonism was deeply influenced by Stoicism.

Paul's call for a day of judgment also can be understood to be compatible with Stoic teaching. The Stoic cycle that ends in fire could easily be perceived as a day of doom for this present existence. However, Paul then presents the "offense" of the gospel to the persons on Mars Hill. He states

---

[5]Plato *Timaeus* 71b.

that a *man* will judge the world and that this man can be known to be divine by the fact that God has raised him from the dead.

At this point the Epicureans can have nothing but mockery for Paul, but the Stoics also are unable to move forward. Their atomist view of the soul makes any idea of the personal survival of any individual after death difficult, though until the conflagration perhaps the good souls may survive for a time. From the return to the divine fire no human or soul can survive. As a result, Paul's placing the man Jesus as judge on the day of doom is incompatible with Stoic doctrine. They cannot accept Paul's teaching.

The philosophical integrity of the Athenians saved some of them from missing Paul's message. Paul argued well, and many wanted to hear more of his message. In this sense they were the pagan equivalents of the Berean Jews, who sought out the truth of Paul's message in the sacred. The Athenian group in the best position to hear Paul would have been the Neo-Platonists. These thinkers could allow for the personal survival of a human soul for all eternity *(Phaedo)*. They had access to creationist language in *Timaeus*. They had a notion of a final judgment in the *Republic's* myth of Er. The unity of humankind was not foreign to them.

What did they lack? They had no concept of God becoming human and then providing a way for humans to become like God. The idea of the incarnation linked to *theosis* (humans becoming like God) was exciting. That the divine Creator should appoint a man to judge the world at the day of doom and by doing so raise this man to divinity was beyond novel. In many ways, the Christology that lies behind this part of Paul's remarks, uniting the divine Logos with humanity forever, is *the* answer to the dilemma of Plato's cave.[6] It is no shock that at least some of the persons on Mars Hill came to faith quickly. In the conversion of Dionysius the Areopagite, we see the model of the Christian Greco-Roman world to come.

The persecution of Christians lasted for three hundred years, but the faith continued to spread. It was particularly successful in attracting tough-minded and rhetorically skillful defenders. Christianity was bub-

---

[6]Plato *Republic* 514-520.

bling with ideas, some heretical and some not. It had the intellectual and
moral energy that paganism and philosophy had lost. As a result, it began
to attract the first-rate intellects of the day. More and more frequently,
Christian bishops would make spectacular advances in theology, appro-
priating the philosophical language and techniques of the pagans to their
own ends. These dazzling intellectual structures, such as the formulation
of the two natures of Christ and the doctrine of the Holy Trinity, would
become the basis for Western and Eastern Christian thought.

In the face of this accomplishment, Constantine the Great, a saint in
the Eastern church, became convinced that only Christianity could preserve his empire. Though inconsistent in his practice of the faith—after
all, there were no Christian emperors to serve as role models—he established a Christian foundation for an Eastern Roman Empire that would
preserve learning, philosophy and faith for one thousand years, eventually passing along these riches to the Islamic empire and the West.

WILL THERE BE A REVIVAL OF DELPHIC RELIGION?

Paul defeated Delphi and its religious system by providing an alternative
to a religious and philosophical synthesis that had successfully defeated
all other foes. Delphi and Homeric religion had adapted to other points
of view while preserving the essential idea that humanity lives in a world
of chaos controlled only by chance. Paul was victorious because he came
with a greater spiritual power and a better set of ideas. Paul was willing
to adopt the language of the philosophers and their ideas where they were
helpful, but he was unwilling to compromise the central tenet of his
faith: the gospel.

The oracle worshiped a god that was subject to the fashions and passions of men. It spoke soothing words that varied depending on the political and social conditions. In contrast, while Christianity allows for an
increase in sophistication and growth in understanding, this happens on
the unchanging foundation of the revelation of God in Christ Jesus. The
only center at Delphi was the fact that there could be no ideological center in the cosmos. Delphi gave humans answers to the questions they
asked. Christianity gave humans answers to questions they did not know
to ask, and so it triumphed.

As humanity tires of the materialism of Darwin and the Victorians, there is some risk that it will return to the polytheism and the intellectual fuzziness of Delphi. An uncomfortable number of moderns, even Christians, desire a polytheistic world where gods can be selected to match popular taste, and theology can be trimmed to match the mood of the moment. This is the religious spirit that motivated Delphi. In the end, the wars of the West are always the old battle of the ancient gods versus the Ancient of Days.

11

A POSTSCRIPT

Where Do We Go from Here?

CLASSICAL EDUCATION

Our brief tour of Athens is done, ending on Mars Hill with Saint Paul as did my trip with the Torrey students. Like tourists who see Europe in fourteen days, we have seen too many things too quickly. Such tours are not all bad, however. They cover what millions of better travelers have discerned to be the high points. A wise traveler docs not think he has "done London" after a three-day stop, but he does have a richer view of the world having seen things that previously were just shadows in the mind. Where does our brief tour of Athens leave us?

Even such a brief tour of Greece shows how much we moderns have lost by ignoring the past. Such ignorance threatens humankind with a new dark age. The fact that this ignorance is sometimes planned is the worst part of it. We need alternatives to the threats of scientific materialism and postmodern irrationalism. The ancient world can provide such alternatives. The modern world faces a twofold crisis, both individual and cultural, occurring in the sciences and the humanities in our major universities. This book tries to renew interest in the classical approach to texts and human problems. It cannot do more than point in a direction for the solution to the problems of the scientists laboring under the tyranny of materialistic philosophy. Ideally one would read a book like this with another book such as *Darwin on*

Trial or *Christianity and the Nature of Science.*

Still, the battle lines drawn in the ancient world remain, and the competing stories of Delphi and Saint Paul still struggle for the imaginations of postmodern people. When summarized, the long struggle of philosophers to either escape or make their peace with the religion of Homer and Hesiod is valuable both in retracing our own journey (like a photo album to reflect on that whirlwind tour) and in sketching out where a longer stay might be of interest and importance.

HOMER, HESIOD AND DELPHI

In the West there is no escape from the battle with Delphi. The religion of the oracle adopts new vocabulary, subsumes strange gods and absorbs new ideas. Fundamentally, Homer and Hesiod do not change. It is still chaos and dark night at the bottom, even when Delphic oracular wisdom comes "new and improved" in postmodern vocabulary.

Homer and Hesiod created a penetrating analysis of what it means to be human, one that still resonates with modern readers. The meaningless warfare of the *Iliad* and the lost man far from home of the *Odyssey* are themes that will continue to be used in books and films. This world began in chaos or darkness and ended there as well. This view of reality allows for diversity as long as there is no claim to have found a meaningful end to cosmic existence for gods or humans.

Delphi as a symbol for the great religious enslavement of the imagination of the ancient world is the python that choked the life out of Greek culture. It could change its mind as it was captured by different philosophical schools, but the basics of the mythology never changed. The commoners were given their Homer straight, while the philosopher tried to rationalize its chaos and justify the quest for wisdom.

THE FIRST PHILOSOPHERS

Philosophy was a response to this culture, and yet philosophy failed. The first philosophers of the Ionian revolution, such as Thales, Anaximander and Anaximenes, tried to fit cosmology to an inadequate theology. They sought natural causes for natural events and expelled magical explanations from philosophy. Each of these first philosophers tried a different beginning point in order to simplify natural explanations. Each attempted to create a "theory of everything."

Pre-Socratic philosophy was willing to consider "intelligent causes" from personal agents (the souls of humans and gods) but lacked a good explanation of the powers of the soul. As a result, it could not distinguish between natural and psychological actions—which is not surprising, since this is a problem that still bedevils science today.

Eventually the Sophists discovered that philosophy could be a lucrative business if it turned from cosmology to more practical matters. Of course, philosophy had also reached a dead end in trying to write the final book *On Nature,* and so the motivation did not have to be totally selfish. Perhaps turning from the entire cosmos to humanity in particular would narrow the field enough to allow for less argument and more development. Sadly, it turned out that humanity was more complicated than the rest of nature.

SOCRATES

Socrates was the response to this philosophical mess. He broke through the tendency that everyone has but that is especially pronounced in intellectual elites—the tendency to mental complacency. Intellectuals often are blind to their own reactionary tendencies because they challenge so many things that are not part of the deep, unseen, status quo of the culture. Socrates restored the idea of philosophy as a *search* for wisdom. He did not pretend to have answers he did not have.

Philosophy is not theology. Without the aid of divine revelation, it must remain incomplete and blind. Since humans cannot command revelation to come from the gods, this search was the best humanity could do. Pretending to hear from the gods was a useless delusion.

Socrates did not pretend to know what he did not know. He did know that there was something out there that he loved, and this something was very great. This known unknown was the passion of his life. Socrates left behind the legacy of his martyrdom as well as his best student, Plato, both of which meant that he would be remembered as long as this culture endures.

PLATO

Plato is the master of all who wish to know, realize they do not and then want to begin learning. His works contain truths that are easy to grasp and those that might take years of careful study to find. Plato wrote in a style he perfected, the dialogue, in order to tease his reader into discussion and argument with him. He did not want his dialogues to contain doctrines; instead, he wanted to lure his readers into working out their nature by wrestling with his text. Interaction with the puzzles in the dialogues would create a dialogue between the reader and Plato's text.

His early dialogues focus on the methods of Socrates and on the need for ignorance. Careful students must first determine what they know and what they do not know. If they claim knowledge they do not have, then their arrogance will only lead them to foolish bewilderment.

Plato's middle years brought his great dialogues, culminating in the majestic *Republic*. There Plato moved from questions to hypothesis and then on to the construction of a grand myth that would unify human understanding. Plato had a unified vision of reality in which his theories about knowledge, politics, the cosmos and the nature of the soul all reinforced each other.

In his maturity Plato challenged his own ideas and further refined his great philosophical story in *Timaeus* and *Laws*. His school, the Academy, would debate his works for centuries and would become an inspiration for many of the educational institutions that followed him. Most important, Plato left behind his complete works and his greatest student: Aristotle.

ARISTOTLE, HELLENISM AND THE COMING OF PAUL

Aristotle proposed answers to the questions of the Academy. He surpassed Plato by carefully defining his terms and trying to make the premises of his arguments plain to the reader. His discovery of the initial rules of logic would by itself have made him of great importance in the growth of culture. He also refined Platonic ethics by allowing for weakness of the will and through his useful ethical tool the golden mean. Add to that the organization of all of knowledge and some of the first attempts at genuine scientific investigation, and Aristotle could rightly be called "the master of all who know."

Many different religions and philosophies exist in modern America and Western Europe, and in a free society it is important to persuade people in a language they can understand. Aristotle's *Ethics* is very valuable in this context to a Western Christian. It provides a vocabulary for the defense of traditional ethics that can be understood by those who do not accept Christianity. Of course, Aristotle assumes ideas that can no longer be assumed (such as the fact that all educated people will just "know" that some things are bad). Centuries of thought have demonstrated that ethics needs an ultimate grounding in the existence of God.

Aristotle wrote as if his answers were final. His lecture notes are unappealingly self-confident, though his intellectual brilliance kept him mentally alert and growing. His dogmatic tendencies were not healthy, but then neither was the doctrinaire and universal skepticism that the Greeks often used to oppose him. It is obvious why humans craved final answers, but the effect was negative when the answers were repetitively insufficient or even harmful to Greek culture.

The Greek world of the tyrant Alexander, the confused world of Hellenism and the great Roman Empire were a succession of failed answers. Alexander in particular is a warning that success is not sufficient for happiness. One can literally conquer the known world and still be miserable.

The ancient world was alive with competing theories, but nothing managed to supplant the religion of Delphi in the minds of the common people or in the imaginations of the philosophers. Philosophers could reject the doctrines of Delphi privately, but they still thought in the language of Homer and Hesiod. The religious categories presented by Homer and Hesiod could be resisted by thinkers as cantankerous as Heraclitus or as brilliant as Plato, but some possibilities were difficult for even a brilliant Greek to imagine. A God who loved his creatures and who would care for them at his own cost was not likely to occur to a person raised on the stories of the squabbling gods of the *Iliad*.

Delphic religion had great strengths. It could adapt to almost any form of philosophy, or it could claim any god, as long as two things were respected: First, any acceptable deity had to allow for other expressions of worship. The exclusivity of the Jews was acceptable only if they did not claim that others should join them. Christianity, which proclaimed only one God and one way to that God, was tantamount to atheism.

Second, philosophers could challenge old ways as long as they did so with care and did not disturb the simple paganism of the masses. This was easier to do before modern communication and nearly universal literacy. It was easier in the ancient world to say one thing in the temple and another thing in the Academy.

State power grew as neither the god of the philosophers nor the gods of the people could act as a check to the demands of the state. When the government was in the hands of an Alexander or an Augustus, there was no power capable of opposing the state. The squabbles between church and state after the coming of Christianity may have been unseemly, but they were ideal for the growth of liberty. State and church could check each other. The Roman state had no such effective competition.

Fortunately for the survival of the individual in ancient times, Greek and Roman governments lacked the power to enforce their demands. They had no mass communication, no weapons of mass destruction and no ability to travel at the speed of sound. Government claimed all power ("Caesar is Lord!") but could not efficiently enforce its demands. This created a gap that allowed some functional liberty. A totalitarian government without modern scientific powers could not utterly choke off the innovation of the individual.

The Greco-Roman world sought unity in the political world, which it eventually achieved under the caesars, but it gave up on truth in the metaphysical realm. It could develop competing schools of thought, but not the university. That had to wait for a solution far outside the Delphic mainstream.

Saint Paul, a Roman who was also outside the religious mainstream, had the answer. As a Jew he brought the truth about the metaphysical world to Athens in his great sermon on the Areopagus. Jesus was God; he had revealed the truth about the divine nature to humankind and guaranteed that truth through his resurrection from the dead. Christianity would bring a metaphysical unity to the ancient world, one that would allow for the creation of the university. The good news was that this unity did not end the joy of dialectic or of the human journey. God is good, and so he hides himself to allow humanity to grow!

A FINAL QUESTION

Paul was right. The God-man provided the unity with liberty that the Hellenistic and Roman world craved. The Neo-Platonists had wanted to forget about the body and climb out of physical reality to a purely spiritual world of ideas. The hedonists and Roman men of affairs were happy to embrace naturalism and functional atheism in order to escape the madness of Greek religion. Meanwhile, most Greeks and Romans were trapped between fear of the gods and hopelessness in this life.

It is common in modern atheistic or agnostic communities to claim that a "god-man" is not unique to Christianity. The dying god who comes back to life with the spring was certainly not a new idea. However, the similarity of Jesus Christ with Osiris or Dionysus is all at the level of generality or coincidence. In this case, the deity is found in the details.

In none of the myths that predate Christianity does God himself, Creator of the cosmos, become flesh and dwell among humankind. Jesus Christ did not just claim to be *a* god (he was a Jew, after all) but *the* God. This God was all powerful, all knowing and eternally existent. There was nothing like him in the Greek and Roman pantheon. The philosophers could imagine such a God, but they could not imagine that this God would love humankind enough to become human.

Jesus Christ was fully God and fully man. A Greek hero could become a god, but not even Heracles could become Zeus, the greatest of the gods. The God of the Jews made claims infinitely greater than those the Greeks made for their greatest god, Zeus. It was this awesome Jewish God who became flesh. Comparing any previous story to the incarnation and life of Jesus is as superficial as confusing Michelangelo's *David* with the crude sketches of the cave dweller because both are of men. The similarities are there, but it is the genius behind the artifact and the differences he placed in it that make all the difference. With eyes ready to see these differences, read the Gospel of Saint John and compare it to the myths of Orpheus or Heracles.

Jesus Christ took on flesh not as the Greek gods did, by wearing skin to experience human pleasures, but by emptying himself of divine powers and becoming a real human in order to *know* our pain. The best of the gods before Jesus Christ might have suffered because of us, but Jesus Christ suffered *for* us.

The God of the Jews was equal to the god of the philosophers in power, wisdom and knowledge. He was equal to the gods of the Homeric myths in passion, and more than their equal in his ability to know our desires and our pains.

> The Word became flesh
> and dwelt among us,
> and we have seen his glory,
> glory as of the only Son from the Father.
> (John 1:14)

This is a good story, a myth, and Plato is correct when he says that if we believe this kind of story, it will save us from the dangers of intellectual complacency and stagnation.[1] There was a man who went to the place of the dead and who returned to report on what he found there. He is still alive, and he is not silent.

Christianity is so complete and so utterly true that it is a severe temptation to give up on mental growth. And yet God has not seen fit to give Jerusalem a complete guide to everything. Christians do not yet live in paradise. There is still a vital role for philosophy.

God delights in allowing his children to grow into his image by thinking as he thinks, with liberty based on his absolute freedom. Knowing revealed truth leads to better questions, not to the end of questions. Stagnation and mere repetition of the truths of revelation risk making this good thing the enemy of natural, God-created, human development.

When I read Homer, Plato or Aristotle with good friends, it is the mental interaction with the Bible that saves me from two twin errors. Reading Scripture in tension with other books in a strong community saves Scripture from being removed from the life I live. Wicked ideas in the ancients illuminate the power of Scripture. True ideas in the ancients expand the world presented in the Bible or illuminate in a fresh way truths already present there.

---

[1]The last line of the *Republic*.

It also redeems the ancient texts as sacred Scripture assimilates all that is good in them while purging all that is bad. The good and the bad in a great book are not always easy for my simple mind to see, and often what seems bad in Plato (on my first reading) turns out to be most Christian.

When God walked with Adam before the Fall, God saw that Adam was still lonely. Religion and even contact with the divine are not enough for human beings. God completed man by creating woman and bringing the woman to the man. Humans are lonely when isolated from other humans.

Death has created a chronological isolation for each generation of humans. We are cut off by the Grim Reaper from those who came before us, and we become lonely in our own time—bored with the same assumptions, virtues and errors in every face we see. In reading old books, we hear the voices of other men and women brought to us over the gulf of death, and our chronological loneliness is decreased.

Philosophy is never a solitary journey. Men and women of all times and all conditions have been pilgrims on this path to God. Books are conversation starters, but true conversations have to be between living people. One good friend is more valuable than *Republic* or the Gospel according to Saint John because the books are for the living, and not the living for the books.

The books come alive only when discussed, and they are truly discussed only when they impact the life of an authentic community. It is this living dialogue, an incarnation of the story, which in the end, by God's grace, brings me back to the blessed Trinity. The nature of that eternal communion between three persons with one essence is the final truth: the Known Unknown. The deepest dialogue for humankind is between humans created in his image and a God who can be known in the incarnation of his Son, Jesus.

READING LIST

The following is a list of some of the texts written by the ancient authors I have spoken of in this book, along with some more recent texts that have helped me think about those authors.

PRIMARY SOURCES

Aeschylus. *The Complete Greek Tragedies.* Translated by David Grene. Chicago: University of Chicago Press, 1992.

Aristophanes. *Frogs.* Translated by Kenneth Dover. Oxford, U.K.: Clarendon Press, 1997.

Aristotle. *Complete Works.* Edited by Jonathan Barnes. 2 vols. Princeton, N.J.: Princeton University Press, 1984.

Hesiod. *Theogony.* Edited by M. L. West. Oxford: Oxford University Press, 1999.

Homer. *The Iliad.* Translated by Richmond Lattimore. Chicago: University of Chicago Press, 1961.

———. *The Odyssey.* Translated by Richmond Lattimore. New York: Perennial, 1999.

Kirk, G. S., J. E. Raven and M. Schofield. *The Presocratic Philosophers: A Critical History with a Selection of Texts.* Cambridge: Cambridge University Press, 1983.

Plato. *Complete Works.* Edited by John M. Cooper. Indianapolis: Hackett Publishing, 1997.

Plotinus. *The Enneads.* Translated by Stephen MacKenna. Harmondsworth, U.K.: Penguin, 1991.

Sophocles. *Three Theban Plays.* Translated by David Grene. Chicago: University of Chicago Press, 1991.

Xenophon. *Memorabilia.* Translated by E. C. Marchant. Cambridge, Mass.: Harvard University Press, 1979.

SECONDARY SOURCES

Annas, Julia. *An Introduction to Plato's Republic.* Oxford, U.K.: Clarendon Press, 1981.

Cohen, S., et al. *Readings in Ancient Greek Philosophy.* Indianapolis: Hackett Publishing, 1995.

Cornford, Francis. *Plato's Cosmology.* Indianapolis: Hackett Publishing, 1997.

————. *The Republic of Plato.* Oxford: Oxford University Press, 1945.

Fine, John. *The Ancient Greeks.* Cambridge, U.K.: Belknap Press, 2003.

Furth, Montgomery. *Metaphysics.* Indianapolis: Hackett Publishing, 1985.

Geier, Alfred. *Plato's Erotic Thought: The Tree of the Unknown.* Rochester, N.Y.: University of Rochester Press, 2002.

Grant, Michael. *The Rise of the Greeks.* London: Weidenfeld, 2001.

Graves, Robert. *The Greek Myths.* 2 vols. Harmondsworth, U.K.: Penguin, 1990.

Kahn, Charles. *The Art and Thought of Heraclitus.* Cambridge: Cambridge University Press, 1983.

Kingsley, Peter. *Ancient Philosophy, Mystery and Magic.* Oxford, U.K.: Clarendon Press, 1995.

Kitto, H. D. F. *The Greeks.* New York: Penguin, 1950.

Lane, Fox. *Pagans and Christians.* New York: Knopf, 1987.

Long, A. A. The *Cambridge Companion to Early Greek Philosophy.* Cambridge: Cambridge University Press, 1999.

Long, A. A., and D. N. Sedley. *The Hellenistic Philosophers.* 2 vols. Cambridge: Cambridge University Press, 1987.

Luce, J. V. *Introduction to Greek Philosophy.* London: Thames and Hudson, 1992.

Modrak, Deborah. *Aristotle's Theory of Language and Meaning.* Cambridge: Cambridge University Press, 2001.

————. *Aristotle: The Power of Perception.* Chicago: University of Chicago Press, 1989.

Pelikan, Jaroslav. *Christianity and Classical Culture.* New Haven, Conn.: Yale University Press, 1993.

Rice, Daryl. *A Guide to Plato's Republic.* Oxford: Oxford University Press, 1998.

Sambursky, Samuel. *Physics of the Stoics.* Princeton, N.J.: Princeton University Press, 1987.

————. *The Physical World of the Greeks.* Princeton, N.J.: Princeton University Press, 1987.

————. *The Physical World of Late Antiquity.* Princeton, N.J.: Princeton University Press, 1987.

Stone, I. F. *The Trial of Socrates.* Garden City, N.Y.: Anchor Books, 1989.

Strauss, Leo. *The City and Man.* Chicago: University of Chicago Press, 1977.

Taylor, A. E. *A Commentary on Plato's Timaeus.* New York: Garland Publishing, 1987.

————. *Aristotle.* New York: Dover, 1955.

————. *Plato: The Man and His Work.* Mineola, N.Y.: Dover, 2001.

————. *Socrates.* New York: Foley Press, 2007.

Taylor, Thomas. *The Commentaries of Proclus on the Timaeus of Plato, 1820.* 2 vols. New York: Kessinger Publishing, 1997.

Veyne, Paul. *Did the Greeks Believe in Their Myths?* Chicago: University of Chicago Press, 1988.

Wallis, Richard, and Lloyd Gerson. *Neoplatonism.* London: Duckworth, 1995.

Index